Praise for
Disrupt Together

"*Disrupt Together* addresses how teams leverage individual skills to multiply their innovation power. This book elegantly instructs us how to compete in a world that demands change as a normative function."

—John Couch, Vice President of Education, Apple

"Steve Spinelli and Heather McGowan rock because they get one simple fact: If you are not disrupting, then you have no chance to change the world, and even better, when you are done disrupting, you can do it all over again. Can you tell I love these guys!!"

—Governor Craig Benson, Former Governor of New Hampshire, Founder of Cabletron

"Change means looking at *everything* to see how to make it better. You have to disrupt the current state of a product or service as a way of life. *Disrupt Together* will help you understand how to be an innovator."

—Maurice Kanbar, Inventor, Entrepreneur, Philanthropist

Disrupt Together

Disrupt Together

How Teams Consistently Innovate

Stephen Spinelli, Jr., Ph.D.
Heather McGowan

Vice President, Publisher: Tim Moore
Associate Publisher and Director of Marketing: Amy Neidlinger
Operations Specialist: Jodi Kemper
Cover Designers: Maribeth Kradel-Weitzel, Chuti Prasertsith
Cover Image: Andre B./Fotolia
Managing Editor: Kristy Hart
Senior Project Editor: Betsy Gratner
Copy Editor: Cheri Clark
Proofreader: Paula Lowell
Indexer: Suzanne Snyder
Senior Compositor: Gloria Schurick
Manufacturing Buyer: Dan Uhrig

© 2014 by Stephen Spinelli, Jr. and Heather McGowan
Published by Pearson Education, Inc.
Upper Saddle River, New Jersey 07458

For information about buying this title in bulk quantities, or for special sales opportunities (which may include electronic versions; custom cover designs; and content particular to your business, training goals, marketing focus, or branding interests), please contact our corporate sales department at corpsales@pearsoned.com or (800) 382-3419.

For government sales inquiries, please contact governmentsales@pearsoned.com.

For questions about sales outside the U.S., please contact international@pearsoned.com.

Company and product names mentioned herein are the trademarks or registered trademarks of their respective owners.

Printed in the United States of America

First Printing December 2013

ISBN-10: 0-13-338411-X
ISBN-13: 978-0-13-338411-6

Pearson Education LTD.
Pearson Education Australia PTY, Limited
Pearson Education Singapore, Pte. Ltd.
Pearson Education Asia, Ltd.
Pearson Education Canada, Ltd.
Pearson Educación de Mexico, S.A. de C.V.
Pearson Education—Japan
Pearson Education Malaysia, Pte. Ltd.

Library of Congress Control Number: 2013949086

Contents

Acknowledgments

When we met as professor and student more than ten years ago, there was an instant curiosity and affinity. Heather, as a design student pursuing an M.B.A., was not the norm in 1999. As an entrepreneur, Steve became intrigued by the design-thinking approach of inquiry in which problem finding, problem framing, solution criteria, and solution selecting cycle in an iterative process until the opportunity becomes more defined—this was a potential breakthrough in creating more rigor around the fuzzy front end of the entrepreneurial funnel. When Steve became President of Philadelphia University and was exposed to a broad spectrum of design disciplines and the related collaborative course experiments, the idea was born—to build an integrated college that formalized the teaching of innovation with design thinking at the core. In this book we attempt to share the insights we uncovered from the many advisors who guided us along this path. Here we attempt to thank them all because without them, neither the college nor this book would be possible.

Thank you to the faculty, staff, and students at Philadelphia University, notably Provost Randy Swearer and the entire provost office—Dr. Lloyd Russo, Maryellen Woltman, Lilly Krupsha, Mary Clare Venuto, Dr. Marilyn Roydhouse, and Gwynne Keathley. The college would not have evolved into the reality it is today without the DEC Leadership Team—Dean Ron Kandar, Dean Michael Leonard, Dean Susan Lehrman, Associate Dean of Graduate Studies Jack Klett, Assistant Dean Phillip Russel. Thank you to the brave and tenacious faculty that built the DEC core curriculum and the students who helped us and continue to help us shape and refine the curriculum, especially the faculty who led the launch of the first core course—Tod Corlett, Dr. Evan Goldman, Dr. Ron Kander, Gwynne Keathley, Dr. Barbara Kimmelman, Maribeth Kradel-Weitzel, Dr. Natalie Nixon, Dr. Christopher Pastore, and Leslie Samoni. Thank you to Pat Baldridge and her team in the PR office who were instrumental in telling our complex, interlocking 100,000-foot story with the invaluable guidance of Ed Sirianno and his agency, Creative Communication Associates.

Thank you to the donors who believed in us and supported the vision, notably Maurice Kanbar, Eileen Martinson, Bill Whitmore, Mo Meidar, Bill Finn, Walter Cohen, and many others.

Thank you to our speakers and advisory network, notably Mickey Ackerman, Ryan Armbruster, Dr. Banny Bannerjee, Dr. Sara Beckman, Dr. Lisa DiCarlo, Dr. Michael Fetters, Heather Fraser, Dr. Natalie Hanson, Kenneth Jewell, Saul Kaplan, Peter Lawrence, Roger Martin, Dr. Mark Schar, Nathan Shedroff, Helen Stringer, Jeffery To, Rachel Warren, and Dr. Harry West.

Special thank you to our fellows, Jeremy Bowes, Kipp Bradford, Lisa DiCarlo, Ellen di Resta, Dr. Nabil Harfoush, Yvonne Lin, Tara Marchionna, Erik Molander, and Sarah Rottenberg.

This book would not have become a reality without the team at Pearson, especially Jim Boyd, Amy Neidlinger, Betsy Gratner, and Russ Hall.

About the Authors

Stephen Spinelli, Jr., Ph.D., current President of Philadelphia University, led the university's strategic transformation. The university's capital campaign of over $50 million included a $20 million single gift to endow the Maurice Kanbar College of Design, Engineering, and Commerce. Dr. Spinelli previously held several leadership positions at Babson College and serves on a number of boards, including the Berwind Corporation, Nextworth, and Planet Fitness. Dr. Spinelli is actively engaged in the community, serving on the boards of the VNA of Pennsylvania, the Episcopal Academy, and the Science Center. Dr. Spinelli is a national expert and frequent speaker and consultant in the area of franchising. Steve received his Ph.D. in Economics from The Management School, Imperial College (London), his M.B.A. from Babson College, and his B.A. in Economics from McDaniel College. He began his professional life as a co-founder of Jiffy Lube.

Heather McGowan is an entrepreneurial strategy consultant who works in both corporate and academic environments to lead and communicate transformational change through crafting a vision of future state while identifying, assessing, and addressing challenges to realize the goal. At Philadelphia University she was charged with creating the strategy, architecting the curriculum, and developing the advisory network for the innovative Kanbar College of Design, Engineering, and Commerce (DEC), which won the 2012 Core 77 international competition for innovation in design education. Heather has advised senior management in several start-up companies in strategy, business modeling, and financing and has brought more than 25 products to market. Heather holds a B.F.A. in Industrial Design from Rhode Island School of Design and an M.B.A. in Entrepreneurship from Babson College.

About the Cover Designer

Maribeth Kradel-Weitzel has an M.F.A. from Tyler School of Art and a B.A. from the Pennsylvania State University. She is an Associate Professor of Graphic Design Communication at Philadelphia University and has lectured internationally about her interdisciplinary teaching techniques. She serves as coordinator for the Integrative Design Process course, an interdisciplinary, team-taught course required as part of the core sequence for all undergraduates in the Kanbar College of Design, Engineering, and Commerce. This core sequence received the top honor in Core 77's 2012 Professional Educational initiatives category. She is principal of the internationally award-winning firm Kradel Design, and is a former President of the Philadelphia chapter of AIGA.

Section 1
Foreword

Innovation comes from those who see things that others don't.

A lot has changed since I wrote *The Four Steps to Epiphany* just over a decade ago—a book about the Customer Development process and how it changes the way start-ups are built. *The Four Steps* drew the distinction that "start-ups are not smaller versions of large companies." It defined a start-up as a "temporary organization designed to search for a repeatable and scalable business model." Today its concepts of "minimum viable product," "iterate and pivot," "get out of the building," and "no business plan survives first contact with customers" have become part of the entrepreneurial lexicon. When I first conceived of these notions, I wanted to change the way start-ups were built, the way business models were tested, and the way customer feedback was integrated. Over the past three years our Lean LaunchPad/NSF Innovation Corps classes have been teaching hundreds of entrepreneurial teams a year how to build their start-ups by getting out of the building and testing their hypotheses behind their business model. Through this body of work, I believe we have fundamentally advanced the process of crafting and refining business models.

In *Disrupt Together,* Steve Spinelli, Heather McGowan, and their team of experts dissect the customer development process by unpacking the customer-discovery and customer-validation phases with tools from the fields of design and ethnography. Most entrepreneurs begin with solving a problem better than anyone else. In this book, Spinelli and McGowan bring a team of experts from a broad range of fields such as ethnography, design, medicine, engineering, and business to show how finding the right problems to solve yields superior entrepreneurial insights—making for better ideas to bring through the start-up funnel. For example, ethnography offers methods to peek around corners and understand concepts like shifting cultural norms and the impact these dramatic shifts have on customer desires and expectations. Tools from the design fields offer means of better probing emerging opportunities spaces through culling insights from latent customer needs and desires. Design thinking also offers superior tools to prototype products, services, and experience for better customer validation. They dive deeper into understanding how interdisciplinary teams bring diverse learning styles offering multiplicative rather than additive impacts to the challenge at hand, often identifying, isolating, and addressing later-stage hurdles earlier in the process when the stakes are lower.

Full disclosure: Philadelphia University's current president, Stephen Spinelli, was one of my mentors in learning how to teach entrepreneurship. At Babson College he was chair of the Entrepreneurship department and built the school into one of the most innovative entrepreneurial programs in the U.S. In 2008 Steve became president of Philadelphia University. Steve, Heather, and their team have taken the approach articulated here in *Disrupt Together* to transform university education through a new model of professional undergraduate education based on instilling skills of interdisciplinary problem solving, innovation, and agility. In 2011 I was so moved by their vision and progress that I wrote a blog posting about called "College and Business Will Never Be the Same." This posting was so popular that Fast Company and Xconomy picked it up, and soon Pearson/The Financial Times came knocking—asking them to codify their vision and process with their advisors into a guidebook for both the academy and the corporation. Here, Spinelli and McGowan assemble a dream team of experts who offer sage insights into the process of opportunity recognition.

Steve Blank
Menlo Park, California
2013

1

What You Will Learn from This Book

Stephen Spinelli, Jr., Ph.D., current President of Philadelphia University, led the University's strategic transformation. The University's capital campaign included a $20 million single gift to endow the Maurice Kanbar College of Design, Engineering and Commerce. Dr. Spinelli previously held several leadership positions at Babson College and serves on a number of boards and in leadership roles for community, business, and professional associations. Dr. Spinelli received his Ph.D. in Economics from The Management School, Imperial College (London), his M.B.A. from Babson College, and his B.A. in Economics from McDaniel College. He began his professional life as a co-founder of Jiffy Lube.

Context

With insights from founding Jiffy Lube and through my 14 years of teaching experience at Babson College, I co-authored nine editions of the entrepreneurial guidebook *New Venture Creation,* which focuses on shaping opportunity, market entry, managing risk, enterprise growth, and harvest. In the past six years as President of Philadelphia University, I have been exposed to a broader set of disciplines, notably the design fields, which has dramatically shaped my thinking about the front end of the entrepreneurial process: opportunity recognition and opportunity development. Entrepreneurship and innovation have historically been taught through the lens of business education. From my experiences with this broader set of disciplines, notably design, engineering, and the social sciences such as ethnography, I have discovered that interdisciplinary collaboration, rooted in design thinking, yields superior opportunity recognition and opportunity development, thereby making for better ideas in the front end of the entrepreneurial funnel. At Philadelphia University, we were so convinced that this interdisciplinary or transdisciplinary perspective is the key to generating superior innovation that we reorganized the University from six traditional schools to three integrated colleges, with one of the colleges focused exclusively on formalizing a pedagogy that teaches disruptive innovation. The Maurice Kanbar College of Design, Engineering and Commerce (DEC) is named for the serial entrepreneur, tireless innovator, and PhilaU alumni Maurice Kanbar, who, among many accomplishments, both founded Skyy Vodka and invented the multiplex movie theater. In creating DEC, we assembled a broad international network of thought leaders in innovation, design thinking, disruption, and education. Part of this team assembled again here to create this book as a guide to disruptive innovation and teamwork. A companion guide to *New Venture Creation, Disrupt Together* refines the art and science of being innovative.

A Note on Integrated Teamwork: Cross-Disciplinary, Multidisciplinary, Interdisciplinary, and Transdisciplinary

Throughout the book, you will see the four terms used at times interchangeably because our authors each prefer a different term for various types of integrated teamwork. As a basic overview, we offer this explanation: Cross-disciplinary and multidisciplinary are both additive (2+5=7) and imply both a dependency across functions for performance and a cumulative impact from integration. Interdisciplinary and transdisciplinary both refer to the fuller integration of functions and as such are multiplicative (2×5=10), offering a transformative impact. In both interdisciplinary and transdisciplinary endeavors the whole becomes much more than the sum of its parts. This book offers examples, tools, frameworks, and tactics for all cross-disciplinary/multidisciplinary and interdisciplinary/transdisciplinary endeavors.

Inspirations for This Book

"Creative destruction"[1] is a concept of new and better replacing old and tired. The long-term benefits to this birth-and-death entrepreneurial process are substantial. But it is not a linear positive trend, and the pace of change appears to be causing heightened tumult. New behaviors clash with societal norms or political constructs. Economic cycles, notably the 2008 recession and the years of continued economic malaise that followed, punctuate the high-risk environment that might be the new normal. Therefore, we believe innovation becomes a required core competency for survival, let alone gain! Teams provide the breadth of perspectives, knowledge, and skills that is virtually impossible for the individual to achieve. Most important, the process of incremental improvement that historically builds economic success for individuals, organizations, and economies before "the new norm" won't win in today's environment. That process occurs too slowly. We believe that pacing imposes a requirement for wholly new solutions. Let me state simply that you know you are being innovative when your solutions outperform the normative techniques as measured by the stakeholders. When your solutions change ways of behavior for entire cultures, you are leading a revolution.

Let's look at the evolution of the "phone" as an example of the pace of change, as shown in Figure 1.1.

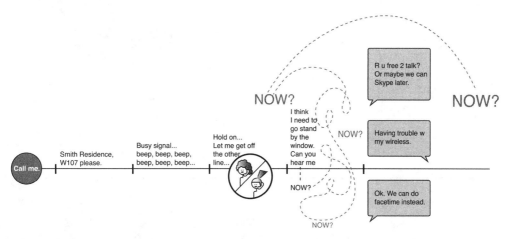

Figure 1.1 *The evolution of "call me."*

The evolution of human communication has been a shift from primarily face-to-face to a broad and deep array of intermediaries. The telephone remained basically the same for generations of users. Incremental advances like answering machines and call waiting made an impact for a few decades. Digital, mobile, and visual interfaces change communications every few years. All require more human time and technology investment and increasing costs. As our human involvement (we are our own tech support), cultural expectation (available 24/7), and technology complexity increase, so does our service provider engagement. Where we once had one phone in the home, and one phone company, we now have multiple devices, multiple accounts, and multiple cost layers. The blur among service provider, product, and technology requires a multidiscipline perspective.

This transformation blends and bends human interactions in terms of what's expected of us for engagement, value expectations as we expand our cost of living from a single phone line for connection to a mobile phone, ubiquitous Internet access for videoconferencing, technological self-reliance as we become our own technology support, and cultural expectations as we are available 24/7, as depicted in Figure 1.2.

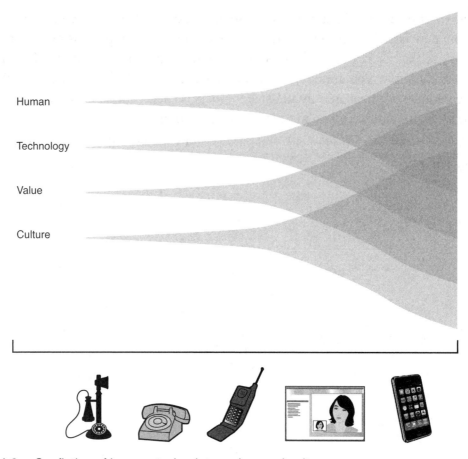

Figure 1.2 *Conflation of human, technology, value, and culture.*

This is where design thinking helps us understand a phenomenon like human communications and presents stepwise (versus incremental) changes. Design thinking is inherently multidisciplinary because it does not adhere to strict theoretical constraints typical of many disciplines. Design thinking asks "what if" questions across disciplinary boundaries and therefore often plays best at the nexus of those boundaries. That is why design thinking is the underpinning of the learning nexus of design, engineering, and commerce. We are fond of asking, "Is your solution desirable, feasible, and valuable?"

A powerful consequence of design thinking and a rapidly changing environment is that the customer becomes an intimate partner in the creation of the solution. For many consumer product experts this has been the Holy Grail for a very long time. Today, with the breakneck pace of change and the ability to share information among large groups and diverse domains, the customer literally becomes the co-innovator.

As we expand the players in the process of innovation, we also increase the magnitude of the problems we can solve. I can't stress enough that design thinking as a strategy spends as much time in the problem-finding domain as in the solutions domain. This time is spent iteratively, not sequentially: problem, solution, problem, solution. Stanford Associate Professor Pamela Hicks calls this "learn, return, and refine." This makes the team expert in the dynamic environment they are working. The classic version 2.0 is a natural phenomenon instead of a tedious incremental next edition that tries to get the first one right.[2]

Design thinking as a sophisticated opportunity recognition process is a game changer.

We conceived this book with the simple proposition that humanity seeks improvement as a natural phenomenon. Education can and should support those instincts. Indeed, the world is filled with imperfections that demand action. Ask a random group of people whether the world is perfect and we predict 100% agreement that it is not.

Therefore, we believe that a basic objective of education is to stimulate the individual to solve problems. The "average" person is reasonably equipped to deal with problems when presented. However, education seldom prepares people to critically assess the current condition and add value.

The value-creating possibilities of a better process, one that innovates as core competency, will result in an improvement in the successful launch and growth of businesses and a sustainable improvement in the human condition.

The authors assembled for this book are inspired believers in the capacity of collaborators to find problems and map solutions when they are prepared with pathways and insights. Because I have spent my entire professional life in entrepreneurship—as an entrepreneur, teaching entrepreneurship and advising start-up companies, and as an entrepreneurial (I hope) university president—my thinking always starts with the question "Is there an opportunity?" Critically, I've always worried that the conception of opportunity was too often random. I cannot count the number of times someone has said to me, "I have a good idea," and how infrequently it really was!

The book is organized into five sections and 16 chapters that begin with crafting the vision and strategic framing and move through to assessing your innovation capabilities and teaming issues to tools for innovation discovery and into shaping opportunity. The final section is a series of stories from the field that illustrate key aspects of disruptive innovation best told through example. Each section begins with an interview with one or more experts from the field that offer salient insights that frame the section's chapters. In this chapter I will share my experiences that led to the reorganization of Philadelphia University and walk you through how this book can help guide your organization for better opportunity recognition and disruptive innovation through teamwork.

Section 1: Architecting the Vision

In the first section of the book, we walk you through crafting a vision and strategic planning.

In too many organizations strategic planning has become a routine process of validating the current vision and direction. Entrepreneurship teaches us to first focus on the nature of the opportunity and then marshal the resources and team appropriate to exploiting that opportunity. Design thinking insists on understanding the environment to allow for optimal crafting of an opportunity by involving many perspectives for leveraged decision making. Bringing together the opportunity focus of entrepreneurship and the problem finding and solving of design thinking is a powerful strategic planning method.

It is during the strategic planning process that the cultural acceptance of interdisciplinary decision making takes root. In this section we see how the foundation for innovation is an intentionally designed dynamic phenomenon.

Organizational change is aligned with the dynamic nature of innovation. That is, for innovation to become manifest and create value, people and processes must adapt their behavior to the needs of the output desired.

In the diagram of strategic planning (see Figure 1.3) for the innovation organization, we begin with organizational involvement to understand and shape the mission through assessing the fits and gaps in capabilities. Many organizations are not structured to accept change and therefore have to change structure to induce new and desired behaviors. That new structure allows for people and processes to develop, evolve, and implement new and different output.

The result of output is, not surprisingly, called outcomes. A well-defined strategic planning process adds discipline to innovative behavior. That's why the Mission-Strategy-Critical Long-Term Initiatives are important. They set the metrics by which innovation can be measured. But, as you'll discover in this book, the effect of these outcomes might very well change, or influence, organizational behavior. I recommend you monitor behavior with a rigorous assessment that we call "action research." Often, myths and misunderstandings about mission and strategy are revealed in this process and can be addressed by leadership.

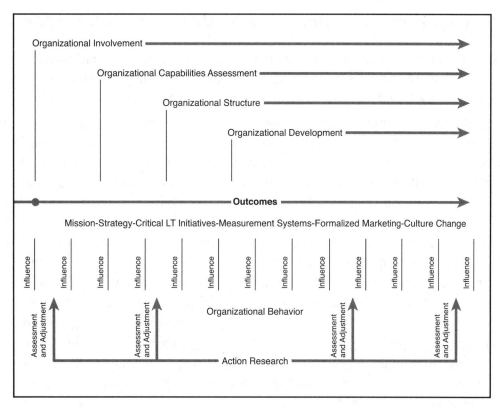

Figure 1.3 *Strategic planning model.*

Section 2: Assessment: Opportunity Recognition and You

This section begins with assessing your innovation capability, which covers types of innovation and understanding the underlying motivations of your team members and cognitive barriers to and lubricants for creativity. This section also covers learning styles, team formation, and managing conflict for gain.

Teams are groups of people assembled to achieve something an organization deems important. Often teams are created to perform tasks or solve problems. Sometimes teams are formed because it seems easier than placing the entire burden on an individual. Teams can be temporary or semipermanent. When transdisciplinary teams are intentionally created, there is an implied disruption of normative disciplinary thinking. We suggest that explicitly transcending your field of knowledge to learn from and leverage colleague perspectives can be explosive. Managing that tension is the key to your success, as Sarah Singer-Nourie points out in Chapter 6, "Your Team Dynamics and the Dynamics of Your Team."

Section 3: Opportunity Recognition: Discovery and Formulation

This section of the book covers the process of reading the landscape and anticipating key cultural shifts, employing design thinking for opportunity finding and development, and an overview of tools and techniques for discovery and probing customer development.

Opportunity is the nuclear center of the entrepreneurial process. It is motivated by innovation and is central to new venture creation. An idea can be a real opportunity if it improves the current solution by being a new, better, faster, or cheaper offering. As the creator of new ventures, a scholar, and a teacher of entrepreneurship, I have always been bothered by the Darwinian approach to opportunity recognition. "I have a good idea" tends to be the starting point of businesses. The idea often begins as a result of the aspiring entrepreneur having an experience that is less than fulfilling. The idea for improvement leads the entrepreneur to search for a business model that will launch, nurture, and sustain the idea. But success rates tend to be dismally small (as low as 9%) and failures personally devastating.[3] This Darwinian process is effective for survivors but not optimal. With design thinking as a process for ideating, shaping, and creating opportunities, we can do better, especially in the opportunity-scoping phase, as shown in Figure 1.4, where failure rates are the highest. In Chapter 8, "Design Process and Opportunity Development," Tod Corlett delves into application of design thinking as a key driver in better opportunity development.

In my entrepreneurship textbook I write about the "3M's"—market demand, market size and structure, and margin analysis—as defining characteristics of an opportunity. In this book you will find a close association of thoughts and practices that bring sophisticated methods to the understanding of the 3M's.

Design thinking is the integration of the teaming in a transdisciplinary approach to opportunity. It is a better way of developing and shaping ideas that create value. We can teach people to be intentionally observant to the surroundings and empathetic to the needs of a larger demographic. In Chapter 9, "Navigating Spaces—Tools for Discovery," Natalie Nixon offers a deep inventory of tools and tactics for this type of probing for discovery. Honed observational and analytical skills enable the innovators to iteratively assess interactions and map the intent and result of the ecosystem being analyzed. By creating this map of understanding, you can observe whether the intended outcomes are achieved and begin to shape better solutions. Opportunity can emerge in a set of changes or in entirely new systems.

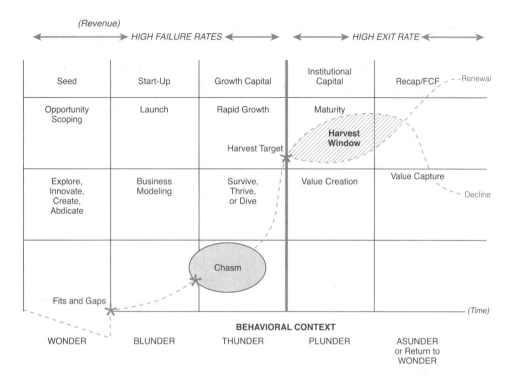

Figure 1.4 *Capital markets context.*

Why Design Thinking Is a Strategy for Creating Value

Increasing rates of technological change, rise in globalization, increasing economic pressures, and environmental concerns create shifting cultural norms, as Sarah Rottenberg points out in Chapter 7, "Leveraging Ethnography to Predict Shifting Cultural Norms." These shifting norms are ripe for disruptive innovation, and design thinking is a unique approach to sense making in this ambiguity and chaos.

The twenty-first century has introduced rates of socioeconomic change that are new to the world. This exponentially increases the need for new and better solutions, which require different approaches. As people increasingly rely on Google and Wikipedia, their engagement creates a valuable digital exhaust.

"Until recently, big data made for interesting anecdotes, but now it has become a major source of new knowledge. Google is better than the Centers for Disease Control at identifying flu outbreaks. Google monitors billions of search terms ("best cough medicine," for example) and adds location details to track outbreaks. When Walmart analyzed correlations using its customer data and weather, it found that before storms, people buy more flashlights but also more Pop-Tarts, even though marketers can't establish a causal relationship between weather and toaster pastries. Wikipedia has been proven to be as accurate as, if not more accurate than, the previous standard, Encyclopédia Britannica.

Design thinking is a methodology that is uniquely qualified to navigate through the ambiguity brought by these shifting cultural norms to find new meaning and new opportunity.

Section 4: Value Creation: Opportunity Shaping

To effectively disrupt the status quo, a transdisciplinary team must have a vehicle to transport their idea to people, markets, and communities. This section covers the entrepreneurial process of shaping that framed opportunity into a sustainable business model and includes execution issues such as pivoting. Attention to shaping an opportunity and business model can have a dramatic effect on business survival rates.

Design Thinking and Entrepreneurship

Opportunity recognition is the nuclear core of the entrepreneurial process. As an entrepreneur and entrepreneurship educator for 35 years, I have been vexed by the randomness of the ideas that are seen as opportunities and ultimately the very few that create value. Part of the problem is the way we teach in general and the specific lack of attention to teaching opportunity recognition.

Colleges and universities are typically organized around disciplines like economics or art or history. Innovation crosses disciplinary boundaries, and therefore scarce few colleges and universities have established curricula that teach it. Domain boundaries do not support collaborative education. Although a significant effort for interdisciplinary education has been made in the establishment of entrepreneurship curriculum, the fact that they are primarily in business schools limits the boundaries that can be crossed. Also, colleges tend to teach entrepreneurship as an implementation process more than ideation. The effect is to spend far less time building opportunity recognition skills. Less well-developed ideas search for a business model, risking resources along the way.

We believe that the new paradigm for organizations is pervasive innovation, and it is an approach that can be taught (see Figure 1.5). The traditional perspectives remain an important skill set. But the new perspectives are required cultural competencies.

New Organizational Paradigm
Innovative thinking and action throughout all organizations

Traditional		New
• Resource allocation model	→	Opportunity-driven model
• General management	→	Entrepreneurial leadership
• Cost-oriented	→	Growth-oriented
• Embraces stability	→	Embraces innovation
• Bound by resources	→	Framed by creativity
• Local focus	→	Global perspective

Figure 1.5 *New organizational paradigm.*

Section 5: Putting It into Practice: Stories from the Field

This section of the book offers some intriguing true stories about interdisciplinarity and disruptive innovation, from branding to designing products and services for women, to technology adoption in healthcare, to launching disruptive innovation business models from within established companies.

Examples from Philadelphia University

As a lifelong entrepreneur and entrepreneurial educator, I have seen my share of real-world projects, largely rooted in business. My role as president at Philadelphia University affords me a view across a broader set of disciplines, notably those working in interdisciplinary projects, that yields an interesting set of examples of the power of collaboration and disruptive innovation even at the student level.

Following are three recent examples of industry "problems" that were solved by transdisciplinary teams of students. Fortune 500 firms presented the assignments to students in the broadest form, and teams were given great latitude in their responses.

DuPont: "Define beauty."

Armstrong: "Think vertically."

Federal Mogul: "Make a mother's life better."

Define Beauty

DuPont dominated the kitchen countertop market for many years with their Corian product. As markets and tastes changed, instead of yielding to competitors they began to innovate, embracing design thinking and the educational system. In a one-week "Sprint" competition students conceived of and prototyped a dozen new uses of Corian. Through discussions with customers and DuPont executives, the teams believed they needed to connect to customers through an aesthetic lens before considering the practical. The teams consistently heard customers talk first about beauty before any other issue such as utility and cost. The teams constantly probed for the connection of beauty in the new products students were designing. The discourse continued with each product feature and characteristic. There were dozens of iterations during the week yet the pace didn't seem frenzied. During the final presentation of the concept prototypes to a team of DuPont management, Philadelphia University faculty, and potential customers, the judging panelists asked as many questions about the process as they did about the final output. Several innovations went on to the next steps in commercialization.

Think Vertically

Armstrong World Industries, Inc.,[4] is a global leader in the design and manufacture of floors and ceilings. In 2012, Armstrong's consolidated net sales totaled approximately $2.6 billion. Based in Lancaster, Pennsylvania, Armstrong operates 32 plants in eight countries and has approximately 8,500 employees worldwide. Armstrong ceiling tiles are a ubiquitous presence in architecture, construction, and the built environment.

In this project students had six weeks to investigate spaces and people that could benefit from a vertical spacing interface. They had to conceive of an improvement of a space using a "vertical perspective," create drawings, make a prototype, and estimate the potential market. Armstrong has been in the tile business in one fashion or another for more than 150 years. Virtually everyone in the U.S. has experienced the horizontal Armstrong ceiling. The mental model of an Armstrong tile is a drop ceiling. Breakthrough thinking could occur only if the old perceptions were abandoned.

Transdisciplinary student teams argued intensely about the potential for vertically improving space. Each argument seemed to break down another preconception. When the silos are removed, a new palate is formed. We found that when team members transcend their own disciplinary understandings, the team achieves breakthrough innovation. We found that statements or questions that imposed definitive strictures blocked creative solutions. "It must" as a beginning of a sentence typically meant the team member was imposing his or her disciplinary perspective on the solution. It is the death knell of new ideas.

In the Armstrong example our methodology of team interviews in a broad ethnographic perspective triggered innovation that transcended individual disciplines.

Make a Mother's Life Better

Our third example required the students to "make a mother's life better." This was the most interesting challenge because of the historical perspective of the company presenting the project and the experience of the teams accepting it.

Federal-Mogul Corporation is an innovative and diversified $6.7 billion global supplier of quality products, brands, and creative solutions to manufacturers of automotive, light commercial, heavy-duty, and off-highway vehicles, as well as in power generation, aerospace, marine, rail, and industrial. That's right. They are a supplier to industry. Their brief was a message to us—and to themselves—that innovation was a cultural requirement that stretched their organization beyond their traditional markets and focused on the needs of customers. The leadership of the company was impressing on both students and management that Federal-Mogul's culture of innovation has to be constantly renewed. None of our students was a parent. The issues presented by motherhood are so vast and complex that I thought, "They'll never get this one right."

I was wrong.

The students met with young and old mothers, single and married mothers, poor mothers and rich mothers. They went to cities and suburbs, racially diverse neighborhoods, and ethnically rigid communities. A disciplined approach to "talking with customers" is integral to the design process and becomes a distinct competitive advantage in creating valuable innovation. The students proudly delivered their answer. The clear and unequivocal problem was...a lack of sleep.

Federal-Mogul has deep expertise in materials science and an intimate understanding of lightweight materials. The team conceived of a wall that was thin and lightweight but virtually soundproof. Noise external to the baby's room would be greatly muffled. Because the wall was thin and lightweight, a fiber-optic wire was easily threaded through the wall for a video and audio monitor inside the baby's room. The baby would sleep better and the mother would sleep better. The solution is patent pending.

How were teams of undergraduate students able to define the opportunities, map solutions, and recommend a pathway to success?

The Disruptive Innovation Approach

We believe that the answer is simple but not easy to implement or master.

Interdisciplinary teams trained as design thinkers to look for problems and iteratively map solutions innovate more efficiently, effectively, and consistently than any individual or organizational construct. The effect is a higher probability of success in the context of a new or improved product or service in an existing organization or a newly created one. In essence, this process is designed to elevate the probabilities of success through improved opportunity recognition. The vehicles for taking that opportunity to the marketplace are not constrained to new or existing ventures. Both forms will have higher rates of success.

In this book, we offer insights into collaboration, teamwork, and disruptive innovation, including navigating ambiguity, applying design process, leveraging learning styles in innovation, managing creative conflict for gain, the process of discovery, opportunity shaping, business model formation, and execution—including execution tools such as the pivot. We offer a series of case studies from branding to healthcare to illustrate our viewpoints in action.

Endnotes

1. Joseph Schumpeter, *Capitalism, Socialism, and Democracy* (1942).
2. Thanks to former Governor Craig Benson of New Hampshire and co-founder of Cabletron for this thinking.
3. http://sbaer.uca.edu/research/asbe/2004/PDFS/23.pdf.
4. Armstrong markets the most extensive portfolio of residential and commercial floor products available—hardwood, laminate, linoleum, vinyl sheet and tile, ceramic, and BioBased Tile—under the brand names Armstrong, Bruce, and Robbins. The company's global acoustical ceiling and suspension systems business is 90% commercial—offices, healthcare, education, retail, transportation, and other segments—and 10% residential.

2

Becoming a Strategic Organization

"Adventure is just bad planning"
Roald Amundsen, Antarctic Explorer

"I may not have proved a great explorer,
but we have done the greatest march
ever made and come very near to great success."
Robert Falcon Scott, Antarctic Explorer

Dr. Geoffrey Cromarty, Ed.D., is Vice President and Chief Operating Officer at Philadelphia University, where he has also served as Vice President of Planning and Institutional Research, Interim Dean of the School of Design and Engineering, and Executive Assistant to the President. At Philadelphia University, Cromarty led the University's first strategic planning effort as well as the University's master plan, landscape plan, and capital plans. He has worked at the University of Pennsylvania, Drew University, and the State of New Jersey. He has earned the Ed.D. and M.G.A. from the University of Pennsylvania and the B.A. from Western New England University.

Until 1911, the South Pole was still one of the last explored places on earth. The dramatic race to the pole ended on December 14, 1911, when a Norwegian explorer, Roald Amundsen, accomplished the goal, one month ahead of fabled British voyager Robert Falcon Scott, who died on his journey back, just 11 miles from his base camp. Amundsen's success is not only one of endurance, but, most significant, one of intentional strategy and planning.[1] Though Amundsen did not announce his intention to reach the pole until 1908, he began preparing and planning for the journey nearly a decade earlier, in 1899. Scott's failure, however well-planned his attempt had been, was the result of poor implementation and the "Fallacy of Detachment."[2] Scott did not fully understand the environment and therefore failed to develop a plan that would enable him to succeed (or, in this case, live).

Becoming a successful, strategic organization, like polar exploration, also requires the strength and discipline to foray into areas outside comfort zones while respecting and understanding the environment, including history and competencies. Transformational success, however, takes place when the strategic plan supports the mission, it is intentional and flexible, and implementation is adaptable. Preparation, execution, and the ability to adapt have a critical impact on success and achievement.

Telling Stories

We learn best through stories. Storytelling is not a reliable strategy for transferring skills, but it is effective in sharing information that cognitive scientists say will be more memorable—and therefore more effective.[3] In this chapter, our approach will be to use the Philadelphia University story as a tool for any organization to use in developing, refining, or improving their process—through either planning or implementation—to become a strategic organization.

A Model for Planning: Philadelphia University

Philadelphia University's emergence as a strategic organization was born of necessity, change, and market demand. Higher education accreditation standards necessitated a strategic plan.

The reason for change was simple: a change in University leadership after the retirement of a longstanding president and the selection of a businessman/scholar who was committed to transforming an institution. He made it clear that strategic planning would be his first priority, and he wanted a plan that would honor the University's past but propel it into greatness. Managing strategy, in higher education, government, or business, keeps the organization focused on key objectives and working toward their achievement, particularly in environments (most) with scarce resources. Leveraging resources toward strategic goals enhances the bottom line, whether it is education, services, or shareholder profit. It is critical, therefore, to develop a strategic plan that is supported and supportable.

Philadelphia University's Planning Culture

Until that transition in 2007, Philadelphia University had thrived without a strategic plan. Created in 1884 as Philadelphia Textile School to educate America's textile workers and managers, the College developed into a comprehensive university, granting bachelor's and master's degrees in professional fields, preparing professionals to be leaders in their chosen fields. It enjoyed demand for its diverse offerings, even in the crowded Philadelphia higher education marketplace; it had not needed a strategy to succeed.

For decades, planning at Philadelphia University meant facilities master planning. Campus facilities are important to traditional undergraduate students; the competition to develop better facilities has created an arms race among competing colleges and universities. The successful Disney organization sells experience through its theme parks, much the same way in which higher education sells education; facilities are a key component in delivering on the brand, though not necessarily the primary driver for consumer decision making.

The University had developed a series of increasingly sophisticated facilities plans to address pressing infrastructure needs. A handful, but representative group, of campus leaders organized the planning efforts. This planning history is common in higher education: In 1965, the Society of College and University Planners originally had primary interest in physical and facilities master plans.[4] Integration of higher educational planning, to include budgeting and assessment, followed through the decades, becoming a requirement for college and university by accrediting bodies early in the twenty-first century. Likewise, corporate strategic planning, adopted from military planning, did not become prevalent until after World War II.

Toward the end of the long-standing president's tenure in 2007, Philadelphia University began overtures toward a strategic plan by revising its mission statement[5] through an informal process that allowed widespread input, but maintained control with the senior leadership. The president said, "It is healthy and constructive for any forward-thinking institution to revisit its mission statement, particularly as a tool for developing strategic, institutional goals." The president invited comments from the campus community to get its feedback. The president then shared a draft with the campus and invited final input. The only comments were stylistic.

The campus community reaffirmed the mission: It remained unabashedly committed to preparing students for careers. The revised mission statement provided flexibility to grow, yet remained true to the University's history and tradition. "In short," the president said, "I believe this mission statement provides us with the tools to plan for student success."

The commercial world offers many similar examples.

IBM was once International Business Machines:

- "I think there is a world market for maybe five computers." (Thomas Watson, chairman of IBM, 1943)

- "IBM dreams of a computer in every home and every classroom." (1974)
- IBM sells personal computer business to Lenovo, 2005.

Each statement was strategically sound in its time. IBM survived and even grew because it was willing to reexamine assumptions, question conclusions, and nimbly pivot to meet market needs.

IBM's mission statement:

At IBM we strive to lead in the invention, development, and manufacture of the industry's most advanced information technologies, including computer systems, software, storage systems, and microelectronics. We translate these technologies into value for our customers through our professional solutions and services and consulting businesses worldwide.

Google's more succinct mission statement:

To make the world's information universally accessible and useful.

In 2007, Apple dropped the word "Computer" from its name and became "Apple, Inc." With a portfolio that spanned software, retail, online distribution of electronic media, home entertainment, cellphones, and computers, the name change was a subtle but clear signal that Apple would continue its relentless move into the wider field of consumer electronics.

An organization that is mission-driven is better prepared for change than one motivated by transactions.

Core Competencies

The Board of Trustees of Philadelphia University selected a new president in June. On his first day as the new president in September 2007, he immediately made the adoption of a strategic plan his top priority.

Developing a planning process for an institution that had no experience in strategic planning presented a challenge, yet it proved liberating because the University community had no tradition or allegiance to any planning process. The President's Council explored step-by-step models,[6] consulted with peer institutions, and researched planning methods to find a process that would create an implementable, measurable, and meaningful strategic plan. The new president, who spent more than a decade running a successfully franchised business, and another 14 years teaching entrepreneurship, brought discipline, expectations, and a demand for accountability to the process; however, he wanted the plan to be aspirational. Senior leadership adopted a vision for the plan: Create the model for professional university education in the twenty-first century. That bold statement guided all planning efforts.

Evolution of the Vision

The University established the vision "Developing a new model for the professional university of the twenty-first century" to guide it through the strategic planning process. By the adoption of the plan, the phrase evolved to "Philadelphia University will be the model for professional university education in the twenty-first century" to be more aspirational, and to emphasize the importance of education.

As the University implemented the plan and witnessed its success, the language changed again to mark that success: "Philadelphia University *is* a model for professional university education in the twenty-first century."

The President's Council identified three strategic areas on which a university-wide planning committee would focus—and created committees that would develop plans to support them:

1. Academic excellence
2. Excellence in the student experience
3. Alumni and community engagement

In essence, Philadelphia University was defining the required "core competencies" of the organization. C. K. Prahalad and Gary Hamel, in 1994 in their article "The Core Competence of the Corporation," asked readers to think of a diversified organization as a tree: the trunk and major limbs as core products, smaller branches as business units, leaves and fruit as end products. Nourishing and stabilizing everything is the root system: core competencies.

To make the process transparent, the president invited the campus to volunteer or nominate someone to serve on a committee. Engaged stakeholders created a system of checks and balances and support; this approach also avoided the perception of a top-down plan from the new president. The Board provided input throughout the process. The planning structure was important. Broad participation can become endless debate. Input is good but decision making is essential. Representation, findings, and focus were channeled to a decision-making body.

The President's Council worked with the chairs to identify the Strategic Planning Committee membership; it was a process intended to achieve balance and fairness—to ensure institutional perspective. Each of the committees had the responsibility to establish subcommittees based on the critical areas they identified. There were no constraints, but only the mandate, "Think big." A Strategic planning website carried updates on the progress and substance of the planning process. Each committee approached its task differently: The Chairs managed the committees around their organizational and leadership strengths, not by a process dictated by success at other universities. A mission supported by core competencies was the common platform for planning. Committees were encouraged to be entrepreneurial.

Know Your Strengths

The University invited external academic consultants to initiate and guide the process. The president did not attend: "Presidents have a way of repressing the flow of ideas in the kind of setting [the consultants] have designed."

The University developed a hybrid approach to traditional strengths, weaknesses, opportunities, and threats (SWOT) analysis. At a retreat to begin the process, the consultants provided an overview of the state of higher education (opportunities and threats), and invited the attendees to begin thinking broadly about strategic issues. They asked for adjectives to describe the University (strengths and weaknesses), generated themes around the vision, and surveyed participants on "the University—the way we see it" and "the University—as it should be." This exercise provided valuable data about perceptions and expectations. The participants developed themes that would guide the process. Importantly, the University conducted the "as is, should be" survey every other year for six years.

Integration

In developing initiatives, the committees first asked how the strategic goals would define the Philadelphia University experience. They considered the physical, financial, fundraising, technological, and human resources needed to implement the plan; they also looked for ways to integrate the objectives with those of other committees and developed initiatives that can be measured. In essence, the University was creating a business model.

The subcommittees presented ideas from their deliberations to the relevant committee; the committee prioritized initiatives. Members of the three committees discussed these initiatives with the Executive Committee, which identified major themes for the committees to explore further and to integrate with other committees, as articulated in

Figure 2.1. Critical to this process were the double-sided arrows, which mandated communication and integration by all the committees. Chairs and committee members evaluated initiatives from subcommittees looking for commonality and institutional priority.

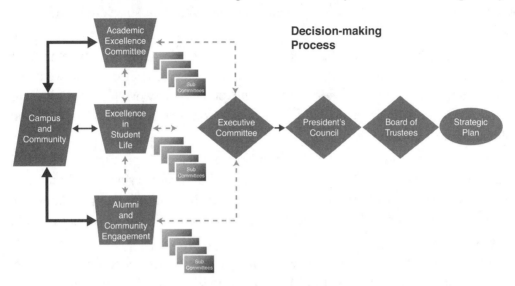

Figure 2.1 *Philadelphia University strategic planning process.*

The president allowed the process to evolve. He was a lively participant in Executive Committee meetings, pressing the Committee Chairs to bring initiatives that did not just improve the status quo but would differentiate the University—"add value"—and make the University the model for professional education in the twenty-first century. It was essential to make the University stretch; it was critical to honor the University's history and strengths.

The subcommittees continued refining their goals with the guidance of the committees, while the Executive Committee directed the committees to work together closely to develop a far-reaching strategy. With a June Board of Trustees meeting scheduled to consider a draft of the strategic plan, the University scheduled a retreat to review the initiatives that had emerged so far.

Two of the themes that presented themselves at the January retreat—"signature" learning and interdisciplinary program opportunities—again rose to prominence at the retreat, to surprise and satisfaction.

The draft plan translated the concept of interdisciplinary learning to a practical "new" concept: the creation of the College of Business, Engineering, and Design—three schools together. One attendee, who had been skeptical about the process, believing there would be a top-down edict from a new, autocratic president, threw up her hands at the proposal. She finally had proof; the idea was a complete surprise to her and reflected nothing that she had heard in her committee.

A 41-year member of the faculty, who had seen more change at the University than anyone at the retreat, corrected the objector. She said that she had been collaborating with faculty from other schools her entire career. This proposal, she said, reflected the best, most active collaborations on campus and what industry sought in hiring employees.

The concept had support; the debate that followed focused not on whether it should be done, but on whether it would require an "über" dean to lead it. In the weeks ahead, University planners further developed the conceptual framework for what ultimately became the College of Design, Engineering, and Commerce, officially spawning the formalization of innovation.

The president shared with the Board of Trustees the draft plan in June 2008. The Board endorsed the concept of the College of Design, Engineering, and Commerce. Many were business leaders who saw the long-term benefit to job opportunities, growth, and innovation from people who could understand the realities of working in and among disciplines.

Throughout the summer, refinement of the initiatives continued; the Executive Committee drafted the plan for Board consideration in a meeting specially scheduled to adopt the University's first strategic plan. The Board unanimously approved the historic document on October 2, 2008.

Absent from the initiatives are the kinds of insular plans of other, less strategic, plans, in which internal stakeholder interests are often included. Although those interests were well represented in the planning process, they were incorporated into the concepts that took shape into the broader university strategy. With so much involvement and communication in the planning process, it was clear to community members how initiatives that individuals proposed became incorporated into broader strategies.

Implementation Begins on Day One

The president used the adoption of the strategic plan as the platform for his inaugural address, which the University intentionally delayed for a year in the interest of preparing the strategic plan. Exhausted after a five-day celebration, the president welcomed the campus community on Monday morning with an e-mail, exhorting faculty and staff to begin implementing the strategic plan. The president called on his senior leadership team to develop a detailed implementation plan. He asked for a plan that would include champions, timelines, and measures of success. He asked that the document be made public and progress be reported quarterly to the Board. The objective was to transform planning into action.

Becoming a Strategic Organization

The planning, research, integration, communication, and structure of the strategic planning process created—and can create—a disciplined culture focused on goals and committed to achieving them, as depicted in Figure 2.2. The University leadership continued to show its resolve by taking actions to support the initiatives:

- Developed a budget process that rewarded new initiatives and encouraged reallocating funds in support of strategic plan initiatives, particularly those that resulted in collaboration among disciplines. To further support the process, the university created a budget advisory committee with university-wide representation that advised the CFO on budget priorities and communicated to university constituents.

- Began a process of "action research," using tools from the first strategic planning retreat to monitor community perceptions about the University's success in implementing the plan. Critical to this process was the action university leadership took in addressing the opportunities revealed in the data: When, for instance, the data suggested a lack of progress in advancing applied research, the president and others made personnel and funding changes to support the initiative. This process continued to keep the university focused on its core competencies and direction; the data provided valuable market data that enabled the university to respond.

- Initiated a comprehensive fundraising campaign to support the strategic plan. The strategic plan created the "case" for seeking outside investors/donors and further refined the narrative for communicating the message of the strategic plan; again, the fundraising campaign provided an opportunity for the university to tell its story in a memorable way. As a result, donors exceeded the ambitious goals of the campaign well ahead of schedule.

- Communicated frequently. By distributing laminated cards with the strategic initiatives, posters, and intentional, frequent formal and informal communications, leadership enabled the university community to understand the strategic plan and the direction of the university. Soon after the adoption of the strategic plan, one faculty member proposed a new academic program at a meeting of the faculty, making a strong case for support of the program with language in the strategic plan. Language is a powerful tool in shaping a culture and achieving success.

- Continued planning and implementing. By measurable, objective measures, the university had accomplished many of the goals in the strategic plan. Continuing to monitor progress and the external market, campus leaders developed a deeper understanding of where the overall strategy still needed support. The strategy was still critical; over five years of implementation, and with changing external market conditions, the tactics changed. The University developed a "Strategic Build" to continue with the strategy, but to pivot implementation in ways that would support the strategy better. Again, the University created a plan and funding priorities to support the initiatives of the Strategic Build, closing the circular process of renewal and growth.

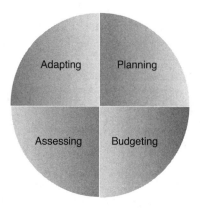

Figure 2.2 *Success and growth require all parts working together.*

Philadelphia University's success in becoming a strategic organization is the result of hard work, discipline, and support, not by a few but by the organization. An organization can have success by knowing its strengths, developing an aspirational vision, gaining commitment to it, continually assessing the plan, supporting the plan with the budget, and changing the plan when conditions require.

Recommendations

Becoming a strategic organization requires an agile and nimble mindset, constant assessment and adjustment, and frequent refinements as conditions, inevitably, change. Specifically we recommend the following:

- Define what is important, possible, and consistent with your mission and vision. Be aspirational and intentional, but be honest and realistic.
- Allow input and delegate decision making; it builds consensus, ownership, and accountability—and results in success.
- Ensure open and constant communication; a well-informed community will be a supportive advocate.
- Test all assumptions: Ask, "So what?" when developing the plan. Ask, "So what else?" when implementing the plan. Assumptions must be translated into measurable goals in order to have an impact on success.
- Be prescriptive, but flexible: adapt the plan instead of forcing the goals, especially if they will not work; know your market and audience.

Endnotes

1. Roland Huntford, *The Last Place on Earth* (Random House Digital, Inc., 2007).

2. Henry Mintzberg. *Rise and Fall of Strategic Planning* (SimonandSchuster.com, 1994).

3. Walter C. Swap, Dorothy A. Leonard, Mary Shields, and Lisa Abrams, "Using Mentoring and Storytelling to Transfer Knowledge in the Workplace," *Journal of Management Information Systems* 18, no. 1 (2001).

4. Jeffrey Holmes, *20/20 Planning* (Ann Arbor: Society for College and University Planning, 1985).

5. M. F. Middaugh, *Planning and Assessment in Higher Education: Demonstrating Institutional Effectiveness* (San Francisco: Jossey-Bass Publishers, 2009).

6. Michael G. Dolence, Daniel J. Rowley, and Herman D. Lujan, *Working Toward Strategic Change: A Step-by-Step Guide to the Planning Process* (San Francisco: Jossey-Bass Publishers, 1997).

3

Framing the Vision for Engagement

Photo credit: Linda Davis.

Heather McGowan is an entrepreneurial strategy consultant who works in both corporate and academic environments. At Philadelphia University she was charged with creating the strategy, architecting the curriculum, and developing the advisory network for the innovative Kanbar College of Design, Engineering and Commerce (DEC), which won the 2012 Core 77 international competition for innovation in design education. Heather has advised senior management in several start-up companies in strategy, business modeling, and financing and has brought more than 25 products to market. Heather holds a B.F.A. in Industrial Design from Rhode Island School of Design and an M.B.A. in Entrepreneurship from Babson College.

Introduction

Strategy is not planning—it is the making of an integrated set of choices that collectively position the firm in its industry so as to create sustainable advantage relative to competition and deliver superior financial returns.[1]
—Roger Martin

You have been handed a strategic directive; now what? How do you take the statement and make it actionable for the enterprise? How do you engage the talent that your organization comprises to "collectively position the firm," whether it is an academic institution, a nonprofit service organization, or a corporate entity? In this chapter we offer the example of the forming of the Maurice Kanbar College of Design, Engineering and Commerce (DEC) at Philadelphia University to articulate a process for taking a strategic initiative and framing a vision to engage your talent to achieve the directive. The process followed a nonlinear, iterative sequence of discover, formulate, develop, and optimize phases, as articulated in Figures 3.1[2] and 3.2. When the directive can be explicitly stated as an actionable vision, the value creation phases of develop and optimize ensue, offering problem solutions and value creation. This innovation process framework serves as the touchstone for this chapter.

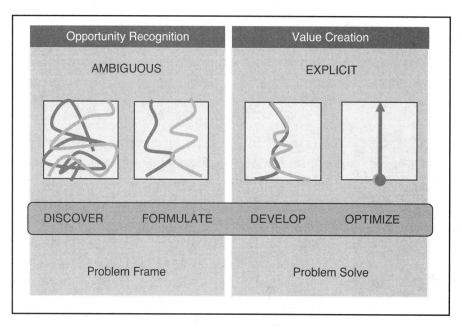

Figure 3.1 *Innovation process framework: The process from opportunity recognition to value creation includes periods of ambiguity with divergent and convergent perspectives in phases of discover and formulate. The opportunity becomes more explicitly understood in the phases of develop and optimize. This process framework will be used throughout the chapter.*

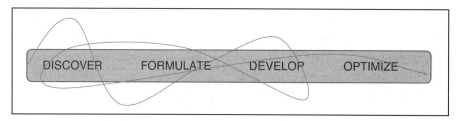

Figure 3.2 *Innovation process phases: Although depicted in a sequence of phases, the process is iterative and often requires divergence and backtracking to check assumptions before advancing to the next phase.*

Although this process is from the example of building an integrated college at a university, similar processes have been employed at both nonprofit and for-profit entities in start-up, turnaround, and growth settings. This is clearly a process for change applicable beyond the academy.

Market Conditions in Industry and Academia 2008 and Beyond

With the increasing rate of change from globalization and related natural resource scarcity coupled with rapid technology innovations, career domains began to span greater professional breadths with increasingly transient boundaries. The term VUCA (volatile, uncertain, complex, and ambiguous), which has origins in the military in the 1990s, became an emerging concept in strategy in industries from consumer products to healthcare to education. As a result, increasingly companies call for employees that are T-Shaped Thinkers with hybrid skills that have great depth in an area of expertise while maintaining profound breadth in understanding the connections, gaps, and interstitials among their expertise and coordinating functions in the value chain or customer experience. The days of the single career trajectory comprised exclusively of discipline expertise are over.

In 2008, design thinking was a well-established concept in design and business circles, thanks to the strides made by thought leaders from IDEO CEO Tim Brown, and *NY Times* best-selling author and Rotman School of Management Dean Roger Martin. As it became clear that economic growth from operational efficiencies, consolidating functions, and outsourced inexpensive labor was nearing an end, leaders focused more on innovation. This notion is illustrated by the example of the transformation of the consumer product giant, Proctor & Gamble. Under the leadership of CEO A.G. Lafley, the company launched its Connect + Develop, Open Innovation strategy, which leverages internal and external ideas and capabilities to expand the core competencies of the enterprise into new brands, new customers, and new offerings. This resulted in doubling of sales, more than doubling of the number of billion-dollar brands in their portfolio, and doubling of the company's market capitalization in under a decade—all in the shadow of the dot.com bubble.

In global university education, collaborative courses, particularly those that linked design to business and design to engineering, many of which were 10 to 20 years in existence, increased in demand and focus. Most substantial collaborative courses and in some cases collaborative degree programs occurred at the graduate level because many educators believed that the student must possess a strong disciplinary viewpoint before inter- or cross-disciplinary collaboration was possible.

This all suggested the need for an immediate transformative shift in professional education. The Philadelphia University Strategic Planning process suggested the formation of an integrated, undergraduate college linking programs in design, engineering, and business with the goal of formalizing education in innovation. To be clear, focus here was on rethinking content and pedagogy first as opposed to optimizing the delivery system.

The focus was to educate students to work collaboratively to probe the gaps and overlaps among disciplines; these are the key skills of the future necessary for successful leadership in the VUCA world.

Due to decades of opportunistic growth, the university was organized in six separate and, to some degree, disconnected schools. Collectively, there were 18 undergraduate programs, and half the undergraduate enrollment, to be integrated into this new college, as depicted in Figure 3.3, which shows the organizational structure in 2008. It is not uncommon when crafting a new directive from a strategic plan to require a new organization structure to realize that directive most efficiently. We expected that creation of a single integrated college among three remaining schools would spur the reorganization of the entire university into integrated colleges, but we did not lead with this reorganization. As we strove to create an organizational structure born from informed need, we began with engaging the stakeholders in crafting the vision through the phases of discover and formulate. We planned to roll out the new organizational structure, with new leadership, for the value creation phases of develop and optimize where it would be most useful. Upon embarking on the ambiguous phase of discovery, we understood that the notion intrigued some, and we also were informed that it scared some, and even angered a few stakeholders resistant to change. No one really knew what the creation of an integrated college focused on innovation meant. Fears included the closing of schools and programs, and the abolishment of majors. In 2008, the current provost was departing and the deans of all three schools were new or interim; in the end, they all departed within 18 months. So we had a big idea, ambiguity, a lot of confusion, and considerable leadership changes. Where to begin?

In this book, throughout the chapters by our various experts, we address all phases from discovery to optimization with an emphasis on the importance of problem framing and the impact of design thinking in opportunity recognition, all of which is reliant on the power of interdisciplinary collaboration for disruptive innovation.

Although the example from this chapter is about the creation of an integrated college at a university, the process, insights, and recommendations have direct applicability to organizational change at any organization.

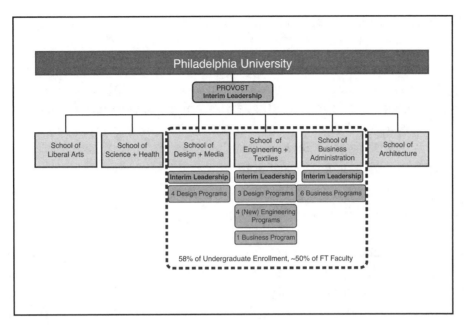

Figure 3.3 *Philadelphia University organizational structure 2008: The structure was one of six schools focused on silo program delivery. A new organizational structure and leadership team were needed to realize the strategic vision.*

Discover

If you always do what you always did, you will always get what you always got.
—Albert Einstein

As Einstein's summation suggests, to get different results, you need different processes and approaches. The discovery phase begins with an assessment of where you are. In this assessment, understanding language differences, the range of expectations, your capability fits and gaps, and the various mental models for your stated objectives is essential.

Starting Point—Snapshot of Philadelphia University 2008

Using the framework from Figure 3.1, we understood we needed to discover four key things:

1. The various mental models and perspectives for the vision
2. A common vocabulary
3. Existing collaborative and interdisciplinary activities

4. The broad capabilities and ecosystem of expertise within the 18 undergraduate programs and nearly 50 faculty members

From these perspectives we needed to formulate a collective vision. This required navigating the ambiguity in the gaps and overlaps among disciplines and making those fits and gaps explicit in order to move the team from the opportunity recognition phase with a shared vision into the value creation phase. This full process resulted in a new core curriculum, new academic planning with new degree programs, a new building, new organizational structure, and new leadership.

Discover: Common Language, Perspectives, and Expectations

First, the job was to understand the various perspectives, languages, and expectations of the faculty and staff. Second, we needed to understand current activities, which included Philadelphia as well as other university student experiences with interdisciplinary pilots around the integration of one or more of the disciplines of design, engineering, and business. Third, we needed to understand the market demand from current and prospective employers of both early graduates and more advanced professionals. To augment this PhilaU market demand viewpoint, we spoke with noncustomers, those who do not hire PhilaU graduates yet but are thought leaders in the relevant fields. Begin with a 360-degree discovery view—assess your internal resources, understand your customers, and probe your market space to understand your noncustomers as well as your competitors. In the chapters by Philadelphia University faculty members Natalie Nixon and Tod Corlett, they will offer greater detail and examples about tools to probe this internal and external space.

Discover: Mental Models for the Strategic Initiative

One of the most valuable first steps in framing a strategic directive for action is gaining a textured understanding of the mental models among the team members. Creating a common model is the key goal of framing the strategic directive for action. As depicted in Figure 3.4, the strategic plan offered a Venn diagram for DEC that depicted three overlapping circles of design, engineering, and commerce with an arrow toward the center of concentrated overlap labeled "Innovation." When probing for a deeper understanding of what that diagram meant through listening to the leadership and faculty, we found that what emerged were two different dominant views. Some perceived the integration of the three disciplines as the coordination of value chain of delivery as design it (design), build it (engineering), sell it (commerce). Similarly in terms of discipline coordination, others saw the circles and overlaps as a visual representation of the time. They perceived a series of three discrete experiences in which one was the discipline skill acquisition in isolation, two was the collaboration of two disciplines learning the connective points among their functions, and three was where innovation happens as the trifecta comes together, presumably in the later stages of the education where synergy can be realized from acquired skills.

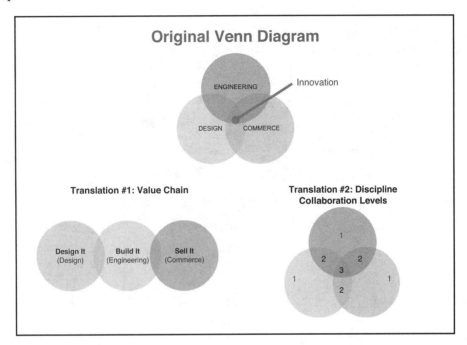

Figure 3.4 *Mental models for DEC: In the discovery phase, two mental models for the integrated college emerged from the original Venn diagram. The value chain depiction indicated discipline coordination in value delivery. The depiction of collaboration levels was an operational view of the curriculum in terms of one, two, and three discipline combined courses.*

Discover: Key Insight: Belated Collaboration

Philadelphia University is a professionally oriented institution of higher education. As with many professionally oriented schools, students declare their major upon entry, which results in a very directed, dedicated, and sometimes rigid focus on the major. Students often self-identify with their major even before the skill acquisition that constitutes such identity, which can result in discipline *"clanning"* and related us-versus-them views of collaboration. Upon review of years of collaborative courses at Philadelphia University as well as other institutions, we discovered that most collaboration occurs in the junior and senior years based on the assumption that interdisciplinary integration is more productive and meaningful when there is a disciplinary base and identity among the collaborators. The delay in beginning collaboration coupled with the entrenchment in the major and solidification of discipline identity results in gaps in language, understanding, and expectations that handicap the potential of the collaborative experience, as articulated in Figure 3.5.

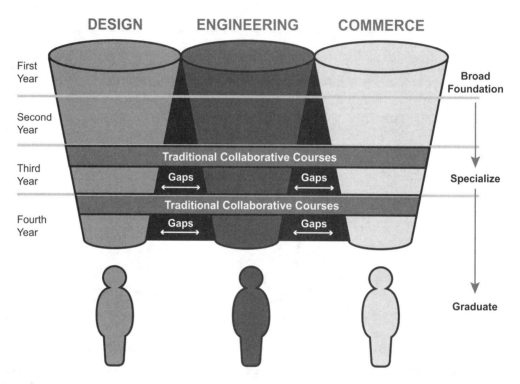

Figure 3.5 *Gap effect of belated collaboration: Our research uncovered that most undergraduate collaborations occur too late in the progression to discipline specialization. This delay in collaboration results in gaps in language and understanding. This depiction also predicts a future in a professional silo.*

Discover: Key Insight: Limitations of the Silo Career Professional

From conversations with the varied stakeholders, it became clear that the university, like many other professional education institutions, does an excellent job in training graduates for their first job with outstanding discipline knowledge and skills required for the task and execution levels of employment. We discovered, however, that advancement beyond entry level was not dependent on discipline skills. We found that the gaps we saw in belated collaboration became pronounced in later stages of the career trajectory where the ability to coordinate in tactical management and collaborate in strategic leadership are essential, as articulated in Figure 3.6.

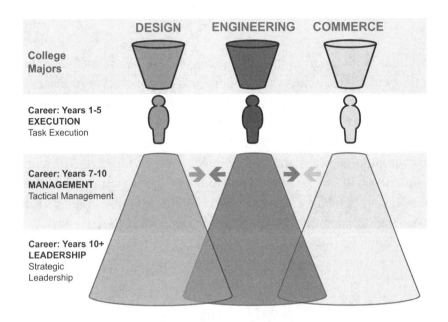

Figure 3.6 *Limits of the silo career trajectory: Our research uncovered that traditional professional education is well-suited preparation for years 1-5 when the focus is on tasks and execution of discipline skills. Years 5-10 focus on tactical management and discipline coordination and years 10+ are about discipline integration in strategic leadership.*

In the recently published book *College Unbound: The Future of Higher Education and What It Means for Students,* the author, editor at large for the *Chronicle of Higher Education*, Jeffrey J. Selingo, dedicates an entire chapter to the "Skills of the Future," which questions the need for a major given the importance of developing cognitive abilities versus consuming subject matter content. Americans switch jobs on average every four years.[3] Given our increasing life expectancy, a career could span 40 years or more, resulting in ten or more jobs and perhaps half as many careers. We kept this top of mind, particularly after viewing the viral video "A Vision of Students Today,"[4] which left us with this tag line directive:

"How do we prepare students now for jobs that may not exist today?"

These are the key insights from the discover phase:

- Collaboration occurs too late in the educational sequence.
- The silo career professional trajectory is limited.
- Skills for success in the future are in the gaps and overlaps.

Formulate

Returning to the initial Venn diagram, the new focus became the overlaps, gaps, synergies, and interstitials among the majors. We embraced the notion that innovation is in the overlaps and the translation of skills and portability of process and knowledge from one domain to another. A great historic example of this is Gutenberg's printing press, often recognized as the most important innovation of the modern period. Gutenberg's press was possible only through the integration of his professional knowledge of metals from silver and blacksmithing with his personal knowledge of the region in which he was raised, wine country, from which he derived understanding of winemaking's screw-press operations. He was able to integrate movable metal type with a superior press, creating unprecedented knowledge liberation.

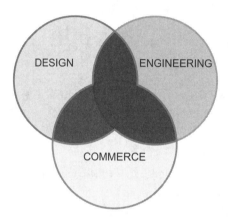

Figure 3.7 *DEC Venn diagram—overlap focus: This depiction emphasizes focus on the overlaps and the design of curriculum to maximize "skills of the future" in the overlaps.*

We knew we had to address gaps in the curriculum. We also knew we had to address the organization to create structural parity across the university. This structure needed to include systems within each college both to enable continued strategic development and to facilitate collaboration. We focused the formulation stage on curricular development with three parallel efforts: faculty development charrettes, curricular outcome mapping, and network engagement. In other organizational settings this is akin to off-site workshops, product and service mapping, and engaging your consulting network. In Chapter 9, "Navigating Spaces—Tools for Discovery," Dr. Natalie Nixon offers extensive tools for discovery, including more in-depth information on use of charrettes.

Formulate: Talent Engagement

We ran cross-disciplinary charrettes, or short intense workshops, that brought a diverse spectrum of faculty together to explore discipline complex challenges such as healthcare and the aging. These charrettes required the faculty members to shed their protective "sage on the stage" mode and dive into a wicked problem that required interdisciplinary collaboration. As illustrated by the authors in this book, this is similar to fieldwork conducted by design or innovation strategy consultants. When corporate anthropologists and innovation consultants such as Jump Associates and Continuum conduct fieldwork with clients such as Proctor & Gamble, Target, and L.L. Bean, they often begin with exercises that ferret out language gaps and barriers and reframe the problem with a common understanding for the various functions assembled on the innovation challenge.

Formulate: Product Mapping

The second formulation effort was a curriculum mapping exercise. Faculty members are familiar with the method of measuring competencies by program outcome statements like "Student will demonstrate...." This integrated model derived from the outcomes from the 18 majors that were to compose DEC offered a single view of our potential synergies, fits, and gaps. For example, Figure 3.8[5] depicts the synergies in engineering students understanding issues related to the operator of the proposed solution, while design students are focused on understanding the latent needs and desires of users, and while commerce students are gaining an understanding of how to influence consumers. When it was presented this way, the potential to collaborate earlier and better integrate the liberal arts became clear.

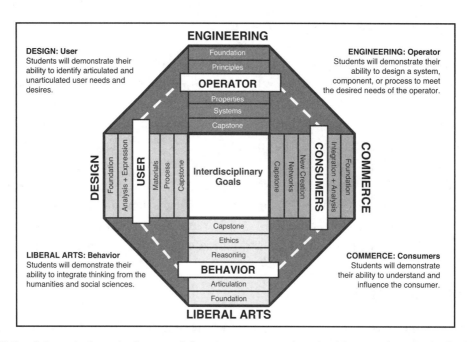

Figure 3.8 *Integrated curriculum model: outcomes mapping. In this exercise, we boiled the learning outcomes from 18 different undergraduate majors into six core learning outcomes per discipline area. The six steps offered a reframing that afforded formulation of curriculum to address gaps and capitalize on fits such as the connections among operator, user, consumers, and behavior.*

Formulate: Advisor Network

The third formulation effort involved tapping our growing network of advisors. Over the course of developing the new college, we met with national and international experts on interdisciplinary education from Stanford's D School to Rotman School of Management's Integrated Thinking Courses and Design Works efforts. We also conferred with the thought leaders behind the groundbreaking new programs such as the M.B.A. in Design Strategy from California College of the Arts and the M.S. in Strategic Design from Ontario College of Art and Design. We also sought the counsel of a large network of innovation consultants, many of whom are authors of this book, from Continuum, Smart Design, and Jump Associates. This network offered insights into the key skills for successful leadership in innovation.

Key Insights from the Formulate Phase

Through the first two phases, we began to associate design with what is desirable, engineering that which is feasible, and commerce that which is valuable. This three-adjective description became the benchmark for a successful solution, be it a product, service, business model, or technology.

Actionable Next Steps for the Develop Phase

At the culmination of our formulation phase, we identified four areas of focus to better leverage the synergies we found in curricular mapping, to address the gaps we discovered in our charrettes, and to build the skills of the future identified by our network of advisors. These became the areas of focus for new curriculum:

1. **Process:** Shared processes for navigating uncertainty and probing ambiguity through tools for problem finding, framing, and propositional thinking.
2. **Value Creation:** Shared framework for understanding business models and functions.
3. **People:** Shared tools for probing users, operators, and consumers to discover latent needs and desires, as well as self-awareness to improve teamwork and collaboration.
4. **Systems:** Shared set of tools to experiment with complexity and consequence.

The formulation stage should end with a descriptive directive that is actionable. The statements should clearly state the goals and focus for the development phase. In many organizations, the discovery/formulation team might not be exactly the same team that carries the solution through develop/optimize phases. It is essential that the group culminate the problem-finding phase with an actionable, clear, descriptive directive. In the case of Philadelphia University, it was now time to address the organizational structure to realign the university for the future. This new organizational structure would call for new leadership and a new team to carry through development and optimization.

Develop

Moving from opportunity recognition to value creation requires substantial development lifts, notably around organizational structure, product development, and teaming.

Develop: New Organizational Structure

Leadership crafted the new organizational structure. We considered legacy organizational structures that offered a single track from faculty member to assistant dean to dean. We realized that in a small resource-constrained university, under this structure, we saddled our academic administrators with operational responsibilities, leaving little time for strategic planning. At the same time, we realized we had some outstanding faculty and staff members who would prefer to focus on operational optimization. Additionally, we had created a center of Nexus Learning to codify and institutionalize our signature learning approach of active, collaborative, and real-world as well as extensive resources for assessment, workforce readiness, and accreditation. In short, we had the talent but had conflated responsibilities and job functions in a linear path. It was clear that we needed to establish matrix management, as detailed in Figure 3.9, to allow focused expertise on these three core competencies of operational expertise to enable collaboration, academic/strategic planning, and advising/assessment. We mirrored these capabilities and resources in the Provost Office for knowledge capture and sharing across the University.

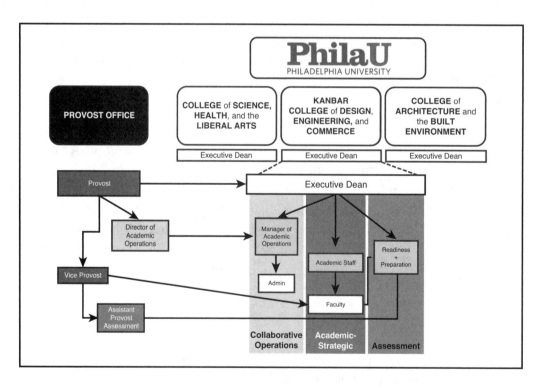

Figure 3.9 *New organizational structure: matrix management for Growth + Collaboration. Once organized into three colleges from six schools, each integrated college included three core competencies: Academic Strategy, Collaborative Operations, and Signature Learning Assessment. These three foci emerged from the needs discovered in the discover and formulate phases.*

When you look at your own organizational structure, consider the goals of your activities, the core competencies of your team, and how they need to optimally interact to achieve your strategic directive. Section 2 of this book, "Assessment and Leadership," and notably both Ellen di Resta's chapter on assessing your innovation capacity and Dr. Sara Beckman's chapter on learning styles and innovation, should give you much greater depth of information on teaming and organizational structures.

Develop: Product Development

In academia, curriculum development is the process and student learning is the product. Through an examination of desired skills for the future, designed to address the gaps and capitalize on the overlaps, we crafted a four-course sequence designed to create synergies across the disciplines and create desirable, feasible, valuable solutions. This curriculum covers the discipline-neutral yet connective focuses of process, value creation, people, and systems. The core curriculum sequence is as follows, as depicted in Figure 3.10:

1. *Integrated Design Process* focuses on probing ambiguity, propositional thinking, and problem finding and framing, and introduces learning styles, teamwork, and collaboration.

2. *Business Model Innovation* introduces value creation using the business model canvas as a tool. This course teaches students how to create and deliver value with an introduction to the various functions of business.

3. *Ethnographic Research Methods* is a deeper dive into understanding people, which was introduced in the first course. The course emphasizes the study of people, which affords students further opportunity to consider their own assumptions in collaboration and teamwork, as well as their assumptions about the VUCA world in which they are proposing solutions.

4. *Science System Thinking* considers issues of complexity and consequence and introduces students to systems thinking with nature as a metaphor. At this point in their professional major, students have crafted solutions to real-world problems, and as such, focus on systems, consequence, and complexity have more application.

5. *Advanced Collaborative Courses* follow the four core courses and offer real-world challenges, including industry engagement.

6. *Integrated Senior Capstone* is both a writing- and research-intensive liberal arts capstone combined with a semester-long thesis project in the professional major. This capstone requires integral consideration of design, engineering, and commerce to illustrate solutions that are desirable, feasible, and valuable.

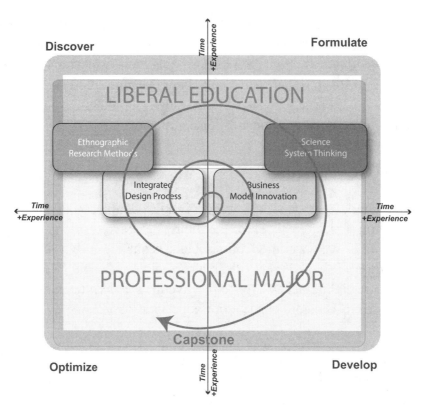

Figure 3.10 *DEC core curriculum: The DEC core curriculum is designed to focus on the skills for the future in opportunity recognition and problem finding and framing. The core curriculum has heavy emphasis on the discover and formulate phases to complement the develop and optimize rich curriculum in the professional education major.*

Develop: Learning Launches

Given the scope of the effort in reorganizing half the university in a short time frame, there were a handful of opportunities to test pilot curriculum or learning modules. We formalized some of our network of advisors into DEC Fellows that provided custom workshops for faculty development and to test learning modules with highly engaged honor students for maximum feedback.

Develop: Product and Process Development Teams

In the development phase we created a number of working groups of interdisciplinary teams of faculty focused on core issues such as curriculum development, core curriculum integration, facilitating collaboration, and industry engagement. All DEC core curriculum courses are team-taught by faculty members from two different backgrounds or specializations. The team teaching afforded two very different views on development of the course, the subject matter, and, most important, relevant connections back to the professional majors. The core curriculum integration group was charged with overseeing connection among the core courses, overseeing linkages from the DEC courses to the professional major, and overall ensuring that the DEC curriculum reflected the University's Nexus Learning Approach, the brand promise of active, collaborative, and real-world infused with the liberal arts.

In your company an innovation might have been discovered and formulated by a consulting firm or brought into the company through an acquisition or a merger. In any case, it needs to be integrated into the core operations of the business to be developed, optimized, and, essentially, monetized with dedicated advocates for the overall brand experience.

Key Insights from the Development Phase

1. *Identify Core Competencies* of your organization essential to your innovation effort. Review your organizational structure to make sure you are leveraging those core competencies with focus and knowledge sharing across the entity. What are your core competencies?

2. *Craft Multidisciplinary Development Teams* to carry the insights key to your innovation from the phases of discover and formulate through to realization (optimization). In the case of the DEC curriculum, we crafted multidisciplinary faculty workgroups and team teaching pairs to develop and deliver the early versions of the curriculum. Is there stakeholder parity in your development teams?

3. *Create Brand Advocates* to disseminate your messaging. Every product or service your customer experiences should reinforce your brand promise. In the instance of the DEC curriculum, it was designed to be the first signature manifestation of Nexus Learning. What is your brand promise?

Optimize

In most organizations, movement into optimization is a focus on maximizing profitability and minimizing risk. In an academic organization, the optimization phase is a ramp-up often scaling a course or courses or broadening the scope of the potential audiences for the learning. In our case, given our focus on building a learning environment of continual improvements, our optimization phase is designed to institutionalize the practices that enabled the changes. As such, we sought to embed methods for enabling collaboration into operations and methods of streamlining our learning and faculty/talent development processes while maximizing our branding efforts to increase the national reputation of the university.

Optimize: Embed Innovation Responsibility in Operations

Given the new organizational structure and the creation of a new leadership level with executive deans and new positions in operations management, it was time to take DEC out of the Provost office and hand it over to the academic leadership to execute, optimize, and iterate. The new organizational structure and new talent assembled to realize DEC were charged with further course development, curriculum deployment, assessment and iteration, new program planning, and overall academic growth.

Optimize: Brand and Capital Investment

Running alongside this effort, the university rebranded itself with new brand stories, marketing plans, logos, website, social media strategy, and overall recruitment strategy to realize the investment in making DEC a unique value proposition. The university also embarked on the largest capital campaign in its 127-year history and, as a result of DEC, secured the largest single donation to name the new college from alumni Maurice Kanbar.

Optimize: Streamline Development and Delivery

The new leadership team is in the process of crafting long-term processes for continued academic planning, curricular development, curriculum and learning assessment, and optimizing delivery—all leveraging the matrix management organizational structure. The university has undergone extensive analytics assessment, optimized class section sizes and teaching loads, and partnered with outside technology partners for launching key programs online to reach a broader audience and extend the brand.

At this point in the development, the optimization is underway. Two of the four courses in the core curriculum have launched and the first DEC class will graduate in 2015. As a result, it is difficult to pinpoint the key insights at this time from the optimization phase. Greater insight into the development and optimization phases can be found in Section 4, "Value Creation," notably in the discussion of business model formation, sustainability, and pivoting.

Conclusion—Suggestions

These are the most important things we learned and offer as recommendations about framing the vision for action:

- Understand the various historical and new vision perspectives early in the discovery phase, and share your understandings verbally and visually to engage your stakeholders. This can be very helpful to correct your own assumptions about the enterprise and the teams.

- Borrow language from the various stakeholders and employ that language in early formulation efforts to engage participants and bridge gaps.

- Make experiences tangible as often as possible, especially when you are formulating a proposed hypothesis so that your stakeholders can experience the suggested future. Prototype your products, experiences, systems, and solutions.

- Use the phases of discover and formulate to tease out your true core competencies and check those focuses against your organizational structure. The organizational structure should enable innovation. Most organizational structures were crafted for prior offerings and are designed to optimize legacy products and services. Unfortunately, the structures often protect hierarchy and prohibit collaboration.

- Engage a large network of external thought leaders to offer perspectives from your own market, your potential market, your competitors, and your collaborators. These perspectives are key to developing your internal team.

- Use learning launches whenever possible to test pilot products, services, or business models with users/consumers for quick feedback and co-creation.

- Create consistency from opportunity recognition to value creation through common team members when possible, clear actionable formulation statements, and organizational structures that are designed to enable development and optimization of your innovations.

Success has many fathers. The students, parents, alumni, faculty, staff, and administration of Philadelphia University and the network of advisors, many of whom have contributed to this book, share the parental bragging rights for the successful creation of the Maurice Kanbar College of Design, Engineering and Commerce, but especially the Provost Office and DEC Leadership Team.

Endnotes

1. Roger Martin, "Don't Let Strategy Become Planning," *Harvard Business Review Blog,* February 5, 2013, http://blogs.hbr.org/cs/2013/02/ dont_let_strategy_become_plann.html.

2. This framework was co-developed by Ellen di Resta, author of Chapter 4, "Assessing Your Innovation Capability."

3. Carl Bialik, "Seven Careers in a Lifetime? Think Twice, Researchers Say," *Wall Street Journal,* September 4, 2010, http://online.wsj.com/article/ SB10001424052748704206804575468162805877990.html.

4. "Vision of Students Today" video: www.youtube.com/watch?v=dGCJ46vyR9o.

5. Interactive flash model of this curriculum map is available at www.philau.edu/ StrategicPlanning/DEC/curriculummodel/.

Section 2
Assessment and Leadership

In this section you will learn about the assessment stages of opportunity recognition. This begins with Chapter 4, "Assessing Your Innovation Capability," which details the process of understanding where you are as an organization, including your internal team, aspirations, and types of innovation that suit your organization's core capabilities and competencies. This follows with a detailed description of how different learning styles and cognitive preferences can affect the design of an innovation team in Chapter 5, "The Role of Learning Styles in Innovation Team Design." The final chapter in this section, Chapter 6, "Your Team Dynamics and the Dynamics of Your Team," covers the process of leading, coaching, and managing a dynamic team of disrupters.

To add perspective, we spoke with Mike Arney, Principal at Continuum. Continuum is a 30-year-old, global design and innovation consultancy with offices in the United States, Asia, and Europe. Continuum partners with clients to discover and translate powerful insights into products, services, and brands that improve lives and grow businesses. Their work spans a broad spectrum of industries from healthcare delivery to consumer products to service design for financial services to rethinking religious service in education, and everything in between and beyond. Given this depth of experience in innovation across such a breadth of industries, Mike's perspective on the evolving leadership roles and organizational structures responsible for innovation is particularly insightful.

Design Thinking Versus Design Translation

Most companies were formed around their capability to satisfy a need better than anyone else. In this book we propose that the spark that forms a company is often disruptive innovation, often changing industries, customer expectations, or even cultural norms. This start-up spark includes cycles of discovery and formulation until a business model is formed. After the business is formed, historically, the focus shifts to incremental innovation of solution development and optimization. Clients engage Continuum to help them discover and formulate new ideas, as well as develop and optimize solutions. Mike explains their client relationships this way: "The engagements are partnerships that range from hired expert for delivery of a solution to hired expert with integrated innovation team development around solution implementation to strictly developing innovation capacity absent of the delivery of product or service solution. The third category is the most challenging scenario in which to define success criteria, as there isn't a 'thing' that's delivered. In this category we have found success often depends on developing trust, creating a common language that they adopt, and developing shared processes. On engagements that depend on our clients and their partners to leverage new insights and ideas independently, we will create experiential guides that help them translate and execute what has been learned into actual products, services, and environmental experiences. But these guides only work if they effectively convey both the logic and the emotional connections with the consumer—not just the what, but the why. This translation is a key role for designers as they are uniquely qualified to articulate these subtleties in an experiential way. There is a lot of media attention on design as styling, and as design thinking, but somewhere between the two is design translation. I see this as one of the key capability gaps in organizations. They are often lacking a solid design translations competency, so the insights uncovered by design thinking are carried through to the final product, service, or experience—so the solution reflects both the what and is a manifestation of the why." In Chapter 4, Ellen di Resta unpacks types of innovation—and the difference and importance of understanding both what and why.

Leadership Roles in Innovation

In the past five years organizations have increasingly added innovation roles from vice presidents of innovation to chief innovation officers (CINOs). Often these positions are rooted in the capabilities of the organization. As such, if it is an engineering firm, the CINO or VP is a trained engineer; if the company is a medical organization, the CINO or VP might be a clinician. Many times the VP of innovation or the CINO is a business development person focused on strategic partnerships. As Continuum has a 30-year view on these organizational structures from their point of engagement, as innovation experts, Mike offered his view on the ideal chief innovation officer: "From my perspective, which is likely grounded in the Continuum approach, the ideal chief innovation officer profile is one that is deeply interested in understanding people, has a sensibility and preferably training in design, and a strong command of business. Ideally they would be fluent in these three languages and know when to operate from which perspective. They would be comfortable both diverging and converging to explore a potential insight or opportunity. They would be trained in the company's core capability, but that would be perhaps secondary to their ability to integrate human understanding, design, and business into the company's offerings so they could both see where the organization is strong today and envision where it could go leveraging core competencies." In Chapter 5, Dr. Sara Beckman explores in detail the four core learning styles, notably divergers and convergers and how they come into play in innovation team design.

Rethinking Organizational Structures

Corporations, outside of start-ups and small entities, are generally organized functionally, divisionally, or in a matrix structure. Functionally organized entities have departments of design, engineering/manufacturing, sales, and so on. Divisionally organized entities might have different groups organized by product or market. Matrix organizational structures attempt to blend the functions across the divisions simultaneously. As organizations seek to increase their innovation capacity, what type of organizational structures work best? Mike offers, "Ideally, the organization has depth in the functional areas of expertise necessary to deliver on their core capability, but they also all have an interest in human understanding, design thinking and design translation capabilities, and fundamental understanding of business. When we work with clients, it's ideal if the client's leaders have the ability to knit the three together. The ideal organizational structure or set of people have capabilities that are not in silos but have so much common language, process, and trust such that there is considerable overlap. These overlaps are essential to translating the 'why' all the way through to a best 'what.' At Continuum our strategic thinkers are also often called Envisioners. Envisioners are able to capture and communicate the essence of an idea in a way that can be experienced, and the strategy is clearly actionable and testable. This is a marriage of think and do skills. I believe more organizations need to embed envisioners or those with this set of blended skills throughout the organization. The chief innovation officer or the VP of innovation will not be successful alone. Organizations need to make sure they have, or partner with, a team that can knit the process phases and experiential touch points together so that the potentially large investment in the initial idea is fully leveraged in the actual execution. The right idea is not valuable unless it is captured in the right solution." In Chapter 6, Sara Singer-Nourie explains how to keep the team in a balance of think and do with her pyramid of perspective.

The following three chapters will help you understand your innovation capability, design the optimal innovation teams, and manage the dynamics of your team of disrupters.

4

Assessing Your Innovation Capability

 **Ellen di Resta** has focused her career on creating new sources of revenue for companies seeking to reinvent themselves, aligning market insight to create successful new products and services. She has worked in corporate and consulting capacities, currently with Becton Dickinson, and with clients such as P&G, Tetra Pak, and the Center for Creative Leadership. Ellen founded Synaptics Group to apply broad educational and industry experience to academic, speaking, and writing venues. She is a frequent lecturer and advisor to university and corporate innovation programs, is published in a variety of trade journals, and holds degrees in design, engineering, and business.

Introduction: Preparing for a Changing World

As with Philadelphia University, which was formed 129 years ago to serve a specific need by supplying graduates to fill a void in the textile market, most companies were formed around their unique ability to satisfy a need better than existing alternatives. The company's unique ability to solve this need often disrupted the market in some way, which has been the key to their success. Typically, as they have grown, they have consistently evolved and optimized their processes to stay ahead of competition. This sustained focus on optimization and continuous improvement is necessary, but without conscious attention, the result could be that the company loses the competitive abilities that secured its initial success.

With Philadelphia University, this consistent evolution resulted in fragmented offerings supplying talent to more specific niches. With large companies, this consistent evolution often results in the industrialization of products to serve mass market needs, and an increased focus in maximizing profits in existing markets.

However, the same VUCA factors (volatile, uncertain, complex, and ambiguous) that were embraced by the leadership of Philadelphia University will impact all organizations. The increasing rate of macroeconomic and technology change will drastically increase the impact of VUCA factors on existing lines of business. As a result, the optimization capabilities honed over the years will become less useful as the company seeks to reinvent itself more frequently.

In this chapter it is assumed that companies know how to build their capabilities to continually improve their existing offerings. The main focus is on developing the capabilities necessary to embrace VUCA factors, and to respond to the need to reinvent themselves with greater frequency.

You've Decided You Need to Innovate; Where Do You Start?

Innovation can be defined as doing something new that creates value for a business or an economy. When assessing your company's ability to innovate, it's important to understand where you started, where you are now, and what you need in order to achieve your innovation goals.

Companies that don't innovate well will surely die. Figure 4.1 shows the four main dimensions of innovation, which fall into two main categories: Evolutionary and Revolutionary.

In the lower-left box in the diagram, the product being produced doesn't change. In the box above it the solution is not the same as what was previously produced, although the type of product is the same. In both, the benchmarks for success are clear, or straightforward to define, and measurable. Methods to acquire the type of knowledge required are also well defined.

Both of these types of innovation can typically be managed from within an organization's current manufacturing or product development processes, which is why they are in the broader category of evolutionary innovation. Extensive knowledge about *what* exists today, in both the internal company and the external market, is required to be successful at evolutionary innovation. In Chapter 3, "Framing the Vision for Engagement," this category is represented by the Development and Optimization phases currently underway at Philadelphia University.

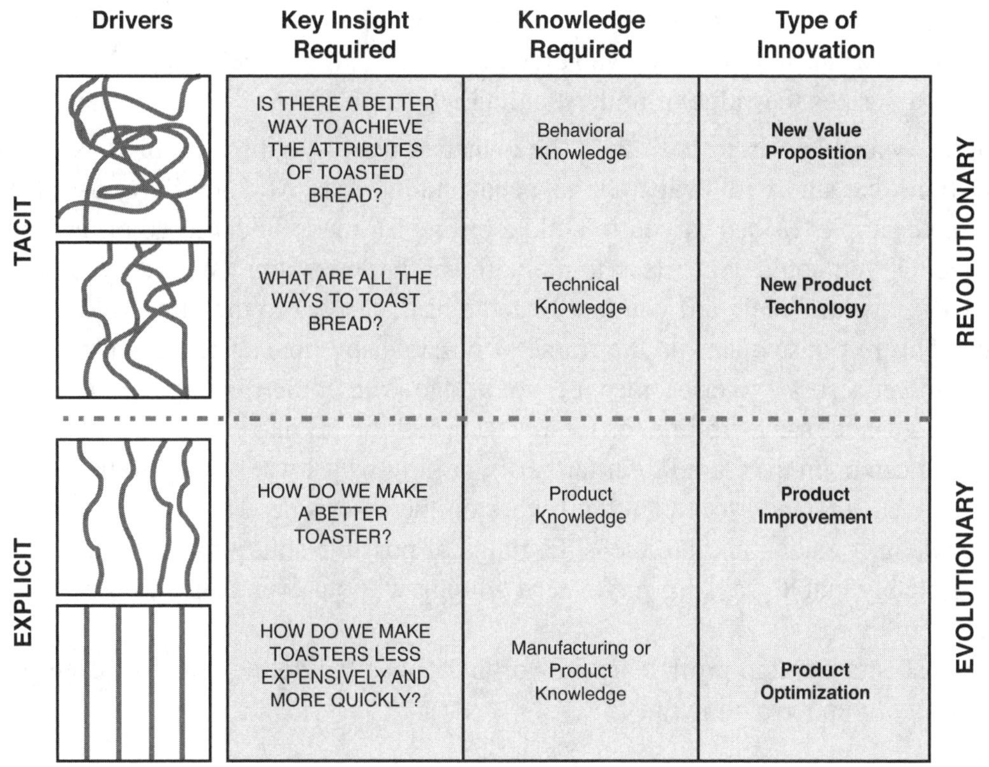

Drivers	Key Insight Required	Knowledge Required	Type of Innovation	
TACIT	IS THERE A BETTER WAY TO ACHIEVE THE ATTRIBUTES OF TOASTED BREAD?	Behavioral Knowledge	New Value Proposition	REVOLUTIONARY
	WHAT ARE ALL THE WAYS TO TOAST BREAD?	Technical Knowledge	New Product Technology	
EXPLICIT	HOW DO WE MAKE A BETTER TOASTER?	Product Knowledge	Product Improvement	EVOLUTIONARY
	HOW DO WE MAKE TOASTERS LESS EXPENSIVELY AND MORE QUICKLY?	Manufacturing or Product Knowledge	Product Optimization	

Figure 4.1 *Dimensions of innovation.[1]*

Where it gets interesting is in the two boxes above the dotted line, which delineates between evolutionary product developments and revolutionary innovation explorations. In the top two boxes, the existing offering is replaced. The end solution might leave both the toaster and even the toast behind. Entirely new value propositions are created, which are often the fundamental building blocks of new category creation. These types of innovation usually cannot be managed from within an organization's current manufacturing or product development processes, which is why they are in the broader category of revolutionary innovation, as represented by the discovery and formulation phases in Chapter 3. Extensive knowledge about *why* current conditions exist within the company and market are required to be successful. For example, instead of understanding *what* the market is doing, it is necessary to understand *why* consumers and the market behave as they do. And instead of understanding *what* technology currently works, it is necessary to understand *why* it works in order to find disruptive alternatives. The core curriculum of the Kanbar College of Design, Engineering and Commerce (DEC) at Philadelphia University was created to build undergraduate capabilities in understanding *why.*

In her article on the need to reframe problems to unlock innovation, Dr. Tina Seelig—Neuroscientist and Executive Director of the Stanford Technology Ventures Program—describes the value of understanding *why* in this way:

> Another valuable way to open the frame when you are solving a problem is to ask questions that start with "why." In his need-finding class, Michael Barry uses the following example: If I asked you to build a bridge for me, you could go off and build a bridge. Or you could come back to me with another question: "Why do you need a bridge?" I would likely tell you that I need a bridge to get to the other side of a river. Aha! This response opens up the frame of possible solutions. There are clearly many ways to get across a river besides using a bridge. You could dig a tunnel, take a ferry, paddle a canoe, use a zip line, or fly a hot-air balloon, to name a few.
>
> You can open the frame even farther by asking why I want to get to the other side of the river. Imagine I told you that I work on the other side. This, again, provides valuable information and broadens the range of possible solutions even more. There are probably viable ways for me to earn a living without ever going across the river.[2]

The goal is to develop proficiency in working above the dotted line, by developing the capability to understand *why*.

How Do You Assess Your Current Skills?

The mention of building revolutionary innovation capabilities might bring to mind thoughts of new technology development, R & D centers, and maybe even skunk works projects. However, the shift from the ability to understand *what* exists today to the ability to understand *why* the market exists requires fundamentally different human capabilities.

What types of skills did the people in the company possess that enabled your company's initial success? What types of skills do the people in the company possess that enable your company's current success?

The answers to these questions are important because they will give you a sense of how far a stretch it will be for you to develop revolutionary innovation capabilities. If you are a large, global corporation, it is not an option to avoid consistent evolutionary innovation, because it is operational excellence that will fund disruptive innovation efforts. Yet trying to achieve disruptive innovation goals with the same mind-set will simply not work.

The skills necessary to understand *why* the market behaves the way it does are different from the skills that are necessary to understand *what* currently exists. We will look at two sources that define the characteristics that begin to describe these differences.

Motivational Drivers

The first source, by N. Nohria, B. Groysberg, and L.-E. Lee, presents a new model for employee motivation based on cross-disciplinary research from the fields of neuroscience, biology, and evolutionary psychology. They define four basic emotional needs or drives that underlie everything we do:

1. **The drive to comprehend:** Some people are driven to make sense of the world around them through creation of frameworks and theories that make events meaningful and valuable.
2. **The drive to bond:** Some people extend common kinship bonding to larger collectives such as organizations, associations, and nations.
3. **The drive to acquire (aka "the carrot"):** Some people are driven to acquire tangible goods such as food, clothing, housing, and money, but also intangible goods such as experiences, or events that improve social status.
4. **The drive to defend (aka "the stick"):** This drive is rooted in the basic fight-or-flight response to real or perceived threats that is common to most animals.

The authors suggest that these four drives must all be addressed, because there is no hierarchy among them. For example, you can't just pay people more money and expect them to be happy if the organization is not perceived to treat people fairly.[3] It's important for organizations to understand that the fundamental motivations of people who thrive in the unknowns of understanding *why* are different from the motivations of people who prefer the knowns of *what.*

DELI: Leveraging Life Interests in Vocational Performance

The second source, by T. Butler and J. Waldroop, describes the impact of DELIs, or Deeply Embedded Life Interests. The authors describe that DELIs are not the same as hobbies, nor are they the objects of topics of enthusiasm. Rather, they are defined as long-held, emotionally driven passions, and they impact the type of work people seek, much more strongly than the topic of the work. They define eight DELIs:

1. **Theory Development and Conceptual Thinking:** These people love thinking and talking about abstract ideas.
2. **Creative Production:** These people love beginning projects, making something original, and making something out of nothing.
3. **Application of Technology:** These people are intrigued by the inner workings of things.

4. **Quantitative Analysis:** These people love to use data and numbers to figure out business solutions.

5. **Influence through Language and Ideas:** These people love expressing ideas for the enjoyment of storytelling, negotiating, or persuading.

6. **Counseling and Mentoring:** These people love teaching, coaching, and mentoring.

7. **Managing People and Relationships:** As opposed to Counseling and Mentoring people, these people live to manage others on a day-to-day basis.

8. **Enterprise Control:** These people love to run projects or teams and control the assets.

Butler and Waldroop suggest that DELIs drive job satisfaction far more strongly than whether or not the employee has strong skills in his job. They cite several examples of people who were excelling at their jobs, but were ready to leave their companies to seek out more fulfilling jobs that more closely matched their DELIs,[4] which underscores the importance of alignment among them. As shown in Figure 4.2, the motivational drivers, when intersected with the DELIs, can provide a good starting point for identifying people best suited to evolutionary and revolutionary innovation work.

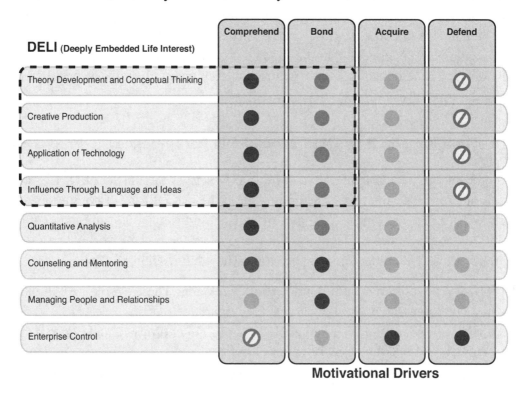

Figure 4.2 *Intersection of motivational drivers and DELIs in innovation planning.[5]*

Toward What Type of Innovation Will Your Employees Naturally Gravitate?

There are two fundamental types of innovation—evolutionary innovation, which refers to making incremental improvements, and revolutionary innovation, which refers to innovation that requires more change across the organization. Revolutionary innovation often requires new processes and approaches, and it may represent an entirely new value proposition to new customers or markets, new sales or production processes, and new financial models. Revolutionary innovation is generally more disruptive. In consideration of your team, consider both which type of innovation is aligned with you today and which type requires talent development or consulting resources.

Evolutionary Innovation

Most likely, much of your business focus and many of your resources are dedicated to the evolutionary end of the spectrum to realize the near-term revenue to maintain your current competitive position. As expected, the team members who thrive here like to work in the known, and they are adept at defining *what* exists today. Here we often find people with an affinity for utilizing life interests in management, enterprise control, mentoring, and counseling to solve known problems. These people want to fully understand the current dynamics in a market, and continually improve on them.

Revolutionary Innovation

On the revolutionary end of the spectrum, we tend to find people with an affinity for inquiry and discovery, seeking to find currently unknown problems whose solutions will shape future market dynamics. For this type of work, it is best to engage people with life interests in theory, conceptual development, creative production, and applications of technology. People here like to work in the unknown, and are driven by the need to comprehend *why* the market behaves as it does.

What Type of Thinking Do You Currently Encourage?

It's clear that to develop capabilities for revolutionary innovation, it is necessary to find people who have an affinity for understanding the unknowns and *why* as described previously. Since most companies have evolved to optimize what is known, unconscious barriers to achieving revolutionary innovation might be embedded in your current work environment. It is unrealistic to expect that even the people most suited to revolutionary innovation work will thrive in an environment designed to encourage and reward evolutionary innovation.

Barriers to Innovative Thinking

In his book *Iconoclast,* neuroscience Professor Gregory Berns of Emory University cites three cognitive barriers to innovation.[6] These barriers are perception, fear response, and social intelligence.

1. **Perception**

   According to Berns, the ability to perceive the world in new ways is the key to being able to imagine new possibilities and come up with new ideas. He suggests that the brain is efficient, and each time it executes a task, it looks for the most efficient way to do it. This tendency needs to be actively broken down in order to think more imaginative thoughts.[7] For example, InSinkErator, the market leader in garbage disposers, needed to shift its own perception from *what* it did ("providing devices that lived at the kitchen sink") to *why* people bought its products ("providing a more clean hygienic living environment through the removal of organic waste") in order to change the market's perception of its value.[8]

2. **Fear response**

   Berns breaks down fear into two components: fear of uncertainty and fear of public ridicule. This response encourages action without thought, as in the primal responses to external threats. When people feel exposed, uncertain, or as if they are being attacked or criticized, their fear distorts their perception, and they cannot imagine new possibilities. Those who cannot tame these fears will not allow themselves to work in the unknown realm of revolutionary innovation.

3. **Social intelligence**

   Berns acknowledges that ideas will not be valuable if others do not accept them. He suggests that the two things key to the acceptance of new ideas is their familiarity and their reputation. "The two go hand in hand. In order to sell one's ideas, one must create a positive reputation that will draw people toward something that is initially unfamiliar and potentially scary." This makes it necessary to network broadly and sell new ideas to the rest of the organization as part of the revolutionary innovation process.

It becomes easy to see how the conditions conducive to supporting evolutionary innovation work can inadvertently create these barriers to revolutionary work.

What Type of Work Does Your Environment Encourage?

After assessing where your employees naturally gravitate, and establishing the right revolutionary innovation team, it is necessary to provide an environment for their work that will lessen the barriers to revolutionary innovation that your current environment might present. At Philadelphia University, the early revolutionary innovation work was managed by creating and incubating the discovery and formulation phases that led to the creation of DEC within the Provost's Office with faculty guidance. When larger-scale development and optimization was warranted, the broader Administration was able to provide more comprehensive faculty oversight of the evolved offering.

The idea of incubating revolutionary innovation efforts until they are defined well enough to be absorbed by the regular business units is a common theme among companies embarking on revolutionary innovation efforts. The extent to which your revolutionary innovation work needs to be segregated, incubated, or completely outsourced should be evaluated on a case-by-case basis. The main point is that revolutionary innovation work requires an environment that is physically and emotionally different from environments that are conducive to evolutionary innovation work in which your company has likely become proficient. The chart depicted in Figure 4.3 highlights these differences.

It is important that the people, process, reward system, and physical environment are aligned for revolutionary innovation work for it to survive. However, it is important that as new ideas are developed to scale and optimized to create maximum market value, the transition from the revolutionary to evolutionary categories must be carefully managed. Even the best ideas cannot succeed if they do not evolve to support their market growth. As with the decision to incubate or outsource revolutionary innovation work, the best way to manage this transition must be made on a case-by-case basis.

After you have the right team in place for revolutionary work, it might seem easy to establish the right process, reward structure, and physical environment to support them as well. However, the difficulty of aligning all of these different components should not be underestimated. The ability to accurately recognize inconsistencies in the alignment of these conditions is often clouded by two main factors.

	Evolutionary	Revolutionary
Team	Multidisciplinary team Consists of functional disciplines (R & D, marketing, finance, etc.) Problem-solving mind-set Adept at understanding *what* the market is	Multidisciplinary people Includes disciplines not represented elsewhere in the company (social science, creative disciplines, etc.) Problem-posing mind-set Adept at understanding *why* the market is what it is
Process	Ensures that product attributes are consistent with currently successful offerings Open approach to well-defined challenges Analysis—break down into manageable parts Linear workflow Ensures analytical rigor that demonstrates reliability	Defines new product attributes that will ensure the success of future offerings Open approach to ambiguous challenges Synthesis of seemingly unrelated data points Iterative workflow Ensures analytical rigor that demonstrates validity
Rewards	Hard skill mastery (necessary within functional disciplines) Adherence to norms, schedules, and processes Achieving clearly defined benchmarks according to a defined process Strong performance in existing market conditions Accepting conventional wisdom	Soft skill mastery (creativity and creation of relevant new connections) Doing what is necessary to achieve a goal, inventing processes as necessary Achieving major milestone dates but not the methods for getting there Creating new metrics for success in new market conditions Questioning conventional wisdom
Environment	Oriented by functional group Hierarchically structured	Oriented by task Functionally structured (separate spaces for team interaction and quiet contemplation)

Figure 4.3 *Key considerations for evolutionary and revolutionary innovation.*

The first factor is based on the potential difficulty of having different operational structures within the company. When this difficulty is perceived, companies often try to change one element, such as the office space or aspects of the reward system, with the hope that everyone will become more innovative and a revolutionary idea might pop out. The problem with this approach is that it often disrupts the current business without fully enabling true revolutionary innovation exploration. Often it is better to segregate, incubate, or outsource early revolutionary work with a plan for transition than to diffuse it throughout the organization.

The second factor is one that is seldom recognized, called the Dunning-Kruger Effect. Based on the work of David Dunning and Justin Kruger, it is a cognitive bias in which unskilled individuals suffer from illusory superiority, mistakenly rating their ability much higher than average. This bias is attributed to an inability of the unskilled to recognize their mistakes.[9] Dunning and Kruger also found that actual competence can weaken self-confidence, because competent individuals might falsely assume that others have an equivalent understanding.[10]

The Dunning-Kruger Effect becomes evident when people will read about the need for revolutionary innovation and how the work is accomplished, and overestimate their ability to undertake such work with current resources and structures. On the other hand, those who are skilled in revolutionary innovation, when acknowledging the uncertainties inherent in the work, will appear to be less competent than they actually are. This also plays out as companies will reward certainty in an effort to reduce risk. What this does is limit their ability to embrace the uncertainty necessary for successful revolutionary innovation.

Conclusion: Meeting the Challenges of Revolutionary Innovation

As mentioned earlier, the increasing rate of macroeconomic and technological change will result in an increased impact of the VUCA factors on existing business environments. As a result, it will be necessary for companies to find ways to embrace this uncertainty, as Philadelphia University did with the establishment of DEC. Ignoring this changing environment is not an option, and companies must be prepared to develop the capacity to embrace revolutionary innovation work.

Whether the task is outsourced or the capabilities are developed internally, it is necessary to recognize the importance of understanding the *why* that drives technology and market behavior as the foundation for successful revolutionary innovation. The ability to understand the *why* is primarily a human capability, which must be enabled by the organization's ability to provide a physical and emotional environment to support it. Without the right combination of human and organizational capabilities to understand the *why,* your company will be pushed into the incremental evolution of *what* exists today.

Endnotes

1. E. di Resta and H. McGowan, "Inspiration for Innovation" in *Global Innovation Science Handbook* (McGraw-Hill Professional, 2013).
2. T. Seelig, "How Reframing a Problem Unlocks Innovation," *Fast Company,* April 19, 2013.
3. N. Nohria, B. Groysberg, L.-E. Lee, "Employee Motivation: A Powerful New Model," *Harvard Business Review,* July-August 2008.
4. T. Butler, and J. Waldroop, "Job Sculpting: The Art of Retaining Your Best People," *Harvard Business Review*, September–October 1999.
5. E. di Resta and H. McGowan, *Global Handbook of Innovation Science* (McGraw Hill Professional, 2013).

6. G. Berns, *Iconoclast* (Harvard Business School Press, 2010), 6.

7. Ibid., 44–46.

8. D. MacNair (VP Marketing, InSinkErator Corporation), interview by author, August 5, 2009.

9. E. Morris, "The Anosognosic's Dilemma: Something's Wrong but You'll Never Know What It Is (Part 1)," *New York Times,* June 20, 2010.

10. D. Dunning, and J. Kruger, "Unskilled and Unaware of It: How Difficulties in Recognizing One's Own Incompetence Lead to Inflated Self-Assessments," *Journal of Personality and Social Psychology* vol. 77, no. 6 (1999).

5

The Role of Learning Styles in Innovation Team Design

Dr. Sara Beckman, CLO of the Institute for Design Innovation, teaches design and innovation at the University of California's Haas School of Business, most recently initiating a course on problem framing and solving that integrates approaches from critical thinking, systems thinking, and creative problem solving that is taught to all incoming students. Her research focuses on the value of design to business and the ability to collaborate to innovate. She also has worked at Hewlett-Packard and Booz & Co., and actively consults with a variety of companies now. Sara has B.S., M.S., and Ph.D. degrees in Industrial Engineering and an M.S. in Statistics from Stanford University.

Innovation Process and Design Thinking

Innovation is a process of problem framing and problem solving. Elsewhere in this book, you'll read about that process, about the tools and techniques that make that process work, about the highly iterative nature of that process, and about getting that process to yield implementable output and sustainable business models. It is a process that is executed by a team, sometimes large, sometimes small, but always by a team. That team has to navigate the process, leveraging at various points in the process the divergent skills, abilities, and styles of the members of the team. In this chapter, we link the phases or key activities of the innovation process directly to the specific skills and styles needed, providing guidance both for the design of innovation teams and for who should lead the activities of the team and when.

There is a wide variety of descriptions of the innovation or creative problem-solving process (today often called "design thinking"), a couple of which are presented in Chapters 8, "Design Process and Opportunity Development," and 9, "Navigating Spaces—Tools for Discovery." At a high level of abstraction, the process simply involves analysis, synthesis, and evaluation,[1] key elements of a general problem-solving process.[2] These abstract terms are made more concrete in the Illinois Institute of Design's description of design (see Figure 5.1) as a process of building and using knowledge that has both analytic and synthetic elements, and operates in both the theoretical and the practical realms.[3] In the analytic realm, the team focuses on discovery or finding, while in the synthetic phases, the team focuses on invention and making. Movement between the theoretical and the practical realms happens as teams draw insights from what they have observed in the world of practice, convert them to abstract ideas or theories, and then translate the resulting principles back into practice in the form of artifacts or institutions.

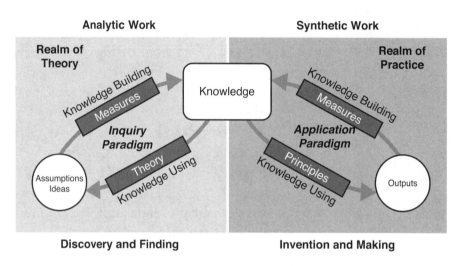

Figure 5.1 *Model of innovation as knowledge management.[4]*

Learning Process

Interestingly, this knowledge-management view of the innovation process maps closely to descriptions of how we learn. In particular, Experiential Learning Theory[5] defines the learning process as one in which "knowledge is created through the transformation of experience" and is characterized along two main axes: how we perceive things and how we process things. The spectrum along which we perceive things ranges from the abstract, where we are conceptualizing or thinking about them, to the concrete, where we are feeling them, from the brain to the gut. The spectrum along which we process things ranges from the more passive engagement in reflective observation to active experimentation or just doing. These two dimensions create a four-quadrant model (see Figure 5.2) that defines four learning styles:

1. ***Diverging*** learners, who live largely in the concrete world and spend time in reflective observation, are particularly able to view concrete situations from different perspectives.

2. ***Assimilating*** learners, who also engage in reflective observation but in more abstract ways, are capable of synthesizing a wide range of information into a useful and logical form.

3. ***Converging*** learners, who are also abstract but prefer doing, excel at finding practical applications for ideas and theories.

4. ***Accommodating*** learners, who also like doing but back in the concrete world, are good at hands-on learning through practical experience and intuitively identifying risks to take.

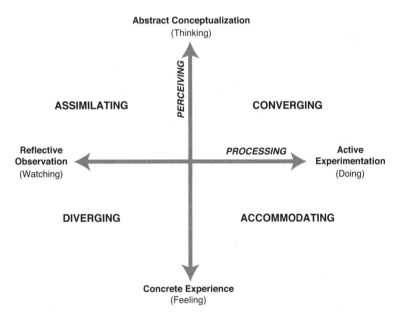

Figure 5.2 *Learning styles.[6]*

We all cycle through this learning process throughout the day as we take in information (diverging), try to fit the new information with our existing mental models (assimilating), adjust those mental models (converging), and then change our behaviors accordingly (accommodating). Thus, we are all capable in all four quadrants, but have particular strength in or preference for one of them. It is these preferences that matter in assembling an innovation team.

Innovation Process and Learning Styles

Now, we can put the two models together to learn something about the ways of processing and perceiving that are needed for the different activities associated with the innovation process (see Figure 5.3). The four key activities are observations, frameworks, imperatives, and solutions.

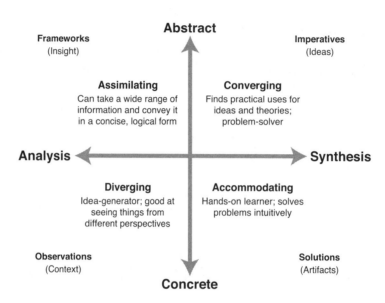

Figure 5.3 *Innovation process with learning styles.*[7]

The Observations phase entails learning in great detail about the lives of the customers targeted by the innovation as described in detail in Chapter 7, "Leveraging Ethnography to Predict Shifting Cultural Norms." It also entails learning about the industry ecosystem in which the company competes; the core competencies the company can leverage; key discontinuities that might provide an opening for innovation; and industry orthodoxies that, if broken, might yield new ways of framing and solving the innovation challenge.[8] All of this work requires empathy and curiosity, both traits of a diverging learner.

Take, for example, a project done for a quick-service restaurant chain that wanted to improve its customer's experiences. Observation entailed spending time following customers through both drive-through and in-store dining experiences and capturing their stories. One observation, for example, followed a mom of three who had little time to feed her two kids between lacrosse practice and a soccer game. She purchased three meals at the drive-through, put the bag with all the meals in it on her lap along with her small dog, and then as she drove 50 miles per hour down the expressway tried to figure out what belonged to whom as she handed items into the back seat.

Observation also identified key trends such as increased emotional (rather than rational) eating behaviors, desire for healthier foods, and family meal opportunities. It identified core orthodoxies of the fast-food industry that, for example, put drink machines rather than human interaction at the center of the consumer experience. It recognized the core competences of the quick-service restaurant, such as its ability to integrate various elements required to provide excellent customer service and the potential competitive differentiation that might provide.

The Frameworks phase requires taking all the messy data captured in the observation phase and extracting key insights from the data. A wide variety of tools is used at this phase, including customer journey maps[9] and perceptual maps[10] that facilitate understanding customer needs; industry maps[11] that help identify alternative bases for competition; and business model canvases[12] that display core elements of a business and their interactions. This work requires the ability to see the big picture, find patterns in messy data, and organize data in ways that clearly communicate the findings to others, all abilities of an assimilating learner.

In our quick-service restaurant example, assimilation entailed identifying common themes across customers, such as the issue our mom had with figuring out what items went to which kid. More important, it required asking "why" enough times to get to the more interesting insight that parents feel guilty about feeding their kids fast food, but don't feel they have any choice in the fast-paced world in which they live. The innovation team also drew customer journey maps for both the in-store experience and the drive-through, which enabled it to identify critical points of interaction and the highs and lows of the customer experience.

The Imperatives phase moves the team into synthesis work where choices are made as to which of the insights generated in the frameworks phase are most important, and then ideas are generated to respond to those insights. In short, the team goes from framing the problem to solving the problem, or as articulated in Chapter 3, "Framing the Vision for Engagement," moving from opportunity recognition to value creation. This requires the ability to come up with multiple concepts that meet customer needs and leverage the other findings of the framing phase, and then choosing those concepts that will be built and tested in the market. Converging learners, who are quick to find solutions to defined problems, fit well at this phase.

Although redesigning packaging to make it easier for parents to deliver food to their kids was certainly among the ideas that came up at this phase, the more interesting imperative was around helping parents feel as though they are still good parents when they feed their kids at quick-service restaurants. Focusing on this meaning-based imperative enabled the team to generate a wider range of options—from more nutritious offerings to a chance for a parent to take a deep breath and relax while in line—around something that was truly important to the customer. These ideas leveraged the capability of the organization to provide friendly and warm customer service.

Finally, the Solutions phase takes the concepts generated in the abstract and makes them concrete, building prototypes—ranging from physical products to storyboards to simulations to business models—and taking them back to customers and users for testing.[13] This requires the ability to make abstract ideas concrete, the willingness to take unfinished ideas out and share them, and the capacity to hear feedback on ideas, even when that feedback is unfavorable. These are areas in which accommodating learners best fit.

After generating hundreds of concepts, the quick-service restaurant design team chose a few representative ones, built prototypes and storyboards to bring them to life, and took them back out to customers to get feedback. They tested different store designs, including color schemes, furniture styles, and presentations of drinks and condiments. They experimented with different approaches to interacting with customers, serving their meals and refreshing their beverages. In a few quick sessions, they identified which of the insights identified in the frameworks stage were of most interest to the customers, and how to tweak the ideas to be even better solutions before rolling them out throughout the chain.

Building Innovation Teams

We have described four activities that are core to innovation, and matched those activities with the learning styles that are best suited to lead and execute them. This should make putting an innovation team together simple: Just find one person with each of the learning styles, put them on the team, let the right learning style lead at the right time in the process, and innovate away. Of course, it isn't that simple. First, not surprisingly, people with different styles are likely to have conflicts. The converging learner, eager to find a solution, is likely to be impatient with the diverging learner who keeps asking questions in an attempt to explore the problem further. The accommodating learner, eager to just make something and see what happens, frustrates the assimilating learner who wants to "think about it" some more. Conflict and the other challenges of working with a diverse team can be dealt with in many ways, such as those described in Chapter 6, "Your Team Dynamics and the Dynamics of Your Team."

The bigger issue, as we've learned through our research in the past few years, is a significant imbalance in the availability of learning styles to construct innovation teams. We have administered Kolb's Learning Style Inventory[14] to more than 3,511 people, including 1,241 MBA students, 113 engineering students, and 1,198 product managers from industry. Table 5.1 vividly shows the challenges for creating diverse, balanced teams. Nearly 50% of the available people are likely to be converging learners, whereas only 3% are diverging learners. Over 70% of the learners are abstract conceptualizers, whereas less than 15% operate in the practical or concrete realm.

Table 5.1 Percentage of Learning Styles Found by Population[15]

Learning Style	MBA Students	Engineering Students	Product Managers	Overall
Diverging	3%	0%	3%	3%
Assimilating	23%	20%	25%	24%
Converging	50%	53%	43%	47%
Accommodating	10%	9%	12%	11%
Balanced	14%	18%	16%	15%

The results are striking, and in stark contrast with other findings. According to early reports by Kolb, young children show an even balance of all learning styles, but move toward more abstract thinking as they grow older.[16] A study of the general population found that 33% of adults are converging learners, another 33% assimilating learners, 20% accommodating learners, and less than 10% diverging learners.[17] A recent study of 179 freshman entering the design, engineering, and commerce (DEC) integrated design class at Philadelphia University found fewer converging (16%) and assimilating (15%) learners, and more accommodating (22%) learners, but still only 1% diverging learners. (The remaining 46% didn't test into one of the four quadrants, and are what we term "balanced learners.") In short, the employee populations in many companies, at least as represented by our data, lack the balance found in young children and in places such as the DEC program.[18]

What does all of this mean for doing innovation in your company? In short, it suggests that you are likely to be dealing with a sizable ratio of converging learners as you assemble your innovation team. The learning styles profile for such a team might look something like that shown in Figure 5.4a. Converging learners prefer problem solving to problem framing, and are thus likely to drive quickly to a solution, perhaps before the situation has been well understood. Our research also shows that having more than one converging learner on a team statistically significantly reduces satisfaction on the team.[19] We hypothesize, supported by anecdotal evidence from teams with multiple converging learners, that this is due to the fact that each converging learner argues for a different solution, sometimes to different problems. Thus, your innovation teams are likely to be dominated by a problem-solving orientation and in many cases by conflict over alternative solutions as well.

The converse also holds, because you are highly unlikely to find a diverging learner on your team. This means you are missing someone who can meaningfully represent the customer (or any other stakeholders) with empathy and perspective. You are missing the person who asks, "What would so-and-so think?" as you process ideas. You are missing the person who brings stories[20] to the innovation effort that create emotional resonance around which a team can rally and create. Arguably, you are missing the fundamental grounding required to successfully launch the innovation process with the required observation work, and thus the key element for properly framing the problem to be addressed.

Overall, your team is likely to operate primarily in the abstract realm, like the team shown in Figure 5.4b, with far less attention to the concrete. You will see much more talking than doing or making. You will see more theoretical conversations about the innovations you might make and less just trying things out. You will hear more abstractions about customer needs and fewer actual stories about real people whose lives you might transform were you to understand them better. Ideally, instead, you would have a more balanced team similar to that depicted in Figure 5.4c.

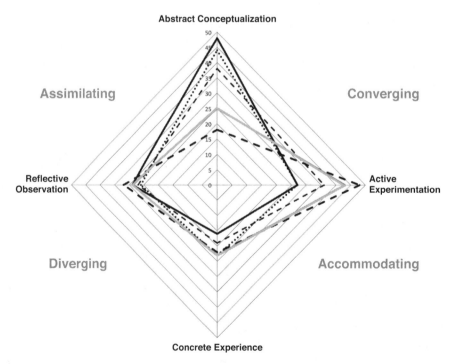

Figure 5.4a *Highly converging-oriented team (actual study team data from anonymous class).[21]*

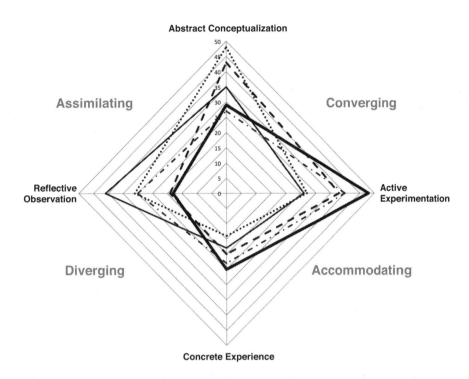

Figure 5.4b   *Highly abstract team (actual study team data from anonymous class).*

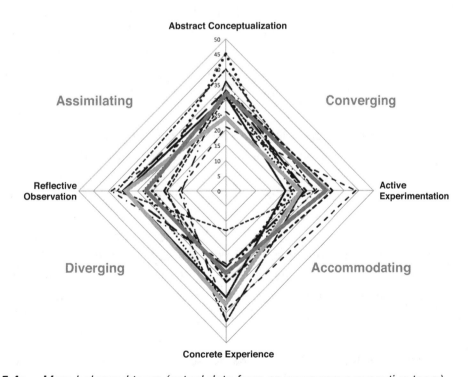

Figure 5.4c   *More balanced team (actual data from an anonymous executive team).*

Suggestions

How might we remedy the imbalance in our organizations and in particular on our innovation teams? First, we need to recognize that we seemingly have a larger problem with how we are teaching students to learn in the first place. Converging learners "have the ability to solve problems and make decisions based on finding solutions to questions or problems,"[22] and have been shown to excel on standardized tests. The U.S. education system is well-tuned to generate such learners[23] with its focus on standardization and testing. There is recognition of these problems, and actions are being taken. Philadelphia University, for example, mindfully created a freshman course, Integrative Design Process, that involves a great deal of ambiguity and divergent thinking to introduce students to problem framing and propositional thinking in their first year. The course is required of all freshman in design, engineering, and commerce (DEC), which represents more than half of the university. More such curricula are likely to be developed as the demand for innovative thinking increases.

Meanwhile, here are some places your company can start to diversity the thinking on its innovation teams:

Acknowledge the learning styles that team members have today. When we launch our innovation teams, we show them their learning style profiles (like those shown in Figure 5.4) and discuss the implications for their ability to get through the innovation process as a team. We advise those teams that are dominated by converging learners to step back and ask what problem they are solving. We teach teams not to jump too quickly to solutions, but to examine a set of options. We encourage them to take options back to their customers and get feedback, which keeps them from focusing too much on their own ideas.

Seek diversity in learning styles when hiring and forming teams. It is likely that finding diverging and accommodating learners will require looking in different places than recruiters typically look, particularly companies in the technology space. Diverging learners, for example, often major in the arts, English, history, and psychology and then go into the social services sector or into the arts. Accommodating learners often specialize in education, communication, and nursing. It is thus possible that you have some of these types of learners in your organization, in the training department, the human resources management function, or maybe in the public relations group. But they are probably not finding their way onto your innovation teams. In the experimental spirit of the innovation process we've described, try putting one of them onto a team and see what happens.

Help the people you have learn the skills needed. Table 5.2 describes the attributes of people with each of the four learning styles, as well as ways of cultivating ability in those learning styles. More attention to the desired abilities in corporate training, team training, and indeed in corporate culture will help you develop the skills you need to innovate. A. G. Lafley, former CEO of Proctor & Gamble, for example, is famously known for his ability to listen with an open mind, not only to customers but also to his own employees. His sensitivity to the feelings and values of others enabled him to be both a lauded leader of innovation and a well-respected leader overall. In short, these innovation skills can help the organization in many ways.

Table 5.2 Characteristics, Strengths, and Means of Improving Learning Styles[24]

Learning Style	Characteristics	Strengths	How to Improve
Diverging	Imaginative	Creativity	Be more sensitive to people's feelings
	Many perspectives	Brainstorming	Be more sensitive to values
	Broad cultural interests	Problem recognition	Listen with an open mind
	Specializes in the arts and humanities	Understanding people	Gather information
	Information seeking		Imagine the implications of ambiguous situations
Assimilating	Ability to create theoretical models	Planning	Organize information
	Assimilates disparate observations	Creating models	Test theories and ideas
	Inductive reasoning	Formulating theories	Build conceptual models
	Likes abstract concepts—basic science and math	Defining problems	Design experiments
		Being patient	Analyze quantitative data
Converging	Practical application of ideas	Design	Create new ways of thinking and doing
	Does well on conventional tests	Decision making	Experiment with new ideas
	Hypothetical-deductive reasoning	Problem solving	Choose the best solution
	Engineering and physical sciences	Logical thinking	Set goals
		Action orientated	Make decisions
Accommodating	Puts ideas into action	Accomplishment	Commit yourself to objectives
	Adapts well to changing circumstances	Goal orientated	Seek new opportunities
	Intuitive; trial and error	Decision implementation	Influence and lead others
	Likes technical or practical fields such as business	Entrepreneurial	Become personally involved
		Adaptable	Deal with people

Leverage the skills you have. After your innovation teams are aware of the learning styles available to them, they can leverage those skills at the appropriate point in the process. If the team is lucky enough to have a diverging learner, for example, it should let that person lead the team through the observation work of innovation. If, on the other hand, the team has no divergers, it might need additional support to learn and execute those skills. In some cases, the team might want to outsource the observation work to others. In other cases, it might simply have to pay more attention to engaging in observation, forcing itself, for example, to avoid jumping too quickly to single solutions.

In this chapter, we've introduced you to a model that integrates the innovation process with the learning styles needed to execute that process. We've warned you about the imbalance in learning styles available to today's innovation teams, in particular the dominance of converging learners and the paucity of diverging learners. Finally, we've given you some actions you can take to provide your teams with the needed skills for each of the innovation activities. We hope this will lead to increased awareness of how to engage in observation, (re)framing, ideation, and experimentation as you strive to improve innovation in your organization.

Endnotes

1. The basics of design have been described in many ways over many years and across many disciplines. For some of the basics, see M. Asimow, *Introduction to Design* (Englewood Cliffs, NJ: Prentice-Hall, 1962).

2. At some level, innovation simply entails framing problems or opportunities in different ways. It thus falls in the category of problem-solving processes such as described in, for example, H. A. Simon, *The Sciences of the Artificial* (Cambridge, MA: MIT Press, 1969).

3. C. L. Owen, "Design Research: Building the Knowledge Base," *Design Studies,* vol. 19, no. 1 (1998): 9–20.

4. Adapted from C. L. Owen, "Design Research."

5. D. A. Kolb, *Experiential Learning: Experience as the Source of Learning and Development* (Englewood Cliffs, NJ: Prentice-Hall, 1984).

6. Drawn from D. A. Kolb, *Experiential Learning.*

7. Adapted from M. Barry and S. L. Beckman, "Innovation as a Learning Process: Embedding Design Thinking," *California Management Review,* vol. 50, no. 1 (2007): 25–56.

8. P. Skarzynski and R. Gibson, *Innovation to the Core: A Blueprint for Transforming the Way Your Company Innovates* (Boston, MA: Harvard Business Press, 2008) describes these areas of inquiry as the five lenses through which a situation can be viewed to generate innovation.

9. There are many good examples of customer journey maps online, one example of which is found at http://blogs.hbr.org/cs/2010/11/using_customer_journey_maps_to.html, July 15, 2013.

10. For more background on perceptual maps, see J. R. Hauser and F. S. Koppelman, "Alternative Perceptual Mapping Techniques: Relative Accuracy and Usefulness," *Journal of Marketing Research* XVI (November 1979): 495–506.

11. Mapping the bases on which companies compete in an industry against the characteristics desired by customers yields new opportunities, or "blue oceans," as described in W. C. Kim and R. Mauborgne, *Blue Ocean Strategy: How to Create Uncontested Market Space and Make Competition Irrelevant* (Boston, MA: Harvard Business School Press, 2005).

12. A. Osterwalder and Y. Pigneur, *Business Model Generation* (Hoboken, NJ: John Wiley and Sons, 2010).

13. For a detailed description of many ways of prototyping, see B. Buxton, *Sketching User Experiences* (San Francisco, CA: Elsevier, 2007).

14. D. A. Kolb, *Experiential Learning.*

15. K. Lau, A. Agogino, and S. L. Beckman, "Global Characterizations of Learning Styles among Students and Professionals" (proceedings of the International Design Forum, ASEE National Conference, Atlanta, GA, 2013).

16. A. Kolb and D. Kolb, "The Kolb Learning Style Inventory—Version 3.1, Technical Specifications" (HayGroup, 2005).

17. D. Kolb, "Learning Style Inventory Technical Manual" (Boston, MA: McBer and Co., 1976).

18. The DEC core curriculum comprises coursework in integrative design process, business model innovation, applied ethnographic research methods, and science-based systems thinking and was created to expose students regardless of major (design, engineering, or business) to all learning styles. One of the main hypotheses of the DEC core curriculum is that greater exposure to a variety of learning styles and experiences, coupled with exposure to the various discipline domains, will make for better prepared teams to integrate divergers, convergers, assimilators, accommodators, and balanced learning styles in practice.

19. K. Lau, A. Agogino, and S. L. Beckman, "Diversity in Design Teams: An Investigation of Learning Styles and their Impact on Team Performance" (proceedings of the Mudd Design Workshop VIII, Claremont, CA, 2011).

20. S. L. Beckman and M. Barry, "Design and Innovation through Storytelling," *International Journal of Innovation Science* vol. 1, no. 4 (2009): 151–160.

21. Each line on the graph depicts the profile of an individual based on the results from the person's Learning Style Inventory test. By plotting all the lines on one graph, you can see the overall profile of the team.

22. D. A. Kolb, *Experiential Learning*.

23. S. Khan, *The One World Schoolhouse: Education Reimagined* (Twelve, 2013).

24. Drawn from A. Kolb and D. Kolb, "The Kolb Learning Style Inventory."

6

Your Team Dynamics and the Dynamics of Your Team

Sarah Singer-Nourie coaches leaders and their teams on how to tap energy, talent, and motivation for accelerated results in school systems, communities, and companies worldwide. Weaving practical application of brain research into team dynamics, personal development, and human performance, her work has sparked clients including Jump Associates, American Eagle Outfitters, Quantum Learning Network, and Bubba Gump Shrimp Company to break through. Founder of Sarah Singer & Company, Sarah loves to open possibility daily as a trainer, facilitator, and coach. Her M.A. is from Saint Xavier University and B.A. from The Ohio State University, yet she attributes her most significant learning to life outside of school.

With a clear assessment of your organization's capabilities and goals, and with a clearer understanding of your team composition by learning style from the previous chapters, you are now looking at leading this dynamic team of disruptive innovators. In this chapter we will give you the tools to lead the team most effectively, with notable focus on maintaining focus and perspective, managing and understanding expectations, mitigating the challenges of pressure, and knowing when and how to reset the team's focus and energy for maximum performance.

Much of the time, the teams' impact will depend on how you as the leader facilitate those elements within your team of disrupters, to make your superstars even better together. Then you can get to the business of disrupting something bigger than all of you.

The big misnomer about teams is that some magical synergistic chemistry just happens when you throw a group of talented, committed people into a project together. In my experience as the coach who is called in to either set up or get teams to the ultimate version of their capacity, although that magic sometimes occurs when just the right combinations of people come together, it's actually rare. In working with hundreds of teams, I can attest that it's also not so natural, especially with the superstar dynamos you're looking to attract. The brilliant dissenters, the mismatching questioners, the mold-breakers...they're the ones you want on your team, wired for creating the shift you envision. And yet they're also the ones who make for a challenging team to lead. Although they have all the right stuff individually to make great things happen in the world through change, they might likely be the most challenged in coming together with others in a way that taps, multiplies, or accelerates talent and changes the way you're envisioning.

Dynamics Defined

As this chapter name suggests, it's important to understand both your team dynamics and the dynamics of your team. As such, we offer clear definitions of these two similar yet different terms:

- *Dynamics* is used to describe what's happening on the team: *the forces that cause change or growth.*

  Referenced as the "team dynamics," the specific kind of interplay happening on your team between these big personalities is an element that requires your careful and constant attention as a leader. These dynamics can attract or repel others to a team, because they're noticeable from the outside. Great disruptive teams attract; they often have a queue of people who want to join them, because people want to be part of the energy a team of that sort creates. Conversely, dysfunctional teams repel; they often experience avoidance, with less buy-in for their impact, and as a result drain rather than generate energy. In short, people would rather be part of something that *gives* them energy. As the leader, you can determine which kind of dynamic your team becomes known for by how you lead them. The bigger the force, intellect, intensity, and vision in your players, the more fiery the team dynamics. Although those characteristics are what drew you to hire each of the people in the first place, they are also what require your deft facilitation and intentional leadership—so that the dynamics don't go off the rails.

- *Dynamic* is used to describe your players: *characterized by energy and/or forcefulness, usually continuous and full of productive activity or change.*

  This is descriptive of both the people you've got *and* the process you're leading them through. You are building a team of disrupters whose dynamic force already creates change and ripples wherever they go, so they're perfect for helping you shake things up. They each bring their unique talent, expertise, and viewpoint to the task. By definition, the process of this team and its work will be anything *but* static or smooth. You'll have moving parts, disparate voices, shifting positions, strong opinions...all of which can yield amazing change if led well.

If it's the right team of disrupters, you'll have some dynamic fire to contain and direct. Your role will be to keep fanning and directing those sparks with the following keys:

Perspective to ground and deepen the work

Process and context to push the team further

Clarity to acknowledge and clear the debris along the way

Nimble ability to strategically reset the team to keep it productive

The Perspective of Team

One of the most effective ways to channel team members' brilliance while grounding it to something solid is to continually give them perspective on their process. Think of it like a Pyramid of Perspective (see Figure 6.1).

So where's your vantage point? Each of the levels on this pyramid represents the distinct components of any initiative, however tactically small or sweepingly large and strategic. Although some are more obvious than others at times, it is important to have a clear understanding of each perspective level for the team to engage and create. The key is to keep each layer clear and in proportion to the others, allowing for the best perspective.

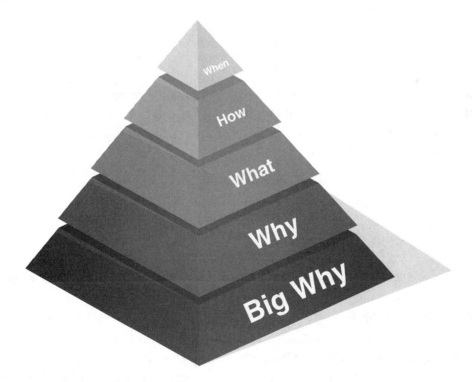

Figure 6.1 *Pyramid of perspective.*

In the way that you lead and communicate, you can come from any of the levels of the pyramid, each one coloring your message and influence differently. The deeper you go on the pyramid, the more foundation of grounded perspective you bring to the team. As a leader, you've got some choices....

When

Coming from this perspective, you're concerned with time (usually never enough), the schedule, optimization, and the deliverable deadlines. For a team of disrupters, *when* is an important and effective driver for them as disrupters who often do their best work under pressure. In disruptive innovation explorations, the ambiguity of the work requires touchstones along the way—moments when you regroup as a team and share the work of the team to those outside the core group. In consideration of the preceding chapter on learning styles, you might find that the convergers on your team are preoccupied with the *when*, which can be harnessed and channeled or destructive if out of balance with the pursuits *(how, what, why)* of the team's exploration. For you as a leader, it's important that you leverage the *when* perspective as a driver for keeping things moving, without becoming the watch-checker. If you cross the line to become overly concerned with time, your team can dismiss you as valuing time over content or process quality, and they'll lose some respect for your input.

Suggestions:

- Build and show timelines to give your team a sense of how their process will play out in concrete terms, and to give them a sense of "we are here" on the map.
- Adjust the timeline as you go, making space for team members' emergent process as they collaborate.
- Strategically, use time and deliverables to create urgency when needed. Deadlines spur action.

How

Here, the focus is on the process, the steps, and the way we get there. If you've got a team of individuals coming from successful yet diverse disciplines and experiences, the *how* will be important to them. They can get stuck on *how* your team is approaching the work, attached to a particular process to achieve results from their previous world. I've seen potentially brilliant teams crumble because they couldn't get aligned on process. Although you might find the assimilators on your team to be very helpful in synthesizing where you are and where you are going, to create a unified process for the team, *how* your team goes about its impressive disruption is ultimately your call as the leader. It's critical, because *how* your team does its magic might be the very thing that sets you apart from your competitors and defines your brand. Yet it's a balance—if you're *overly* skewed on form and checking off every box just so, disrupters will feel micromanaged and stifled.

Suggestions:

- Direct the approach, honoring and incorporating team members' expertise, and then getting their buy-in on why *X* is the best way for the team.
- Get alignment on the process early, and check in and adjust course often, looking to make sure the *how* is tapping their talent consistently and providing a way for it to manifest in great work.
- As the leader, be the keeper of the process.
- Document your process. Innovation work rarely follows the same path twice, but showing the process of a past successful innovation is helpful when you are seeking time, space, and resources for future explorations.

What

This is the outcome or result you're going for. You will always need this to be as clear as possible. If it's not, each participant will come to the team's work with her own interpretation of *what* you're trying to accomplish, which can be problematic when team members clash with one another. Although they each might hold their own important piece in the puzzle, they all need to be working toward the same picture on the box lid to guide them together. You might find that the accommodators on your team are particularly helpful here as hands-on problem solvers, in guiding the team to articulate the solution. Clear focus on the *what* elevates the team's dynamic and conversation to a common goal and a reason to rally in collaboration. The more vividly they're able to envision the outcome they're going for, the more they'll be pulled to it, causing the *how* and *when* to fall into place to make it happen.

Suggestions:

- Get *what* your team is going for—the change you're trying to impact—clear and concrete.
- Have the team articulate the goal, get it visually up on the wall of your workspaces, and keep reiterating it for them.

- If the result you're going for is ambiguous, set shorter-term *what* milestones along the course for them to focus on and hit.

Why

All the layers of the pyramid are key in keeping your team and the work focused on the right things at the right times. And *why* is the one that makes the difference between managing and really leading people. The *why* both trumps and grounds everything above it on that pyramid. Often the *why* perspective, more than any other, includes a view of the broader context—landscape, industry, and so on. The broader view includes an increasing number of variables. The divergers on your team will be very helpful in articulating this perspective, as they focus on the *why*s of the situation, question the question, and generate multiple ideas, incorporating multiple perspectives. For you as the leader, getting the *team why* clear and articulated is the most important thing of all, after which everything else (*what, how,* and *when*) is about execution of the *why*. It's what engages these individual brilliant people on your team, bringing their separate *why*s and visions of what's possible in the world to this work together. This is the conviction that makes the game matter to disrupters.

Suggestions:

- Continuously sort and prioritize the layers of *why* to the work, and then keep bringing it back to focus for your team.
- Lead your team with the *why*. Tell the *why*. Ask the *why*. Every time, every conversation, every day.
- Open with the *why,* and then layer the *what, how,* and *when* on top.

The Big Why

The deepest level of individual personal drive we all have is our *big why*—why we're doing this in the great scheme of life. This is our biggest game, truest purpose, and greatest good, and what gets us out of bed in the morning.

Steve Jobs: "To make a dent in the universe."

As a leader, get clear about your *big why*. When you do, it will come through as the passion that fuels everything else you do, and will serve as inspiration for every person you lead.

You also need to get team members' individual *big whys*. When you know their *why,* it can be very powerful, giving you a way to frame communication with them—an entrance into their world at any moment. When they're in need of motivation, acknowledgment, or perspective, you can frame it in the most meaningful way for what matters most to them. Their *why* is their buy-in, and your *why* can be their inspiration.

After you're grounded in this deepest, most stable part of the pyramid, the others—*what, how,* and *when*—are easy to reference and command as needed, because they're truly held in perspective of the *biggest why.*

Suggestions:

- If you don't already know them, find the *big whys* for each of your key team disrupters—ask them! Although this is getting to what's most essential to people's core, many people don't talk much about their *big whys* or even think of it consciously to the level of easy articulation. Getting them to unearth it will help them get more passionate about what they're doing, and help you to lead them more accurately.

- Give people space to think about this. Know that these questions are the kind that might require them to search a bit internally if they haven't already clarified it for themselves.

- Ask *big why* questions in layers. For each answer they give like, "Because I care about *XXX,*" ask another *why* question ("Why X?") to peel the layers back like an onion.

Using the Perspective Pyramid as a Leadership Tool

Ultimately, it's your role as the leaders to keep zooming in to the *why, what, how,* and *when* as needed to clarify, deepen, or change the focus for the team there. Equally important is your role of panning out from it all to get a vantage point on all of those layers in the right proportion and priority relative to one another. With both approaches, you can bring and hold grounded perspective for your team.

Suggestions:

- In small tactical moves or big strategic maps, start with the *why. Why* first sets context and gives a reason to engage.

- Then add each layer, in order from the bottom up. *Why → what → how → when.* Each layer adds more specificity, ending with *when* as the driver.

- When you or the team is stressed, use the pyramid to check your perspective. Often stress occurs in the top layers of the pyramid, when you get too wrapped up in the execution of *how* or *when*. If so, come back down to the *why*, and then add the others back in on top, keeping them as important, yet back into perspective.

- As a leader, keep zooming in and panning out. The details of each layer are critical for quality of the work, whereas the whole perspective is the clutch for your team's focus in doing the work fully engaged.

Team Under Pressure

Disruption creates shift. Shift at an irreversibly transformative, cellular level is different from a temporary "flavor of the month" change, which doesn't stick. Consider the transformation of a piece of coal into a diamond. Now we get a picture of what true, permanent change to a stronger different entity really looks and feels like. You're building a team to create that kind of change, right? When perturbations (see Figure 6.2), or incidents/forms of disruption, increase, pressure within a team (or an organization or individual) builds to a threshold in its current form, and then...

Everything transforms. Literally. It'll push through the threshold to a stronger, more stable structure, which can withstand more pressure.

The wood turns into coal.

That coal under sustained pressure over time transforms into a diamond.

Water at its boiling point transforms into steam.

Individuals pushed with enough pressure of challenge will transform inalterably, the ultimate learning.

Unrivaled championship teams perform best in the playoffs.

And none of these, like you and your team, go back to their original form.

You, your organization, and your team will go through this. It is simply how irreversible transformative change occurs. You'll know it's happening when the various forms of pressure increase the heat on the team—metaphorically—yet also the temperature of the individuals and in the room literally goes up when the pressure of those dynamics rises. This can happen when team members have been wrestling through an idea or a process in search of a breakthrough, and have been at it a long time. It can happen when they're being challenged by an outside force or time running out, and have to pull out a solution they haven't yet discovered. This is where you come in as the leader. The way you hold and facilitate those dynamics makes all the difference in your team being able to push through to transformative change or not.

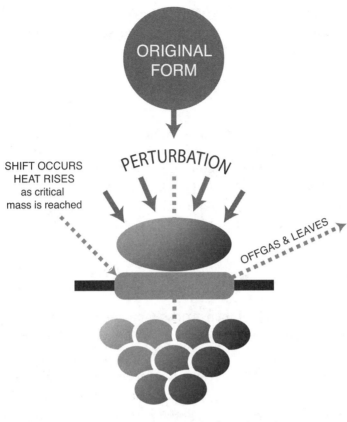

Figure 6.2 *Perturbation.*

Context Holds the Team

Teams either stay together through that pressure or they do not, depending on the agreements and commitments they have in place with one another. In looking at any team that thrives through pressure (sports teams, partnerships, organizations), there's a context of solid agreements there, which hold them all together when things get rough, and become the "true north" on the team's internal compass, to which they can reset with one another and recalibrate. These agreements keep everyone's energy and reflexes in check under pressure, redirecting the players back to one another and the commitment they've made.

"Never leave a teammate alone" and "Work through upset on the team directly, immediately, and out of the public eye" are examples of agreements that call the team back to one another, build solidarity, and enable them to stand in the heat all the way through to the other side.

Blair Singer calls this context of agreement the *Code of Honor,* and it's what makes the difference between teams that fall apart under pressure and teams that step up to their best work under pressure.

Suggestions:

- Create a context of unconditional agreements early in the team's process, before they're in the heat of the pressure. Help them clarify and articulate what they need to be able to count on without question from others in order to be all in, and create agreements to ensure and protect those things.
- Ask, "What gets in the way of your being able to do your absolute best work on a team," and then create agreements to proactively guard against those obstacles.

Navigating Expectation and Upset on the Team

As your team gets into the thick of their work together—along with the perturbation that occurs and the breakthrough that will come out of it—conflict and upsets will also happen. On a team of disrupters, upsets are pivotal opportunities for you as a leader to get them more aligned and accelerate the team's performance rather than slowing it. For truly innovative work, you need all the disrupters on your team to be able to access their absolute best thinking and creativity. To get there, they need nothing in the way—no judgment, no doubt in their teammates, and no nagging upsets to carry around. Upsets must get cleared out of the way deftly, because every unresolved upset creates a layer of conscious or unconscious inhibition in someone's thinking. Left alone, seemingly small upsets collect to create barriers of doubt and restriction to your team's best work, slowing the team. As the leader, you'll need to be the coach to help your team move through upset quickly, leveraging them as openings to pull out clarity and understanding (see Figure 6.3).

There's a lot to be said for how upsets and their resolution are communicated, but for now let's go to the source itself....

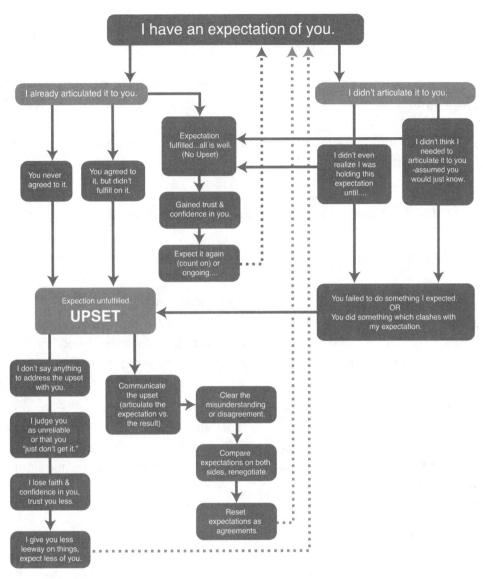

Figure 6.3 *Mapping expectations and upsets.*

We Expect More Than We Think

Upsets exist on a spectrum from tiny annoyances barely worth mentioning to huge stand-offs in avoidance (introverted approach) or blowout confrontations (extroverted approach).

Any upset on the spectrum breaks down to an expectation that didn't get met. Every time.

People handle it in a few different ways. The key for you as a leader is to create a culture on your team of getting expectations articulated clearly and upsets cleared out quickly.

An upset almost always presents itself as an irritation to start, possibly a complaint. Depending on how egregious the upset is or how long it's allowed to compound, it can quickly move to a full-out glaring conflict (see Figure 6.4). The context you set for the team to play by (handling upsets) and the role you take as a facilitator (to move them through quickly) will make all the difference.

Figure 6.4 *Spectrum of upsets.*

In coaching hundreds of these moments, I find that most of time, the person carrying a judgment about the competency/quality of another is doing so from an upset based on unarticulated expectations. What was expected in the first place for "good" or "competent" wasn't ever clearly articulated, so those expectations weren't ever met.

The most problematic and common expectations are ones we either assume or don't even realize we had until they weren't met by someone else. These upsets end up as judgments and decisions about whether a person "has what it takes," or whether an organization is the "right fit" for me and my talent. They can be devastating to a team, because invisible upsets like these insidiously erode trust, collaboration, and uninhibited engagement for people.

Unreasonableness

Now that we understand upsets, consider our expectations. We each have much more specific expectations of one another than we realize. There's what we articulate and agree to out loud versus what we silently expect of one another. A lot of what's left silent is assumed, often categorized as "common sense" or "what's right"—implying that we should all just naturally be in common agreement, without the need to discuss. Common sense is our own self-created filter built from personal experience and knowledge. As such, it is personal sense, not common sense. Considered this way, it's impressive that our unarticulated expectations sync with one another as often as they do, yet perhaps a bit unreasonable to count on that personal sense being common. Expectations crafted from this personalized filter are, unknowingly, often the starting point of many conflicts.

Suggestions:

- Condition your team to identify, own, and clear their upsets with one another.

- Establish a team practice of asking and articulating, "What am I expecting?" in team members' interactions with one another.

- Get as articulate as you appropriately can about your expectations with those you've got on the hook to deliver.

- Get agreement. After someone's expectations are voiced, they need to be renegotiated, adjusted, or accepted, becoming agreements. Then you've got a way to hold one another accountable.

- Articulate assumptions. Make the unstated common sense assumptions explicit.

- Be clear in what you agree to, and teach your team to do the same. If by, "Yes, I'll take that piece of the research," you really mean that you'd like to read more about it, and might do that if you can fit it in, you're setting yourself up for an upset.

- Get flexible about your expectations. The more flexibility in your expectations, the more chances for success, but be honest—our expectations are usually more solid and inflexible than we're willing to admit, let alone articulate.

- Create rigor on your team to dissect upsets down to the expectations beneath and to reset quickly. With each one, they'll get stronger, faster, and more unified.

The Energy and Attention of Team

Timeouts in sports, reboots on your devices, sleep for your body…your team needs resets, too—often when they least realize it. The more passionate and fixated on a result your disrupters are, the more weighed down in their process or fixed in their opinion they can get. Although you want authentic work and passionate creation, you don't want them to get stuck in their thinking, on a position, or in a conflict with another. In helping thought and innovation leaders build ultimate ideating performance cultures, a key we've built into the creative process is the power of reset. Just as your computer, when it has too many apps running for too long, needs to reboot, so do our brains. Especially your team of disrupters whom you're counting on for the big ideas.

That's all reliant on the disrupters' state, composed of the three inextricably linked parts of where one is mentally, emotionally, and physically at any given moment (see Figure 6.5). There's enormous power in monitoring, changing, and maximizing state for every member of your team in the process you lead.

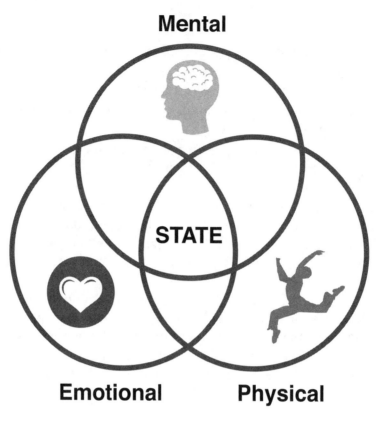

Mental

STATE

Emotional **Physical**

Figure 6.5 *Components of state.*

As a leader, start paying attention as much to their state as you do to their performance output, because it's actually fueling that output already. Your team's state of tired, irritated, or distracted will yield very different results than focused, curious, or excited. This is because attention, learning, and performance are completely state dependent. To maximize your team's flow, start facilitating their states. Your mastery here is directly proportional to their motivation, focus, and productivity. Although there are many ways to do this by causing even the slightest mental, emotional, or physical shift, for now we'll focus on the power of reset within your team's process.

The brain craves clean beginnings and clean endings to its focus and tasks, not never-ending thought loops, like open apps, that drain power. It also has a limited attention span. The average attention span correlates roughly with age (like 5 minutes max for a 5-year-old), up to about 18 to 20 minutes as the general limit of most adults' focused attention span in the work they're doing (outside of gaming and other immersive altered-state activities). All attempts of "plowing through" beyond that window are a waste of time and energy, because after that state is gone, so are their focus, learning, and performance. If your disrupters get stuck on a thought or position in their intensity, they need a way to "unstick." Quick resets of attention—state changes—about every 18 to 20 minutes in the work process or in natural transitions (whichever happens sooner), and the brain/performance/focus stays fresh, keeping it all clear.

Although it might be too slow to get far enough into team members' internal dialogue to reset their thinking, you can quickly and easily change their state from the outside. Change one of the three parts, and they all change. The easiest access for you is physical…by simply getting them to move, you'll break the state they were in and help them reset. You'll see it before they will, because you've got that perspective, right?

Suggestions:

- Build in physical state changes for transition—between topics of a meeting, between phases of a process, and in the moments people don't even realize that they need to move from one mental/emotional place to another.
- Keep and use physical manipulatives for people to handle in the space, such as squeezable balls—they are instruments for fast state change for people as they think.
- Give your team the awareness and language of state, and the conscious practice of state changing.

Parting Advice: The Impact of Team

The disruptive work you have taken on is game changing, the ripples of which will be felt beyond what you can measure. Harnessing the talent, energy, purpose, and alignment of your talent into a truly dynamic team will be the lynchpin of your impact. The dynamics of your team will make it happen because you choose to be the inspiring facilitator and model in the dynamics of your team. Through your leadership, the team can focus perspectives and vision, articulate and manage expectations, navigate and leverage pressure, and, when necessary, reset their focus and energy. In doing so, they will unify their brilliance and push through to the other side.

> *"We choose to go to the moon not because it is easy but because it is hard…*
> *this is an act of faith and vision.*
> *For we do not now know what benefits await us…."*
> —*John F. Kennedy*

Section 3
Opportunity Recognition

In this section you will learn about the search process of discovery and formulation through experts in ethnography, design thinking, and design strategy. This section is focused on the process of navigating through ambiguity, with tools and tactics for probing the VUCA (volatile, uncertain, complex, and ambiguous) world in search of new opportunity. We begin with Chapter 7, "Leveraging Ethnography to Predict Shifting Cultural Norms," an introduction to the use of social sciences to uncover opportunity through greater understanding of human behavior. This is followed by Chapter 8, "Design Process and Opportunity Development," which delves into applications for design and design thinking in discovery and formulation of new opportunities. The final chapter in this section, Chapter 9, "Navigating Spaces—Tools for Discovery," is an extensive inventory of various tools and tactics for probing for new opportunity.

To add additional perspective, we spoke with Rich Radka, founder of Barcelona-based Claro Partners, a unique strategy consulting firm focused on "navigating disruptive change" for their clients. Rich, a longtime consultant, was previously Director of User Experience for Sapient. In his extensive experience operating as an innovation consultant to large corporations, he found the gaps between and among social science research firms that offer insights through ethnographic research, design strategy consulting firms that offer design research-based observations, and management consulting firms that offer analytic frameworks to help firms determine what to do. From these gaps, Rich and his partners, all veterans from innovation consulting firms, founded Claro Partners to help companies both find opportunity and develop strategies to determine how to capitalize on them. They bring together diverse teams of analytical and synthetic thinkers to understand people's actual experiences, service design to envision the desired experience, and business modeling to create real, sustainable opportunities. We spoke with Rich about his experiences in helping companies navigate disruptive change in the search for new opportunities.

Design Thinking, Innovation, and Creativity as an Economic Driver

Innovation has become inextricably linked to design or, rather, design thinking—the term for using tools from design to create "an improved future state." The design thinking approach focuses on the user and the user's needs as the primary driver, and prototypes and iterates potential solutions to better understand the root problem or opportunity. Although the term was coined in the late 1960s, it took a couple of decades to gain broader traction as a viable approach. Today, design thinking is a bit of a buzzword and is seen by some as a magic-bullet solution to complex challenges or "wicked problems." We believe that there is a great deal of merit to the application of both the social sciences and design to understand and solve complex challenges. Designers or those with educational background or experience in design author a great deal of this book, and the three chapters in this section on opportunity recognition are authored from the design and social science perspectives. Rich commented on the current interest in design thinking and what it really means from his global view: "I think design thinking is incredibly important but it is not the be-all and end-all. Unfortunately, corporate culture has a curse of grabbing onto new things and stripping them of their deeper meaning. Corporations are filled with left-brain, analytical people as businesses, in general, are designed to operate most effectively when they mitigate risk and maximize efficiency. But businesses also need to navigate disruptive change and continually generate new ways of providing value. Innovation cannot be managed through the same system or measured by the same metrics. It requires a balance of both analytic and synthetic thinkers. For example, when you look at a set of LEGOs, an analytic thinker can break down a constructed LEGO structure and explain how it was made, but you need a synthetic thinker to look at the pieces and imagine what we can build next. Until we stumble upon an invention for the 'innovation bot,' we will need humans to increasingly be creative; we will need synthetic thinkers. We know creativity and innovation are at the core of our economy for at least the next couple of decades, so we will need to establish better methods of integrating synthetic and analytic thinkers." Tod Corlett's chapter on opportunity development describes the difference between entrepreneurial thinking and managerial thinking to delineate the distinction between managing business operations and leading disruptive innovation and transformational change.

Frameworks and Tools

Throughout the book, we offer frameworks from which to consider your organization, notably where you are, your capabilities, and where you are going. In this section we offer tools and tactics for discovery—the search for the future improved state. Both are very valuable but often conflated, especially when a tool is treated as an algorithm of certainty rather than a guiding compass. Rich said, "To me a framework is something that illustrates something real but difficult to see—it brings in what people do and how they make decisions. It's descriptive but not necessarily prescriptive. On the other hand, a tool is something you can run things through. From a tool you should be able to get some sort of results or insights. A tool should be adapted to the situation. In most situations I would prefer people use tools even if they adhere to them too tightly, but it's best if the tool comes with guidance. It's ideal when tools are adapted to the situation. I am both pro framework and pro tool. In short, if use of a tool or discussion around a framework helps them have multidisciplinary conversations, then it's valuable." In Sarah Rottenberg's chapter on ethnography, she describes the importance of tools and field-work to bridge cross-disciplinary boundaries. Dr. Natalie Nixon's chapter on tools offers several tools designed specifically to bring together diverse perspectives and leverage the creative abrasion to unlock new opportunity.

Innovation Traps

As most businesses grapple with how to simultaneously develop and optimize products, services, and business models based on their current core competencies and customers while also creating new offerings, traps and missteps are inevitable. As an innovation consultant to large multinationals, Rich offers insight that is a broad longitudinal view crossing industries, cultures, and economies. He noted, "The three most common errors we see are (1) the propensity for businesses to convince themselves that they are doing innovative work when they are not discovering but rather just validating, (2) convincing themselves they are taking a user-centric view when they are really just rewording their business impetrative, and (3) framing things in the wrong way. There is a relatively recent propensity to develop leadership positions for innovation—vice presidents of innovation and the like—but often these positions are heads of offices that are unfunded or underfunded. Innovation is creating something new, like a young plant—it is difficult to nurture and grow it in a rainforest like a larger, more mature plant. It needs shelter, nurturing, and a more sensitive environment. Management of innovation teams needs similar shelter and protection to nurture and grow. Perhaps creation of the leadership role in innovation is the first step, but until that innovation is given adequate resources and structure to be effective, it is in danger of being crushed for not hewing to 'how we do things around here.' Discovery, or white space work, cannot be managed and measured in the same way you develop and optimize products and services around current known competencies."

User Experience First, Business Model Second

Perhaps the only term hotter than design thinking is business model innovation. We structured this book to build toward the formation of the business model. We begin with an assessment of the organization's capabilities, talent, and team structures, and then focus on discovery and formulation to probe new opportunity spaces with a focus on the user. We then build into opportunity shaping and business model formation. Rich commented that corporations often do this in reverse:

"At Claro we focus first on the user. We believe the best opportunity lies in the intersection of three key understandings about the user: (1) What do they do, as in what are their current activities? (2) What do they use, which really means what are their tools, routines, and self-made solutions? (3) What do they think, which means what drives them, how do they envision outcomes, what are their biases, perceptions, or mental models?

"Understanding those three things creates better experiences. Once you understand them from these perspectives, you can propose the optimal experience from which the business model can be formed. It is always much, much easier to identify and align a business model to support a real human need than it is to try to get people en masse to change their perceptions and behaviors to match your business model."

The three chapters that follow offer frameworks, tools, and tactics to understand the user, the user's needs, and how to craft solutions.

7

Leveraging Ethnography to Predict Shifting Cultural Norms

Sarah Rottenberg is the Associate Director of the Integrated Product Design Master's Program at the University of Pennsylvania and a Lecturer in the School of Design. Outside of the university, she trains clients in design research methodologies and helps teams design products, experiences, and businesses that are desirable, meaningful, feasible, and viable. Sarah began her career as a design researcher at Doblin and was formerly a Directing Associate at Jump Associates. She has a Master of Arts in Social Sciences from the University of Chicago, where she studied anthropology, and a Bachelor of Science in Foreign Service from Georgetown University.

Context

Enabling an organization to move in a new direction and identify new strategic opportunities requires a vision for what the future could look like. Successful visionaries seem to see around corners, anticipating the ways in which the world is likely to evolve and painting a picture of how the organization can thrive in that future. Very few people possess the skills to develop that vision intuitively. Thankfully, for the rest of us, there are tools and techniques that can enable us to develop that vision based on understanding what cultural norms exist and recognizing how and when they change.

Many new business opportunities emerge when cultural norms shift or evolve. Cultural norms are the rules that govern behavior, attitudes, and values within a society or group. Everything that we do, from how we wait in line at the grocery store, to how we expect our kitchens to be outfitted, to how we run business meetings, is governed by cultural norms. These norms are like glaciers. They are constantly shifting, but slow-moving. Norms often change in ways that are perceptible only over generations.

Infrequently, new technologies or dramatic events cause norms to shift more visibly in a short period.

This chapter focuses on the ways applied ethnographic methods can be used to research white space to help teams identify new, disruptive opportunities for innovation by identifying changing cultural norms. There are things you can do in three parts of the research process to give your team a better chance of not just understanding existing behaviors but identifying those that are on the verge of change. Specifically here's what you can do:

1. In the planning stage, you want to think about whom you recruit and what kinds of activities you observe, and questions to ask.
2. In the research execution phase, you want to follow the trails that your participants lay down, being curious about everything in their lives even when things start to get emotionally intense.
3. In the analysis phase, you can combine highly analytic techniques with those that prioritize your intuitive sensemaking, to provide yourself with multiple chances to see the world in a new way.

We will first discuss cultural norms in greater detail and then move through the ways ethnographic research methods can be applied in each of these three phases.

Cultural Normatives

Just as a geologist can predict a potential glacial shift before it occurs, ethnographers can often predict potential small, subtle shifts in cultural norms that can make large social, economic, and environmental impacts.

Small Shifts in Cultural Norms Can Mean Big Opportunities for New Businesses

When cultural norms change, business opportunities abound. People change their behaviors and adopt new ones. They spend their money in ways that reflect their changing values, buying different products and availing themselves of new services.

Their expectations change.

New products can cause cultural norms to shift. The pervasiveness of the smartphone has dramatically impacted our communication norms. When I began my consulting career, if a prospective client left me a message, it was acceptable to take a few days to get back to him or her. Last year, after I hadn't responded to an e-mail after 24 hours, I received this text: "Is everything ok? I haven't heard back from you." We now expect responses immediately—within minutes or hours, not days. "Quick turnaround" is much quicker today than it was even ten years ago.

Norms that determine the role of products in our lives change, too. Consider the role of cars in our lives. From the dawn of the age of the automobile to the late twentieth century, cars have been a status symbol. As a signifier of freedom, wealth, and taste, the car a person drove spoke volumes about you, and the automobile industry maximized this association, providing makes and models for every market segment. Then changes in prioritization of personal economic expenditures, increases in environmental awareness, an increased focus on personal health, and shifting perceptions about ownership versus access led to a consistent decline in car ownership.[1] Today, the car is no longer a significant marker of identity and status. And for many people, particularly those in urban environments, not owning a car is more of a status symbol than owning one. Although this decline is scary for car companies, it is an opportunity for others who rethink facilitating human movement.

Shifts in cultural norms come about for a number of reasons. Sometimes, as in the shifting communication norms, they're driven by new technologies that enable new behaviors and therefore tee up new expectations. Sometimes, as in the car example, norms change because our values, economic situation, and factors we consider salient to a decision change over time.

Recognizing Subtle Changes in Culture Is a Challenge

In hindsight, it can be easy to identify a shift in cultural norms. They become evident in demographic information, or in surveys, or in data on how purchase behavior changes over time. To take advantage of the business opportunities that shifting norms present, you need to be able to recognize a shift as it is happening, or as it is just beginning to become mainstream.

However, while it is happening, a shift in a cultural norm can be difficult to recognize. Within every organization, established perspectives on customers and their needs already exist. Even when people experience shifts in their personal lives, they might not recognize the implications for their business.

Our minds are wired to pay attention to information that confirms what we know and ignore information that doesn't mesh with our worldview. This bias toward confirmatory evidence makes it hard to see change as it happens.

Tony Salvador, Genevieve Bell, and Ken Anderson, anthropologists working at Intel, have written about what they call contextual asynchrony, the tendency for people to act and think differently in the workplace than they do in their home lives.[2] This phenomenon interferes with people's ability to translate their experiences in their at home lives into implication for the products that they design, engineer, and market in their work lives. Instead, people tend to subscribe to a collective corporate view of "the customer" and his or her behaviors, attitudes, and values, and these views can remain stagnant even while people experience change in their personal lives.

Sometimes, we actually aren't our customers, and therefore won't know about changes in their lives unless we consciously go out and discover them. In his book *Wired to Care,* Dev Patnaik points out that one of the challenges that large companies have with building empathy for their customers is that their experiences are markedly different from those of their customers.[3]

These are experiential reasons why it can be hard to notice shifts in cultural norms. There are also cognitive reasons why recognizing shifting norms is challenging. There is a large body of psychological research that demonstrates that we all suffer from confirmation bias, the tendency to dismiss information that doesn't fit with our worldview and accept information that confirms how we already think. Basically, human beings generally prefer to believe that the way we think of the world is the way the world works, unless forcibly confronted with information that argues otherwise. And, when confronted with that information, we try to ignore it.

Companies Can Use Ethnography to Identify New Norms

In the face of these challenges, identifying shifting cultural norms or new norms seems impossible. Yet companies small and large have had success using methods from social science research to do so. Ethnographic research methods are designed to identify this kind of information.

Ethnography is a qualitative social research method tuned to understand culture, which is composed of what people do, the material people make, and what people think.

Ethnographic research for design or new opportunity identification typically involves observing people in the context that you want to understand, participating in their activities alongside them, and conducting interviews around the topics you are interested in that are designed to elicit stories about people's activities, behaviors, attitudes, and values. These basic methods can be supplemented by a wide range of additional techniques, such as card sorts to identify cognitive categories or mapping exercises to get at social norms. The people who ethnographers study aren't referred to as subjects; instead, they're participants, partners in the research process who collaborate with the researchers as they share their lives.

These social research tools help organizations understand people's behavior, emotions, attitudes, and priorities. They can then translate this learning into implications for what people need today, how those needs are evolving, and how they can create value for them in the future.

Corporate anthropologists, designers, and business process analysts have used ethnographic methods for over 30 years. There is a large body of work written about how to conduct this research in a rigorous way to inform the design of everything from software products to consumer products to business processes to entirely new companies. For an overview of ethnographic research methods and great insight on how to apply it, see Jeannette Blomberg's thorough chapter "Ethnographic Field Methods and their Relation to Design"(Sanoff, *Participatory Design: Theories and Techniques,* 1990). The remainder of this chapter highlights particular ways to conduct ethnographic research to identify shifts in cultural norms.

Using Ethnographic Research Methods to Uncover Evolving Norms

Understanding the importance of detecting even a subtle shift in cultural norms, now let's look at how, more specifically, to do that through applying an ethnographic approach to planning, conducting, and analyzing research.

1: Planning

Recruiting the right set of participants and creating an open-ended research protocol can set you up for more successful research.

Scattershot, but Purposefully So

Picture a target in your head, and imagine that you are the archer. Now, try not to aim for the middle (see Figure 7.1).

Figure 7.1 *This picture from the National Library of Ireland shows a woman looking delighted to have hit the bull's-eye. But notice the arrows on the outer ring of the target too. In my mind, that's a perfect combination of focused and scattered.*

Often, ethnographic research for design of new products or services is structured to study the people in the center of the bull's-eye. The goal is to learn as much as possible about a specific group of people who use a specific product or engage in an activity or a set of activities and understand how that singular group of people interacts with, feels about, and encounters a product or a product category.

So, for example, to grow your line of products for parents of young children, you will identify a relatively small number of parents of young children, perhaps between eight and ten, and get to know them pretty well. You might look for ethnic, socioeconomic, and geographic diversity and possibly representative family composition. This focus would allow a team to study small numbers of people and still identify patterns.

To identify shifting cultural norms, your team needs to understand the needs of people within the bull's-eye *and* the needs of people in the outer rings of the target. So that same company that is trying to understand potential new product categories, or new businesses, aimed at parents of young children will want a few parents of two children under the age of five, but they'll also need to recruit research participants who give them a much more diverse perspective of what parenthood is. They'll want to find people who are distributed all around that outer ring, for different reasons. This requires understanding the current trends that might change behavior over time.

It's critical that the trends are relevant to the category in interesting ways. Robust secondary research in both the popular press and academic journals can help your team identify what those trends are, which different points of view they need to understand, what's considered "normal," and who the interesting outliers are.

When you're looking as much at the edges of society as at the center in your research, it can be easy to dismiss what you see with comments like, "Oh, they're just doing that because..." (insert any reason you can think of as to why the person is just a quirky, unusual human being and you therefore can ignore what you learn from the person). However, these outliers can be the most important data that you identify. The key is to be able to tie the behaviors from the people on the edges of your target to the behaviors of the people in the center, and identify ways in which the same needs, values, desires, or aspirations appear in both groups. When you see that, you have a clue about how cultural norms might be shifting.

Use a Wide Angle Lens

After you've identified the people you want to spend time with, you need to frame your research activities so that you learn their whole lives, not just the parts of their lives that you think your organization is interested in. Although you might think of yourself as a provider of public transportation, in the automotive industry or in the business of manufacturing bicycle parts, the people who buy and use your products don't parse the world in the same way. They think about traveling or transportation, or how they're going to get from point A to point B. The factors that they perceive to be relevant to any single decision they make are not restricted by the boundaries of your industry.

Companies tend to view through the lens of how they construct offerings, and users evaluate based on how they experience the offering, which includes key contextually influencing factors.

When I am deciding how to get to work, for example, I think about the meetings I have that day and what I need to wear or carry. I look at the weather. I consider my family's schedule. Then I decide whether to take the bus, drive, or ride my bike. If you work for a bike manufacturer and want to understand future opportunities, you have to look beyond just understanding my relationship with my bike, my gear, and what my morning commute is like. You have to understand why I choose to ride on certain days and drive on others. You might need to understand my exercise routines, how I feel about my hair and my shoes, my relationship with technology, and a number of other factors that don't initially seem salient to the problem at hand. And you need to frame your research efforts so that you learn about all of those aspects of my life that you don't even know exist.

Of course we need to learn how people engage with, interact with, and experience products related to your business. But to see where those activities were headed, we need to see how those issues relate to the rest of people's lives. Setting up your research plan to enable that requires writing a broad, topic-based research protocol and making sure that you spend enough time with people to understand many aspects of their lives.

2: Execution

While you're conducting your research, use a wide-angle lens, follow your research subject's lead, and embrace their emotional moments. It is also important to progress from hand to heart to head, which means watch what they do, empathize with how they feel, and understand how they think. Document everything because when you get to the analysis phase, the insight moment might come from where you least expect it.

Follow Their Lead

As opportunity recognition is navigating through ambiguity, it can be frustrating to not know the answer, let alone the question. Fortunately, ethnography is best used when companies are aware that they do not know exactly what questions to ask. The observational and interviewing techniques are designed to allow the participant to lead the direction of the encounter. Of course, you can't just go in blindly to someone's home or office without any idea about what you want to see and hear about. The trick is to design observations, activities, and exercises that will give you the best shot at learning something new, and to follow people's lead when you're there. So if you're trying to understand my bike routines and I keep talking about my hair, or my kids, follow up on those parts of the conversation. The environment you're in can also provide prompts for what you need to learn more about. Just as archaeologists use the material culture of past societies to learn about their lives, you can use the material culture of the environments you are in to understand shifts in values. What do people leave out on the kitchen counter, and what appliances do they tuck away? What artifacts surround people in their workspaces (see Figure 7.2)? These are information trails you can follow to understand what matters to people.

Figure 7.2 *If you were doing ethnographic research with this university administrator, you'd learn a lot about both what she does all day and what's important to her through her material culture: the contents of her desk, her technology tools, and the decorations on her walls.*

Embrace Emotional Moments

Conducting ethnographic interviews and observing people as they go through their lives is socially awkward. You're in people's homes or workplaces, trying to get them to open up about their lives without sharing that much about your own life. It subverts our social script for how we behave with people whom we visit. However, you are there for a reason, and with the agreement of your research participant. Often, a good interview becomes a cathartic process for the participant. She gets to talk about something she's interested in, her life, and is asked to reflect on it. I've had participants thank me at the end of an interview and tell me how fun and illuminating it has been for them. If you've done a good job of building rapport with your participant, these conversations can become very emotional, making an awkward situation even more so. When a participant pauses to collect herself, or laughs awkwardly, or even tears up, an interviewer might be tempted to change the subject to keep things comfortable. Instead, let the moment happen. Either stay quiet and listen or find a gentle way to acknowledge the emotion and ask about it. Your participant might be experiencing cognitive dissonance and might be trying to resolve conflicting attitudes, expectations, or needs. This is a clue that the glacier is in motion and cultural norms are shifting.

Progress from Hand to Head to Heart

Often, when we observe others, we focus on what they're doing: their hands. We notice the activities and functions they're trying to accomplish. Dig a little deeper and focus on their head: What are they thinking about what they are doing, and how do they make conscious, rational sense of their behaviors? Why do they do what they do? Then ask yourself to look even deeper: into their hearts. How do they feel about what they are doing and what inner emotional needs to these activities and behaviors fulfill? What is the why behind the why? As you observe your participants, focus your observations from the external to the internal. As you conduct interviews, first ask about the hand, what they do. Then ask about the head, what they think about what they do. Finally, you will earn the right to ask about the heart: how they feel about what they do.

Document Everything

Managing these encounters, making sure you are following the participant's lead and hitting on the topics that you came to the encounter to learn about, is quite hard. It requires the ethnographer to be constantly listening, looking, thinking, processing, and remembering, all while building rapport with the participant. Because of this, it's impossible for any researcher to notice everything that's happening in the moment. Yet sometimes the most important information that can be learned is subtle. It's not what someone says in the moment, but it's the look that passes between two people while it's being said. We often do not see those things in the moment, and we can easily misremember what actually happened a few days, or even a few hours, later. The only way to notice these subtle moments is to go back and listen to the tape of the interview, watch the video (often over and over), or reread the transcript. This requires you to audiotape and videotape as many of your ethnographic encounters as possible. Many companies do great research yet fail to document the process well enough for researchers to go back and revisit the data to dig deeply into what was said or heard. Investing resources in documentation upfront will increase the yield on the time and money spent conducting the research.

3: Analysis

In the analysis phase embrace the large amounts of data and dive in, look for the outliers, and don't be afraid to ideate too early.

Geek Out!

After your research data is collected, spend as much time as possible with it! The goal of analysis is to try to construct a framework or generate an insight that will help you see the world in a new light. If you don't spend time really pushing toward insight, you might not notice the big news, or you might end up coming up with a very complete description of how the world works today without any understanding about how that could be evolving in the future. Ethnographic research methods create lots of information. Every minute of conversation, every gesture you observe, is data. Your first job is to organize it. Your second job is to restructure the way you've organized it so that you can learn from it. I recommend borrowing techniques from grounded theory, a social science analysis method that relies on inductive analysis of information by looking at how bits of information might be connected and creating categories based on those connections, rather than immediately categorizing information into the themes that are already in your head (see Figure 7.3). This opens up the opportunity for you to learn something absolutely new about your area of inquiry.

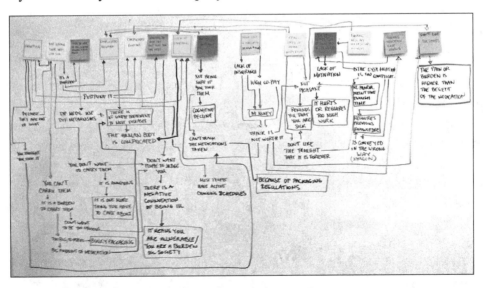

Figure 7.3 *My students Carolina Garzon and Sooyoung Cho created this root-cause map to understand the underlying reasons people don't always take their medications. It took them hours to create an accurate map of the causes, but the detailed analysis gave them a central focus for their project.*

After you have a hunch, created by really immersing yourself in the data, get a little geeky with the information in order to prove or disprove it. Use Post-Its, Excel spreadsheets, and any other techniques you can think of to ensure that your insights are truly grounded in data from the research.

Look for the Problem Scene

The actress Meryl Streep is acclaimed for her ability to step into a diverse range of roles and become the character. When asked about her craft, she talks about how, in every script, there's a problem scene, a scene that stumps her.[4] She can't quite figure out why her character would act that way, in that moment. And although her inclination is just to ignore that scene and not say the lines, she has learned that she can't do that. In fact, she has learned that understanding that scene is the best way for her to finally understand the character, to unlock the core of the story.

Ethnographic research inevitably provides research teams with problem scenes. Those stories that you can't quite figure out, a behavior that doesn't jibe with everything else you've heard about a participant. Like Streep, you will be very tempted to ignore these stories. But if you keep coming back to them, if you spend time trying to understand why that thing makes sense to that person, you will often unlock a surprising cultural norm, or a shift about to happen. Carefully considered, problem scenes can be your key to unlock new opportunities.

Don't Wait to Ideate

The design process as articulated in Chapter 5, "The Role of Learning Styles in Innovation Team Design," highlights four stages: observations (context), frameworks (insight), imperatives (ideas), and solutions (artifacts). It's an apt description of stages that every design process should go through, but it can be misleading. The visual of the diagram might imply that a team moves sequentially from one quadrant to another. Instead, the actual progression through the phases is not so simple or sequential. If drawn, it might look like the drawing of a two-year-old, scribbles all over the four quadrants. Clustering research findings in the analysis phase may simultaneously lead to insights and ideas or ideas that spur insights (see Figure 7.4).

Figure 7.4 *Sometimes, people can articulate big insights better through new ideas than through words. When ideating during the analysis phase of a project, take time to cluster and organize your ideas, as in this picture, so that you can learn from them.*

In an ideal ethnographic research world, we would start our process with observations and then go directly into a frameworking phase, during which we would be able to articulate our key insights clearly and coherently. And then we would ideate. However, the more surprising our insights are, the harder they can be to articulate. Instead of staying in an analytical phase, it is helpful to jump into ideation. If you've been immersed in the data, your ideas will be informed by what you've learned. And you might be able to articulate an insight through an idea that you couldn't quite get to while thinking analytically. Early ideation enables teams to tap into the implicit knowledge that they've gained from the research process. Taking a step back and looking at your idea, asking yourself why it's good, what it is that you've learned about the world that makes you think it's a good idea, can be the best way to prompt you to articulate how cultural norms are shifting.

Parting Advice: Building It into Your Culture

The previous conversation focuses on things you can do in the course of any project to better understand cultural shifts that are taking place and their implications for your business. These activities can be done on a project-by-project basis, but your organization will be stronger if you are able to turn deciphering cultural norms into an ongoing organizational capability.

If you work for a large corporation, you can create a team of internal consultants whose role is to identify shifting cultural norms for the purpose of identifying new opportunities for future growth. Many successful companies have special groups that are tasked to pay attention to the boundaries of their business—groups like the corporate anthropologists at Intel or the i-Squad, a team of senior scientists, marketers, and other specialists who guide business teams across General Mills on new product strategies. To ensure the success of these teams, they must be connected enough to the organization to understand its orthodoxies yet still able to offer a unique perspective and provide a different worldview. To borrow a term from Gordon MacKenzie, they should be able to orbit the giant hairball that is the large corporation—close enough to the organization to feel its gravitational pull yet still apart from it.[5] Don't just outsource peeking around corners to this team. Instead, task them to them facilitate the process for the rest of the organization. Ideally, they will know the best culturally appropriate ways to lead business teams in gaining perspective on cultural shifts and deliver insights in a manner that people within the organization can easily apply.

If you're a small company or an entrepreneur, you won't have the luxury of a separate team to focus on seeing what's next. You'll need to embed it into your activities.

Schedule regular times to get outside of your office and talk to your customers and stakeholders. Do this even when you feel you don't have time for it. Share your pitch and the products and services that you're working on often, even before you think they're ready to be seen outside the company. And then, take things a step further. Train yourself to pay attention to the things you don't yet understand—to look for problem scenes. Keep a good list of these problem scenes in a notebook or on a whiteboard, and revisit the list every month or so to see whether you've learned anything that could unlock the mysteries. Make time to think through the potential implications for your business, or your product.

These methods and techniques take an hour to learn, but a lifetime to master. The only way you and your team can get really good at immersing yourselves into the lives of others, seeing the world from their point of view, and understanding the implications for your business is to do it. And do it again. And again. Over time, you can train yourself to notice shifts in cultural norms.

Endnotes

1. For statistics on the decline of the significance of car ownership, see www.wnyc.org/blogs/transportation-nation/2012/jul/20/percentage-of-young-persons-with-a-drivers-license-continues-to-drop/.

2. Tony Salvador, Genevieve Bell, and Ken Anderson, "Design Ethnography," *Design Management Journal,* Fall 1999.

3. Dev Patnaik and Peter Mortensen, *Wired to Care: How Companies Prosper When They Create Widespread Empathy* (FT Press, 2009).

4. "Meryl Streep," interview by Wendy Wasserstein, December 1988.

5. Gordon MacKenzie, *Orbiting the Giant Hairball: A Corporate Fool's Guide to Surviving with Grace* (Viking Adult, 1998).

8

Design Process and Opportunity Development

Tod Corlett is Associate Professor of Industrial Design at Philadelphia University. He directs the Master of Science in Industrial Design program, and oversees the program's innovation-research and technology initiatives. Before full-time teaching, he was an award-winning lead designer for Cloud Gehshan Associates in Philadelphia. He maintains a design practice, Public Works, focused on design for public spaces. He holds a B.A. from Yale University and B.F.A. and M.I.D. degrees from the University of the Arts in Philadelphia.

Framing statement:

- Design is becoming known as an effective shared process, as well as a set of visual disciplines.
- This process has specific characteristics that let it help organizations understand challenges, articulate value propositions, and reach new markets.
- Now, diverse disciplines are coming to a shared understanding of design processes, one that is well suited to a fast-moving world of diverse teams, accelerated product life cycles, disruptive innovation, and social media.

"Coming Up with Good Ideas": What's Design?

It's widely thought that design is the process of having new or creative ideas. Although this is not completely untrue, the process of actually having more, or more creative, ideas is just a part of design, and it's covered elsewhere in this book, notably in Chapter 9, "Navigating Spaces—Tools for Discovery." Design is an innovation process;

that is, it's expected to develop new value, of one kind or another. Design turns notions and opinions into value. So, if one takes a bountiful source of new ideas as a given, the real task that separates design from mere dreaming is to separate good ideas from bad ones, and to make good ideas better and more effective. Design is to ideation what the polymerase chain reaction is to DNA: It's an amplifier that turns a precious, rare commodity into something that can be worked with on an industrial scale. If design is a way of separating good ideas from bad, it follows that design operates by making ideas real, in order to assess and manage the way those ideas fail. Failures—in particular, fast failures—are the key tools of design.

The Leverage of Upstream Innovation: Failure and Managerial Thinking

Fail early and often is a mantra used by many innovation consulting firms to remind clients of the importance of experimenting and learning earlier in the process. The notion of embracing failure is the antithesis of managerial thinking.

Failing Better

Innovation is inseparable from risk. Anything new stands a reasonable chance of failure. Evolution is built on failure. Most of us appreciate the usefulness of looking at failures in separating good innovation from bad, but we tend to see failure as a mysterious process, clear only in hindsight. Failure has a bad reputation. Certainly nobody wants it to happen to them, and only the pessimistic expect it. In fact, depending on your definition of failure, eight or nine out of ten new ventures fail—a terrifying prospect. Failures can arrive from any direction, without warning. Failures of new ventures can happen because of delivery delays, technology development problems, cash-flow issues, problematic quality assurance, and bad customer service, just to get started. It's important to consider the difference between mistake and failure. Mistake is error without theory. Failure is an experiment tied to a theory from which you can learn and experiment again with new knowledge and insight.

Failure isn't as mysterious as it appears, however. Like fire, it's a frighteningly destructive force that can be used as a tool by those who are canny, cautious, and systematic enough. It also resembles fire in that small, intentional, strategic failures can guard against larger, disastrous ones. In approaching failures, however, there are some important, linked, and rather counterintuitive principles that potential users need to understand:

- Much of traditional management and business practice is based on operating according to a set of fixed assumptions, and aimed at eliminating and delaying small failures.
- In a VUCA environment (see the following section), unexamined assumptions are failures in disguise.
- Small failures prevent large failures, so preventing small failures is bad. Learning from them is key.
- Failing early is smaller and hence better than failing later; thus, delaying failures is also bad.
- Design can be thought of as a versioning and simulation system for making and learning from intentional, small, quick failures, reducing the size of failures, moving failures upstream, and converting assumptions into failures early.

Managerial Thinking and Failure

A really important distinction needs to be made between what can be called "manageable failures" and "wicked problems"—because both are important, but many don't appreciate that they require diametrically opposed strategies to resolve them and learn from them. Spinelli and others have pointed out the basic philosophical difference between "managerial" and "entrepreneurial" modes of thinking and of building and running businesses. The goal of managerial thinking is the elimination of risk and unpredictability, in the service of achieving a smooth-running enterprise. In Chapter 3, "Framing the Vision for Engagement," McGowan notes the difference between opportunity recognition and value creation. Entrepreneurial thinking is key in the problem-finding phase of the process whereas managerial thinking is key in value creation, especially in optimization phases.

Managerial thinking isn't bad by any means; its suitability varies by context. It's simply better adapted to circumstances in which conditions are stable, all the learning has been done already, and efficiency of operation and optimization can be made a primary goal. Managerial thinking can make a business successful, as long as it has a model to follow, but it can't do original innovation or adapt rapidly to change or disruption. Managerial thinking is the key to monetization of an innovation. Manageable failures are those that can be ameliorated by standard managerial thinking: failures to plan, failures to deploy the correct resources, failures to follow known best practices.

Wicked problems, on the other hand, are those stemming from volatility, uncertainty, complexity, or ambiguity within or affecting the new enterprise—the so-called VUCA factors. Traditional managerial thinking is powerless against these.

Of course, moving appropriately between managerial and entrepreneurial modes of thinking isn't just a matter of knowing the difference between them; there must also be an institutional culture robust and flexible enough to support both modes within one organization. Ellen di Resta discusses this foundation further in Chapter 4, "Assessing Your Innovation Capability."

Design and Disruptive Innovation

The failures of traditional managerial thinking aren't hard to find. Sometimes they can be as simple as becoming overly complacent. As part of a business innovation course, Philadelphia University sophomore Elizabeth Benedetti researched Boscov's department store, a family-owned regional retailer based in Reading, Pennsylvania. Boscov's succeeded for decades, and had a sustainable competitive advantage: Their customers were stubbornly loyal. Boscov's conscientiously learned and stocked what their customers liked. However, as the years went by, Boscov's customer base began to skew older and older, and the company proved unable to innovate to bring in younger buyers. Its dwindling customer base forced Boscov's to reorganize and sell out to its creditors in 2008. This enabled it to reduce its costs, but still didn't help it to innovate; as of 2013, it was once again following its loyal customers toward the graveyard.

Disruptive innovations are an especially troubling kind of wicked problem. As defined by Clayton Christensen, these are simple, cheap new products and services that transform their industries, starting at the bottom of a market. By now, disruptive innovations are widely recognized, and means for generating them (and guarding against them) are widely sought. However, habits of managerial thinking can be hard to transcend, or to supplement with more innovative practices, even under severe corporate duress. In 2007, in an interview with *Wired,* Doug Morris, CEO of Universal Music Group, described his company's response to the technological transformation that led to CDs being replaced by digital downloads: "They just didn't know what to do. It's like if you were suddenly asked to operate on your dog to remove his kidney. What would you do?" Universal didn't know how innovation was done. What's more, as Ellen di Resta discusses in Chapter 4, their corporate culture didn't support the changes they needed to make to find out.

The Importance of Upstream

These cases share two common elements of failure: Corporate leaders failed to examine the assumptions they held about the technologies, markets, and customers they interacted with, and they found no way to act, or to build new strategies, while their problems were small. Instead of examining their assumptions about their products, value propositions, and markets—in lieu of predicting, analyzing, and testing responses to trends—they waited until change at a scale that would save them was vastly expensive and difficult, if not impossible.

However, all products and services are developed, launched, maintained, and phased out in cycles, including those at Universal Music and Boscov's, and this cyclical nature of product and venture development gives innovators a key point where change is not just possible but necessary. At the initial, "upstream" end of a product development cycle, anything can happen, and happen cheaply. The cost of changes is low, and they can be made instantly. A product on paper can be revised in a moment. A prototype product, however, even before production tooling, can represent an investment of millions. The farther upstream in your process you can generate and test new ideas, the more quickly and cheaply you can innovate.

This is why design-based processes fare better against wicked problems: They're based on evaluating options and innovations quickly, at the upstream end of the development cycle, using three major tools: prototyping, integrative thinking, and iteration. Risks are minimized by making a series of small, fast, intelligent bets, in order to inform the big risks that must be undertaken downstream.

Prototyping

Prototyping is a practice of making solutions as real as possible through upstream simulation. This can mean making physical representations of new products, but it can also encompass videos, storyboards, interactive mock-ups, and stories. Failures in prototype are inexpensive, instructive learning experiences, which can prevent much larger failures downstream in the development process. Steve Jobs famously said, "Sometimes people don't know what they want until you show it to them." This has been misinterpreted by many to mean, "Trust your instincts, ignore the naysayers, research is a distraction, full speed ahead." To pull off this approach to new ventures, however, you pretty much have to be Steve Jobs. For the rest of us, his aphorism really means customers should be shown more versions of more products more quickly, so as to reliably learn what they want. If you use the right tools and procedures, we can all do that.

Resolution Versus Fidelity

Design prototypes, then, are representations of products or systems, produced quickly and inexpensively, for the purpose of assessing and learning from user or customer response, usability, and interaction. This is very different from the traditional engineering prototype, which is used for final validation of a system in all particulars before tooling up for production.

In 1997, Stephanie Houde and Charles Hill (interestingly, working at Apple at the time) defined the key concepts resolution and fidelity as applied to prototyping. Resolution describes how much detail is present in the prototype. To design any product, service, or business system, all the details have to be defined and prototyped eventually. But because detail tends to be both time-consuming and expensive to develop, prototypes that embody too much detail end up exiling themselves from the cheap, effective upstream end of the design process and becoming expensive, static investments in themselves. Additionally, users tend to react to the details as opposed to the broader experience and potential of the solution. Fidelity is how closely the experience of using the prototype approximates that of using the designed system—in only those areas being assessed. The classic example is a surgical handset designed by the consultancy IDEO. The breakthrough prototype—the one that allowed validation of an innovative, market-changing product—was taped together by a surgeon from office supplies on the table during a discussion (see Figure 8.1).

Resolution of prototypes should always be kept to the minimum necessary for the task at hand. Fidelity, as the example shows, is context-dependent, can be created on the fly, and should be maximized in creative ways where possible. Low-resolution, high-fidelity prototypes tend to engage users in completing the picture, offering the added benefit of user co-creation.

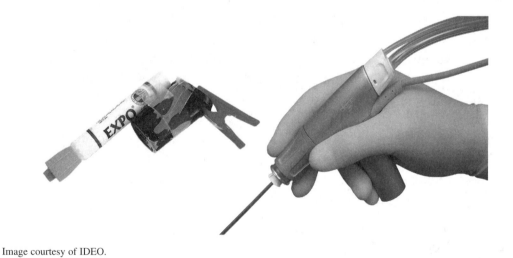

Image courtesy of IDEO.

Figure 8.1 *Surgical prototype from office supplies.*

In-Market Prototyping

Although it's usually true that products and systems that are ready for the market have taken too long getting there and are too expensive to realize the benefits of upstream prototyping, good businesses realize that every product is potentially a prototype—if and only if they can learn enough about their customers' reactions and experiences with it. In addition, recent developments such as 3D printers, third-party logistics, overnight freight, e-commerce, and quick-turnaround manufacturing have made some kinds of product rollouts so fast and inexpensive that what IDEO's Anthony D'Avella calls "in-market prototyping" is becoming commonplace. Some businesses, in fact, have built themselves around the idea of prototyping continually.

Integrative Thinking

Integrative thinking, as defined by Roger Martin of the Rotman School of Management, is the process of adding factors to a problem to achieve solutions that don't rely on compromise. Between them, integrative thinking and prototyping are Kryptonite to unexamined assumptions. Peripheral but unexamined factors are discovered, and failures are forced to happen early.

Iteration

Iteration is the key factor in design that enables quick, effective learning based on generating and prototyping new ideas. In brief, iteration is the cyclic process of the following:

- Studying product/service users and markets to uncover new insights
- Generating credible new ideas quickly
- Visualizing and prototyping them
- Testing and evaluating them in interaction with potential users and customers
- Changing, editing, and improving them based on feedback
- Repeating the cycle

Helical Thinking

The design cycle, of course, would be useless if it just went around. As it revolves, however, it also quickly moves understanding and decision making forward. This three-dimensional dynamic has led Banny Banerjee, of Stanford ChangeLabs, to refer to it as "helical thinking." Helical thinking and iterative prototyping can generate value in novel ways; as design teacher Hy Zelkowitz puts it, "The value lies in where you get off the bus." User research and framing of good problems can generate new product and process ideas. However, believable, prototyped ideas can also be used as the basis for more advanced research.

Philips Electronics doesn't just design thousands of consumer, medical, and industrial products. They intentionally design and prototype future products that can't be achieved at reasonable cost with current technology. Then they use these prototypes to learn which technologies, affordances, and features consumers value—not the things they want, but the things they would want—if those could be possible. Philips uses this information about its extensive nonexistent product lines to make very real, very big decisions. In 1998 Philips funded an exhibition of future products that traveled around the world; in New York it made a temporary home on the second floor of Bloomingdales. In addition to positioning Philips as an exciting leader and innovator in technology products, the show enabled Philips to gather information on consumer responses to products and technologies that it wasn't yet able to offer—to determine corporate strategy by finding out what it did not yet know it didn't know. Several of the prototypes featured flexible, folding display screens—an impossibility to produce, given the technology of the time. Potential customers, however, loved them. In response, Philips made major budget allocations for internal efforts to develop flexible screens; they also bought up several small flexible-display start-ups. Now, although flexible screens still aren't commonplace, it's clear they're coming. For its part, Philips has assembled a formidable portfolio of flexible-display patents and technologies. When the future does arrive, it will need to go through Philips first. As one analyst observed, Philips used the design cycle to "install a tollbooth on the way to the future." In other words, the research side of the design cycle generates prototypes—and the prototypes can be used to generate better research—to amplify the effectiveness of learning, and of institutional strategy based on it.

The Funnel, or Filter, and the Fence

The design process is commonly described as a "funnel" or "filter"—a process of editing or selecting among competing concepts, with a single surviving "best" idea at the end (see Figure 8.2).

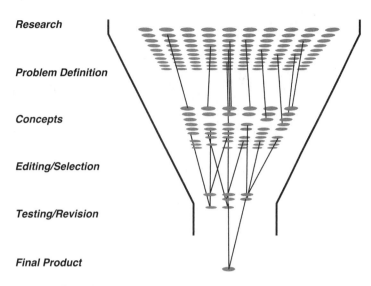

Research

Problem Definition

Concepts

Editing/Selection

Testing/Revision

Final Product

Figure 8.2 *The funnel: traditional design process.*

Although this describes the convergent phase of the design process well, and a single final product often serves the needs of a project—for instance, if the objective is to develop a product—users of design processes should keep in mind their ability to "get off the bus" with more than one finished result when the desired result requires it.

In their "Heimspiel" project, for instance, IDEO Berlin wanted to define a particular "area of opportunity" they had found through user research, one based on products embodying ideas of "play" in their use. A single final designed product would have demonstrated the opportunity's capability to support a single product, but IDEO wanted to build a "fence" around the opportunity, to show its extent, boundaries, and limits, in order to demonstrate its size and validity as a potential market opportunity (see Figure 8.3). To this end, they developed a finished collection of six products, in different product categories and customer segments, to fully define the opportunity. Because it makes use of divergent, as well as convergent, phases, and incorporates both concrete and abstract modes of thought and documentation, the design process is well suited to generate diverse products for different purposes and audiences, not just "designs."

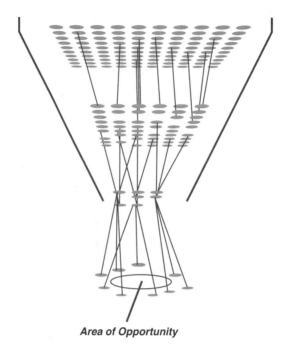

Area of Opportunity

Figure 8.3 *The fence—iterative, multiple-endpoint design process: mapping opportunity.*

Opportunity Development: Design Across Disciplines

The collaborative, interdisciplinary design process described here originated primarily as a way for engineers and graphic and industrial designers to explain and structure their processes and collaborative interactions. Now, however, the process has escaped from the industries where it was born, and spread virally. In the twenty-first century, it has become anachronistic to think of design processes as the exclusive property of designers, but this broad application is a very recent development.

The Age of Agile

In the 1990s, Mark Fowler and other software programmers became dissatisfied enough with established long-term, inflexible, preplanned, and top-down methods of software development that they proposed an alternative, one that would enable them to communicate better and write more robust code more quickly, while allowing rapid responses to changing conditions. In 2001, they published the *Agile Software Manifesto,* which laid out a set of new development processes and principles. These were revolutionary in the software engineering field, but to industrial designers, they immediately seemed familiar: Small teams, working in fast, iterative loops, moving from divergent ideation to quick prototyping to evaluative testing and back again. The agile software revolution quickly spread across Silicon Valley and then the world during the great Internet boom. From there, entrepreneurs in the software industry adapted techniques based in their technology backgrounds to the design of entire new business ventures. Their hope was to reach better-defined markets more quickly, with better-tuned products, and to seize the prized "first-mover" advantage in the fast-changing software marketplace.

This movement, called "lean start-up," was evolved by the technologist and venture investor Steve Blank, in his book *Four Steps to the Epiphany*. Blank added another vital element that united lean development with user-centered design. Frustrated with the failure rate of new ventures, most of which were predicated on "if you build it, they will come" approaches that put technologies first, Blank advocated that entrepreneurs instead "get out of the building," widen their focus, and start with product users instead—study their potential customers' lives, work, and needs closely, in order to frame better-understood, simpler problems for technology start-ups to solve. In other words, Blank completed a process of convergent evolution, as best practices for new business opportunity development became analogous in principle and process with product development processes. Thus, we refer to this interdisciplinary, collaborative process as "opportunity development." Whether the opportunity is a product, a system, a technology, or a business, the steps, the roles, and the kinds of thinking required are the same.

Modes of Thinking in Opportunity Development: A Shared Process

To work effectively in a shared design process, design, engineering, and business disciplines have to understand the modes of thought that lead to success in different parts of the iterative cycle, and the ways diverse disciplines can contribute (see Figure 8.4). Although traditional disciplinary stereotypes are not always true or applicable—the creative designer, the linear businessperson, the analytical engineer—it's really useful to remember that design is as much about editing, organizing, and analyzing as it is about creating. And if there are team members who are strong in a particular thought process, it's good to know where to deploy that thinking within the design loop, as Dr. Beckman notes in Chapter 5, "The Role of Learning Styles in Innovation Team Design."

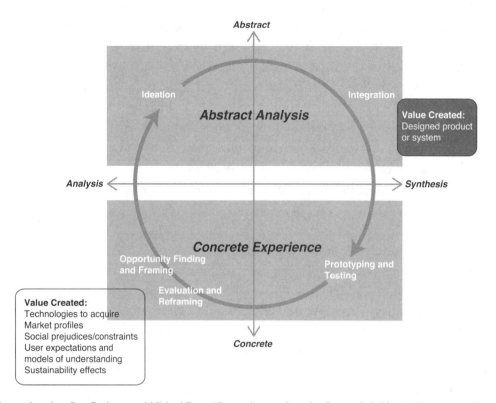

Diagram based on Sara Beckman and Michael Barry, "Innovation as a Learning Process," *California Management Review,* vol. 50, no. 1, Fall 2007.

Figure 8.4 *Design cycle: modes of thinking.*

As Beckman explains, the process begins in the lower-left quadrant with opportunity finding and framing, which calls for skills in analytical thinking, applied to concrete situations. The next phase, ideation, is much more abstract—this is where the brainstorming happens, and serious divergent thinking is required. It's still analytical, though; these ideas can be about visualizing or responding to pieces of a problem clearly, and at this phase it's important that there is no requirement that an idea represent a perfect solution or respond to every identified need. It's enough to get all the ideas out into the world where they can be compared and evaluated in the next phase, called integration. This is a phase that calls for good skills working in abstract, convergent modes, and it's also synthetic—in this phase the whole is more important than the parts, and the team is striving to fit things together. The process then shifts to prototyping and testing, which is concrete and synthetic; it's about making something in and for the real world.

Iteration is simple in principle and powerful in its effects, but can be difficult to build into organizations that are used to linear processes. The usual fear is that iteration will result in needless repetition and cost, as decisions are examined over and over again, or that the process will come to a halt without having generated meaningful results. In fact, this is hardly ever the case. Iteration, in many cases, beats planning, especially if you don't know what you don't know. However, Jump Associates, a design and business consultancy, has found that this fear is consistent enough that they've been able to graph it (see Figure 8.5). Design always requires taking a risk, persevering in pursuit of insights and solutions, and having faith in the process and the abilities of the team members using it. As you use design in your own work, keep this knowledge in mind, and you'll be better able to predict your own, and other stakeholders', reactions and state of mind.

Overview

Exploration is an emotional rollercoaster.

Jump uses an inductive analysis process. That means that halfway through a project, we won't yet have half the answer. It's often not until near the end of a project that the answer emerges. The emotional experience of a project tracks with how fully the problem is solved.

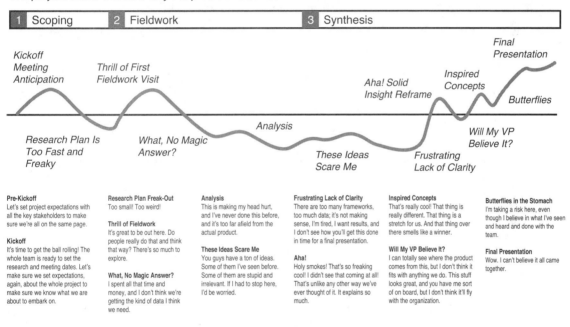

Jump Associates Confidential

©2013 Jump Associates

Figure 8.5 *Emotional rollercoaster of white space exploration.*

Conclusion

This chapter has introduced design as a set of processes, procedures, and ways of thinking, all aimed at taking good ideas and making them better. Although the details will always be evolving, all good design is based on two major principles. The first is what the entrepreneur Steve Blank calls "getting out of the building"—finding new insights directly, by observing and talking to the people who will buy and use the systems being designed. The second is iteration, the process of making small, fast, informed, sequential, and very intentional failures as a way of putting ideas into the real world, while managing the attending risks.

For decades, these simple ideas were thought of as somehow the property of inherently "creative" people—but in fact, those people were probably more creative just because they learned to follow a few simple design processes. As Jump Associates has shown, design still has the capability to discomfit conventional thinkers, because it's impossible to predict the process's end result. In the end, though, the results are generally well worth the discomfort.

9

Navigating Spaces—Tools for Discovery

Photo credit: Janelle Wysock.

Natalie Nixon, Ph.D., is a hybrid thinker, synthesizing the creative and the analytical to arrive at innovative opportunities. A design-thinking researcher, she has 15-plus years' experience as an educator and has worked in the fashion industry as an entrepreneurial hat designer and in sourcing for The Limited Brands in Sri Lanka and Portugal. Natalie's consulting interests are in business design and in applying strategies from the fashion industry to other realms. Natalie earned her B.A. *(cum laude)* from Vassar College, Anthropology and Africana Studies; M.S. from Philadelphia University, Global Textile Marketing; and Ph.D. from the University of Westminster, London, Design Management.

Introduction: What Is the Discovery Process?

Problem solving has become a commodity activity; the real added value is in framing the problem, and being certain that you've even asked the right question. This chapter discusses the tools to frame the problem and navigate the innovation process, with emphasis on the phases of discovery and formulation, as mentioned in Chapter 3, "Framing the Vision for Engagement." If we understand innovation as a discovery process, the best tools to navigate this process are ones that are adaptive, fluid, and accessible. Innovation is grounded in both inspiration and invention, and as such, it cannot be restricted by inflexible contraptions. Think of sailing, cooking, and jazz improvisation. In each of these endeavors, a concrete skill set, structures, and clear parameters are essential. However, those structures are meant to be fluid, meant for rebounding, to be played with and to be tweaked. Similarly, the best tools for innovation are those that allow for structure and flow. Diverse tools are needed, much like the parable of the six blind men and the elephant: Each man described completely different qualities of the elephant depending on whether he was touching the animal's husk, ear, or foot. Using only one tool will only lead us to see a portion of the opportunity ahead of us.

This chapter is based on research and interviews with 12 diverse and distinctive practitioners from innovation firms and consumer products companies.

The Purpose of Tools

We typically think of tools applied to do physical tasks. In environments that are complex and ambiguous, it is important that tools are utilitarian, process-oriented, and also adaptive. Tim Brown has said, "The design process is best described metaphorically as a system of spaces rather than a predefined series of orderly steps" ("Design Thinking," *HBR,* 2008). Extending that notion, innovative outcomes are a result of proceeding through a system of spaces, not linear steps.

We end with definitions of a tool by the 12 practitioners interviewed for this chapter. For simplicity's purposes we'll start by defining a tool as an adaptive device that provides a means to an end. That device could be a tangible object or a process.

The Repertory: An Adaptive Toolbox

What follows is a repertoire of seven foundational tools (see Figure 9.1) to assist you in sparking empathy and curiosity about who your user is, what his or her real needs are, and how you can discover new insights about the extension and capacity of your offering. By practicing and applying these tools to various situations (see Figure 9.2), you will develop and customize your own portfolio of methods that will enable you to adapt to the changing needs of your customer and allow for structure and flow.

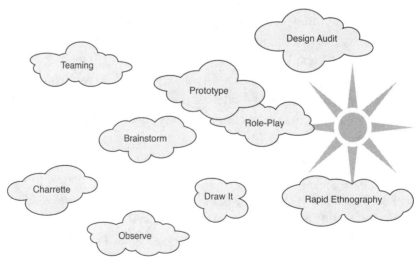

Figure 9.1 *Tools for discovery.*

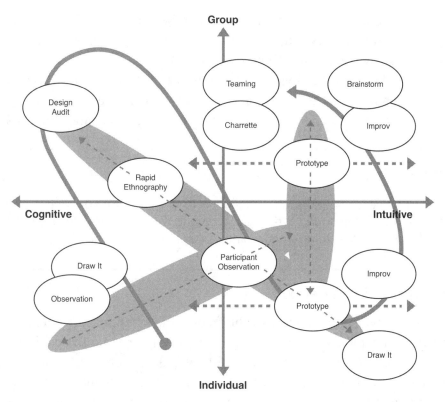

Figure 9.2 *Tools for types of discovery.*

Teaming

As you learned in Chapters 5, "The Role of Learning Styles in Innovation Team Design," and 6, "Your Team Dynamics and the Dynamics of Your Team," getting good at teaming requires an organization to view itself as an organic, evolving ecosystem. The formation and sustaining of teams involves setting up the right human dynamics and the correct problem definition. This is one of the most critical steps in any of the subsequent innovation techniques because the real value comes from the people in the organization. Developing a productive team could take six to eight weeks to allow for latency in conversations to emerge. One of the biggest mistakes in teaming is not allowing for the right diversity in the room. For example, the team should include people beyond the core team working the problem so that the process taps into naive eyes, who tend to help the discovery process. Include skeptics and early adopters on the same team because this causes creative abrasion, a friction between two seemingly opposing ideas that results in more innovative insights.

Lastly, an important part of teaming is tracking the team according to metrics such as safety, support, creative expression, value, and truth. These particular metrics come from the work of Mukara Meredith, whose consultancy, MatrixWorks, outlines a process to help groups view themselves as living systems. If one of those metrics is out of whack, there are corresponding activities to set new ground rules. This example points out the dynamic (not static) way to approach maintaining a team that is part of an ecosystem.

Exercise

Who are the outliers in a particular challenge facing you? Make a list of unusual suspects you might include in the main team and subteams to inform this challenge. Pick two and create an action plan about how to engage them.

Brainstorming and Charrettes

Brainstorming is a synthetic act and its value is that it is a tool for reflection. The important thing to remember about brainstorming is, as Manoj Fenelon of PepsiCo reminds us, "Creativity needs constraints!" Constraints actually make the creative brainstorming process more fun and productive. For example, time limits are helpful constraints. Another constraint might be that you require a particular word (say, "rose," for example) to be included in every proposed solution during the brainstorming session. Not everyone is a proponent of brainstorming because it can devolve into one huge divergent brain dump. The purpose of a brainstorming session is often less about the final idea and more about making people on the team feel as though they are part of the process. As you grow in your brainstorming capacity, it might be helpful to develop a library of exercises.

Brainstorming is an in-out process that speaks to the organizational culture, because it definitely requires an emotional readiness and willingness to expose oneself. Not all organizations are up to the task for brainstorming.

One of the wonderful outcomes of brainstorming is something John Heath, Senior Vice President of Innovation at Chobani, calls "wet paint"—because nothing should ever seem as though it is fully baked. Otherwise, it appears as if you are telling someone what to do, instead of valuing their engagement in a process.

The charrette is a structured brainstorming and consensus-building methodology used for problem solving among diverse stakeholders. It has been used traditionally in the architecture and urban-planning fields to unite stakeholders and engage in conflict resolution. Charrettes are a proven means for generating actionable opportunities for the purposes of innovation. The purpose of a charrette is to share ideas within a succinct time frame in an interdisciplinary setting. Teams are asked to produce multiple variations of an idea, in rapid succession, so that the larger group can review a large quantity of ideas. It is better to have 25 ideas with 3 potentially great ones than to spend many hours coming up with "the one good idea." The structure of the charrette enables you to take advantage of the convergence-divergence process that is key in any creative process. Divergent thinking comes with the free-flow, fire-hose push of ideas outward. Convergent thinking is equally, essentially, for sorting and sifting through all of those ideas, identifying what bigger ideas begin to surface, and acting on particular ones.

A two-day charrette might be structured in the following way, as described by Nick Hahn of Vivaldi Partners: On day one there is lots of divergent, big-picture thinking. On day two convergent thinking occurs utilizing "dot-allocation"—that is, participants place dot stickers on the ideas that they believe are most actionable. Day two is more tactical and involves figuring out how your team will actually do what has surfaced. Cindy Tripp prefers to use dot-allocation to highlight the ideas that scare participants regardless of viability because those spaces tend to debunk preconceived notions and lead to innovative insights.

Teams should also ask, "What is the cost of failure if the idea does *not* work?" and, "Who else is doing this?" Teams need to produce many ideas very quickly in order to create a broad range of ideas that can be vetted by the larger group. Keep in mind that these identified opportunities can be small ideas, and result in subtle shifts that will have large implications for innovation in organizations of any size or scope. Ideally, the charrette consists of at least two sessions of two to three days each, with one- to three-month interims during which stakeholders are exploring the actionable ideas that have surfaced and conducting more research. In this way, the charrette is part of an iterative process.

Exercise

1. **Metaphor:** Sometimes a metaphor exercise is helpful to provide the necessary boundaries. Construct a brainstorming session in which participants are required to plug in related words, for example, "_____ is like a _____."

2. **SCAMPER:** Valerie Jacobs of LPK uses SCAMPER as a way to help teams incrementally build on one idea, instead of jumping from idea to idea. SCAMPER is an acronym that stands for substitute, combine, adapt, modify, put to another use, eliminate, reverse. Ask questions about your existing product or service using each of those seven prompts, for example, "We own a brick-and-mortar clothing boutique. What could substitute for the physical store in which we currently sell our clothing?"

3. **Flip-It:** Mark Raheja of Undercurrent likes to have teams practice intentionally taking an opposing viewpoint of an idea that has been offered, even if it is their own idea!

Prototyping

Prototyping is the process of representing an idea in rough-draft form. As Chapter 8, "Design Process and Opportunity Development," details, prototypes can be low fidelity or high resolution depending on your goals in creating the simulation. Pop-up retail is one way to prototype the tangible and the intangible; improvisation and role-playing are means to prototype new service delivery ideas, brand stories, or a customer journey. Prototyping places value on failing early and often, before millions of dollars have been invested in new hires or new technology. The reason to prototype is to learn things. A prototype gives tangible access to examine three parts of the discovery process: Here is what we are testing; here is our hypothesis; here is what we hope to learn. It is data that can be used to generate more data.

Proximity to the user and the conditions in which you do the prototyping are essential. For example, some companies take the Skunkworks approach and sequester the prototyping team away from the politics and business pressures of the daily work. Prototyping has different uses at different points in a project.

Exercise

A video such as "Powers of Ten" (www.powersof10.com/) can help you think about the scale at which you are prototyping. For example, "How would this department function differently if employees were engaged in metrics based on contentment versus metrics based on performance?" Or "How would our sales team function differently if the members were engaged in metrics based on bravery instead of metrics based on risk taking?"

Prototypes are pilots with specifically defined objectives that can help you examine what you are doing. Watch the "Powers of Ten" video and then brainstorm a new metric that is another way to view the function of your team.

Observation and Fieldwork

Fieldwork is a critical methodology in anthropology and many organizations have begun to hire anthropologists. It requires people to immerse themselves in the environment of the user and utilize skills such as interviewing, observation, participant-observation, and a range of documentation techniques like note taking, photography, and video recording. Greater insight about the use of anthropology and ethnography and specifically fieldwork can be found in Chapter 7, "Leveraging Ethnography to Predict Shifting Cultural Norms."

Mark Raheja of Undercurrent reminds us, "There is what people *say*, and then there is what people *do*!" Observation ends up being many innovative companies' most accessed tools, and the most overlooked in run-of-the-mill organizations. Some organizations incorporate digital tools such as Evernote to tag and reference visual observations, and end up creating a bibliography. Observation is incredibly important and can deliver a tremendous amount of data if done properly; note that it's what you see, not what you interpret. Noting that "a juvenile delinquent is standing around in the middle of the day looking suspicious" is interpreting; noting that "it is 2:15 on a Tuesday afternoon and a boy is sitting with an iPod, headphones, baggy jeans, a T-shirt, and a baseball cap on a corner at a bus stop" is seeing.

Fieldwork is a way to connect to the work at hand, to get to stories and then analyze those stories. It helps you learn the context in which an object, a service, or an experience lives. As Annie Chang of Jump Associates explained, "A lot of the work we do is emergent—when it comes to ambiguous challenges, we need to let those themes emerge over time." Jordan Fischer of Gravity Tank points out that fieldwork allows for the ambiguity that is part of letting themes emerge over time.

Exercise

A-E-I-O-U: After brainstorming, select a site where you can observe a user interacting with your product or service. In one row, write and sketch what you see, hear, and smell in terms of activities, environment, interactions, objects, and users. In the row just beneath, write down how you are interpreting what you have just observed.

Audits

An audit is a detailed cataloging of a product or service from various perspectives. Audits are used in the innovation discovery process by taking inventory of a brand, product, or service; one must conduct detailed observation, interviewing, and secondary research. For the purposes of innovation, "design audits" and "brand audits" are often helpful. Sometimes a good place to start is with what is commonly known as the 3C's of the organization: the company itself, the customers of that product or service, and the competitors. Audits work well because they require narrow focus and detailed attention to aspects of the product or service that you typically might have ignored. For example, if auditing a product, you would note the color, textures, and form that are embedded in the design of the object. It is helpful to look broadly at related products. Additionally, one can use audits when exploring broader, higher-level topic areas that are helpful for business improvement. So, for example, if "convenience" is the topic at hand, an audit is helpful for taking stock of convenience in multiple areas and environments. What are all the ways to be convenient? You might look at fast-food restaurants, public restrooms, or luggage. Each of these is an on-ramp to the field of convenience.

Exercise

Conduct an audit of your organization's brand by cataloging all the ways messaging is communicated about your offering.

Draw It: Visual Mapping and Diagramming

A component of the innovation process involves looking ahead, identifying what artists call "negative space" (that space in between the outlined contours), and attempting to see what is not yet visible to the masses. When done effectively, visual mapping builds consensus around a problem and explores possible solutions in order to articulate the final vision. "If I have a good designer that can draw pictures and articulate the right thing, then I can get people to really work well," says John Heath at the Chobani offices in New York City. He points to a huge chalkboard full of beautiful illustrations of fruits and vegetables and container shapes that illustrate potential new flavor combinations for their yogurts. He explains that Chobani has begun to use this method of live chalkboard drawing to pitch new ideas; instead of using PowerPoint, one of their artists on staff draws the concept and they end up with live, nondigitized infographics: "Once we have identified the new product, story becomes important because that is the envisioning part." Manoj Fenelon of PepsiCo recalls a colleague who presented a strategic plan to a CEO as a visual map, almost in cartoon form. It was effective because it caused people to lean in and engage.

When presented with a sketch or a drawing, people tend to lean in, and engage with the big ideas. Dan Roam, author of *Back of the Napkin* and *Blah, Blah, Blah,* reminds us that we are hard-wired to respond to visual representations, and that she who can draw it gets the negotiation done, gets the deal done, and receives the ultimate buy-in from the team. When clients participate in the pattern emergence, they own their business competencies and have a firm grasp of their own offering as well as those of their competitors. The business model canvas, presented in Chapters 10, "Value Creation through Shaping Opportunity—The Business Model," and 11, "Developing Sustainable Business Models," is an example of a visual mapping tool. Like most visual mapping tools, it is helpful in distilling complex ideas. The canvas helps people see each component of their business to help support their strategy. When you can finesse tools such as the business model canvas, it is easier to break the rules.

Gordon Hui and Mai Nguyen explain how, at Smart Design, "we like real consumers," and because they are driven to put people first, they use "Consumer Snapshots" as a way to highlight key takeaways of a particular user group. These snapshots are three-dimensional thumbnails of real people, not personas that are composites of people, and thus tend to be a simplification of the user. The messiness of consumer snapshots shows the messiness and complexity of the issue as well. Annie Chang from Jump Associates explains how they frequently use the whiteboard and notebooks to visually record meetings; it grants assurance and makes people feel heard.

Another powerful tool is customer journey mapping, which visually charts the physical and emotional touch points a customer has through interacting with your service or product. A complete customer journey map starts before the need and ends after the solution has been consumed and discarded. For example, a user with a potential medical need could begin his journey prior to diagnosis of an illness, at the point of a preexisting condition, and it could flow all the way through the stages of disease progression with a textured noting of emotional and physical considerations for the user, his family, his medical community, and so on. A hotel would begin plotting their customer journey map at the point of awareness of the offering (the Web? word of mouth?), and incorporate the travel to the hotel (airport experience? cab or designated van service?), detail phases of the stay (welcome, room experience, walking through hallways, etc.), departure, and resonance of the stay in the user's memory. Even traditional consumer product journey maps begin with research and awareness and extend through use to customer service when there is a post-purchase issue and on to disposal and reflection. Although many companies focus on product or service performance alone, full customer journey mapping highlights opportunities to meet latent needs in marketing, brand communications, the business model, customer service, and more.

Exercise

Never underestimate the value of the Post-it or the whiteboard! At your next meeting, instead of conducting it with everyone seated with a laptop in front of them, stand up, go to a whiteboard, and begin to draw out, with very basic circles, lines, and arrows, the major points of the discussion. Physically and visually connect the dots between ideas.

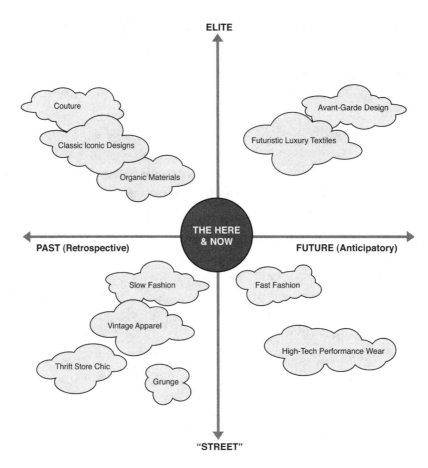

ELITE

Couture

Classic Iconic Designs

Organic Materials

Avant-Garde Design

Futuristic Luxury Textiles

THE HERE & NOW

PAST (Retrospective)

FUTURE (Anticipatory)

Slow Fashion

Fast Fashion

Vintage Apparel

High-Tech Performance Wear

Thrift Store Chic

Grunge

"STREET"

Adapted from the original by Natalie Nixon and Johanna Blakely, "Fashion Thinking—Towards an Actionable Methodology," *Fashion Practice*, Vol. 4, issue 2, p. 159.

Figure 9.3 *"Fashion Thinking Matrix" by Natalie Nixon and Johanna Blakley—an example of visually diagramming by using a 2×2 matrix.*

Improvisation and Role-Playing

Improvisation is a tool that both sparks and helps reimagine an idea, a concept, a conversation, a way of seeing, and so forth. It is a collaborative discovery process that challenges the status quo through exploration and experimentation, and requires participants to make different choices than they typically would make. In this way, new and varied possibilities are created.

Sevanne Kassarjian of Performance of a Lifetime explains that improvisation starts with the "offer"—any new idea, situation, or dynamic that occurs in a scene—and these are the sparks for innovation. Although typically we might respond to new ideas with criticism ("I've got a better or different idea"), in improvisation, "offers" must be accepted and built upon—you say "yes, and...." Improvisation emphasizes the value of building the idea together rather than asserting one's superiority through identifying weakness. And it requires keen and creative listening. This might be a new paradigm for your team. Improvising gets you invested in what others are thinking and feeling, and provides the creative impetus to build and create with their multiple offers.

Bodystorming is a kinesthetic form of brainstorming, in which participants imagine that the product or service actually exists and physically interact with the imaginary product; gaps in function and form come to light. For improv to be used as a tool in a work environment, the organizational culture must be one where employees' emotional component is allowed to be visible.

Exercise

Engage in an improvisational sketch with a colleague: Imagine that the two of you are planning a surprise retirement party for a colleague. Start by having your colleague suggest an idea for the party.

Continue the conversation (no questions; statements only), and every time one of you responds to the other, you begin with the words "Yes, but...."

Try it again, with the only change being that this time, all your responses begin with "Yes, and...." Note how the dynamics and outcome of the conversation change.

Synthesizing the Repertory

There are five key themes that surfaced in interviews with practitioners about adaptive tools for innovation:

1. **See the Latent Need:** Be diligent and self-conscious about seeing emergent patterns that are right in front of you. Valerie Jacobs emphasizes to practice "seeing" to help you identify the unmet, latent need. Use recording mechanisms such as pen, paper, and your smartphone camera; keep a whiteboard in some area of your office. Pattern-finding tools, which facilitate structured, lateral thinking (making connections between multiple data points), and lateral inspiration, are key. The business model canvas, blue-ocean framework, and 2×2 matrices are helpful. For example, Michelle Miller's "whole-system collaboration model," shown in Figure 9.4, is a redesigned 2×2 matrix that helps you to map stakeholders in a holistic manner.

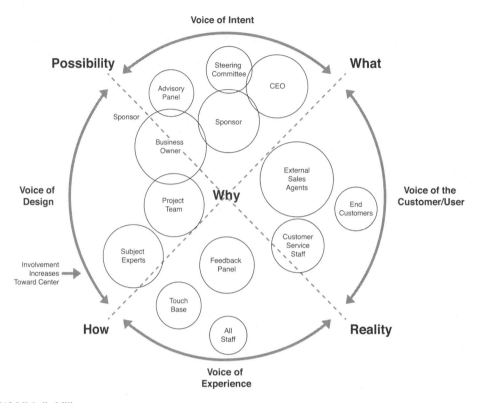

Voice of Intent

Possibility

What

Voice of Design

Why

Voice of the Customer/User

Involvement Increases Toward Center

How

Reality

Voice of Experience

©2013 Michelle Miller

Figure 9.4 *Example of a stakeholder map for whole-system engagement, developed by Michelle Miller (from "Everyone Has a Role: Whole System Engagement Maximizes Collaboration," Michelle Miller, 2013, The XXIV ISPIM Conference).*

2. **People Are Essential:** Harold Hambrose points out that Electronic Ink's added value is in their skilled people, who are keen and focused observers. If you don't have that internally, build out hub-and-spoke models consisting of a tribe of people who can give you that skill set. When you're investigating users, attention has to be put on not only what Hambrose calls "the procedural truth" (planned processes) and "the mechanical truth" (how do I set up my physical space to support the procedural truth), but also the "human truth." Cindy Tripp pointed out the need to get the right people in the room, allow for latency in conversations, and remember that healthy tension, also known as creative abrasion, is good. Have face-level interactions with your clients and your end users—they are who Mark Raheja calls "your co-conspirators." Proximity and immersion into the process are essential. John Heath knows that Chobani's advantage is in its people: "That is the only way you can explain the Chobani product versus some competitor product…we have access to the same machines and technology. Different choices are made about ingredients because a different staff of people are driving different values." Heath refers to this as ecosystem of design where there are

organic interdependencies among departments. Nick Hahn likes to reframe the question in human terms: "It is 'outside-in' beginning with the consumer." Hahn also talks about the need for "strategic intuition": "Intuition is how you get to something based on collective memory. With strategic intuition, you are getting to 'that something' in a more structured way, for example, by using a business model canvas." Since everything has already been invented, one must appropriately scan all that has come before. Manoj Fenelon values ethnography, "even bastardized ones," to help you get out into the real world, beyond the spreadsheet.

Exercise

Create a library of business models, by coming up with 20 business models that exist, and give examples of companies that have successfully illustrated those models.

---

3. **Agile Hybridity:** There are layers of dual processes in tools for innovation. For example, it will always be structured by the constraint of time, so adapt by using both quantitative and qualitative data. It is important to balance the qualitative research of fieldwork with quantitative research so as to not get too far in the weeds. Quantitative research shows us the pattern and the "what"; qualitative research provides the deeper story and the "why."

   Gordon Hui points out the "internal-external" dynamic: Strategy's legacy has been to focus internally, but this focus doesn't stretch one's capacity; design's legacy has been to look externally, at the customer. When integrated, these two lenses become a dynamic duo. Alain Sylvain reflects that the main tool for his "nonprocess" is creativity, or organized chaos, in which simplicity needs complexity.

4. **Story:** Each of the foundational tools described in this chapter can contribute to developing story for the product and service in order to give narrative, shape, and form and can be used as a helpful guide for the company. Story from the inside of the corporation out can also be effective in branding and messaging to the public. The increasingly popular use of transmedia storytelling utilizes multiple platforms to tell a brand's story, annotated by the user: in a movie, a novel, a graphic novel, a website, and an animated short film. Think of the Batman franchise, Mike and Ike candy, and the Old Spice franchise, which allow for open-source additions.

5. **What-If Money:** One of the things that these tools point out is the need to budget for instinct and "latent ROI" or "not-asked-for money" in budget lines, enabling your team to play with resources, time, and the unexpected discoveries.

This requires an acknowledgment for time and space to allow for failure of 99% of the ideas. How does one cultivate and get better at instinct? Some of it is about time on task and repeatedly allowing for structures in the work practice that enable people to engage in instinct. Instinct also comes from immersion in the right context and observing different ways of practice. As Mark Reheda says, "Are you a sponge or Teflon? Are you listening or hearing?" Instinct is a muscle that has to be developed.

Applications of the Adaptive Toolbox for Innovation

In summary, we offer an overview of which tools to use when (see Figure 9.5). Frameworks are helpful to use alongside tools because they offer a snaphot at complexity that is otherwise difficult to articulate. Frameworks are descriptive, and tools are prescriptive. It is important to understand the intent behind the use of the tool.

	Application
Tools for:	**How (Examples)**
Reframing the Question	Fieldwork Observe Teaming
Identifying the Gap	Brainstorm
Who Are the Stakeholders? Who Are Our Users?	Fieldwork Observe
What's Next?	Design Audit of Different Industry Fieldwork Teaming
What Problem Does Our Product/Service/Experience Solve?	Prototype Fieldwork
How Do We Know What We Are Providing Is Still Relevant?	Design Audit Teaming Charrettes Prototype
Starting with Why You Exist--Not What You Do *See http://www.startwithwhy.com	Charrettes Learning
Show Me; Don't Tell Me	Visual Diagrams + Mapping Prototype
Ignite Different Brain Synapses *See http://marshmallowchallenge.com	Get Physical (Kinesthetic Learning) Improvise
Fail Often and Early	Prototype Improvise

Figure 9.5 *Adaptive toolbox guide.*

Acknowledgments

The author would like to acknowledge the following practitioners for making the time to be interviewed for this chapter.

Here are their own definitions of a tool:

- **Annie Chang,** Strategist, Jump Associates: "A known/defined way to approach something."
- **Manoj Fenelon,** Director of Foresight, PepsiCo: "A tool is anything you can use again and again, and that allows for the tool itself to change."
- **Jordan Fischer,** Lead Strategist, Gravity Tank: "An artifact that performs a series of functions."
- **Nick Hahn,** Senior Partner, Vivaldi Partner Group: "A thing, idea, or construct that accelerates your ability to accomplish something. I don't like the word *tool,* because it isn't about the tool, it's about the builder!"
- **Harold Hambrose,** President, Electronic Ink: "A tool is anything we can leverage to move us a step forward. A tool might be a conversation, a technique, an object. But like any tool, these things are consciously used and we've got to demonstrate your ability to effectively manipulate them."
- **John Heath,** Senior Vice President of Innovation, Chobani: "When used properly, a tool can help accelerate the process of identifying problems and solutions."
- **Gordon Hui,** Global Director of Business Design and Strategy, Smart Design: "A tool is just a process, a framework, a deliverable output that allows you to enable a set of insights that are external or internal—allows you a lot of flexibility in thinking of a what a tool is."
- **Valerie Jacobs,** Vice President, Managing Creative Director, Trends, LPK: "A tool is anything that helps somebody get their idea from their head into reality, or on paper."
- **Sevanne Kassarjian,** Lead Trainer, Performance of a Lifetime: "We talk about improvisation as a tool that both results in innovation, and it's an innovation in and of itself."
- **Michelle Miller,** Organizational Architect, Synexe: "It's like having a quiver full of different arrows. Like how a handyman has a box carried around, or a toolbox on their waist....You have to pick your favorites—a virtual but fairly lightweight tool kit!"
- **Mai Nguyen,** Business Development Director, Smart Design: "It is simply something that enables you to discover."
- **Mark Raheja,** Strategy Director, Undercurrent: "A tool is something that you draw on to help you achieve a goal, and carry out an objective. Sometimes it's a person, sometimes it's a lens, sometimes it is specific, hard and tangible. There is a thrill for us in building the plane in midair, versus having a 'research tool kit.' There is a moment when every strategist invents their own tool."

- **Alain Sylvain,** Founder and CEO, Sylvain Labs: "I don't really believe in tools. Tools are more for the client than for the process. My un-process is my tool...creativity is my tool and validates my un-process."
- **Cindy Tripp,** President, Cindy Tripp & Company, LLC: "A tool is something that is useful. Unlike gardening tools, which are specialized and rigid, a tool for discovering innovation can be created in the moment, for the moment. They are not static."

Section 4
Value Creation

In this section you will learn from a team of experts about their academic and entrepreneurial experiences in incubating, launching, and scaling new ventures. They specifically offer insight here in how to move an idea from the lab or garage to the market with focus on business modeling, sustainability, and execution issues, notably the art of the pivot.

To add additional perspective, we spoke with Kris Clerkin, Executive Director of the College for America (CFA) at Southern New Hampshire University (SNHU). Although SNHU is 80 years old, in the past ten years alone it has grown from a small regional university to a national player in innovative online education, with revenues rising from $80 million in 2005 to over $200 million in 2012. Fast Company recognized SNHU as the 12th-most-innovative organization in 2012, ahead of more well-known brands such as LinkedIn and Starbucks. CFA was born in the Innovation Lab at SNHU under the direction of President Dr. Paul LeBlanc, who stated, "We want to create the business model that blows up our current business model." The CFA program is unique in that it lacks most traditional higher education components: There are no instructors, there are no textbooks, there are no grades, and degrees are based on competencies as opposed to consumption of credit hours. The program is grounded in go-at-your-own-pace, peer-to-peer, project-based learning. Rather than paying per credit hour, it's an all-you-can-learn with a set entry price per six-month term of learning consumption. CFA is designed for those without prior college experience and for those whose schedules and finances would otherwise prohibit higher education. CFA was the first competency-based higher education program approved for federal financial aid under direct assessment rather than the credit hour. Kris, former President of the College Division of the publishing company Houghton Mifflin and SNHU Board Trustee, was hired by president Dr. Paul LeBlanc to take the concept from the lab to the market—essentially to craft and execute the business model. Kris's experience in taking this radical innovation live offers unique insight into the process of value creation and business modeling.

Engaging the Market for Clarity of Value Proposition

In keeping with D. R. Widder's chapter on business models, which stresses the importance of market feedback in shaping the opportunity, when Kris entered CFA, her first order of business was to assess the potential customers for CFA. SNHU offers three business models to three market segments of customers:

1. *On its Manchester campus:* The traditional college-aged student taking face-to-face classes.

2. *The College of Online and Continuing Education:* Mostly nontraditional, older students taking traditional online classes in nearly 200 degrees and programs.

3. *CFA:* Employed working adult enrolled in an online competency-based degree.

Each segment is fairly distinct with some crossover between the first two segments since many traditional campus students now take online courses. When Kris looked to bring the concept of CFA out of the Innovation Lab and into the market, she had to clarify their value proposition as distinct from the other SNHU offerings: "As Paul said in Fast Company, we knew that the all-online model, although disruptive to the traditional educational model, would itself soon be disrupted and we wanted to be the ones to do it. When I arrived, the business model in the lab was largely articulated in the application for the Educause Next Generation Learning Challenge grant funded by the Bill and Melinda Gates Foundation. The main components were reduced cost of delivery and a competency-based curriculum. We needed to take that out to clarify our target market and value proposition. We soon discovered that our target market sweet spot was not a business-to-consumer play but rather a business-to-business play. The online market is saturated with both nonprofit and for-profit providers seeking students (customers) in need of bachelor's degree completion. Because we began with an associate degree, we looked at the non–college student in consideration of future labor demands for mid-skilled workers and current and anticipated skills gaps. This shifted our focus toward workforce development, where the pain point is at the employer perhaps more than the employee. So what began as conversations with employers about their interest in our offering for their employees became a partnership with employers to develop their workforce." This shift in focus to the employer and workforce development is a pivot, as described by David Charron in Chapter 12, "Business Model Execution—Navigating with the Pivot," and is a great example of how changes in a target customer segment can also be a shift in channel through which you approach them and the nature of your customer relationship, as described in Chapter 10, "Value Creation through Shaping Opportunity—The Business Model."

Symbiotic Relationship between Customer and Value Proposition

As all three of the upcoming chapters explain, there is interdependency between the customer and the value proposition that sometimes elevates to a level of co-creation. When CFA approached the market of employers to gather feedback on the CFA product for their employers, the conversation shifted to how the CFA could serve the employers as customers first. This shift in customer focus changed the attributes of the offering. As Kris explained, "Instead of focusing only on traditional metrics by student with individual progress as the primary unit of measure, we are also tracking competencies mastered by employer and by sector. We are building analytic dashboards for employers to see the return on the investment in developing their workforce as a whole. This alters the conversation from the cost of a benefit offered to an employee to an investment in enterprise itself via the employee."

Crafting the Right Team, Aligning the Right Resources

As the old investment expression goes, "You bet on the jockey, not the horse." The team is the most crucial asset brought to an opportunity. Section 2 of this book, "Assessment and Leadership," is dedicated almost entirely to assessment of teams, crafting teams for innovation, and managing a dynamic team of innovators in the opportunity recognition phases of discovery and formulation. When moving into value creation, crafting the execution team is equally important. Kris noted this as one of her most important focuses in building CFA: "One of my first priorities was finding the right people and molding them into a high-functioning team. In our situation, Paul LeBlanc was the visionary and innovator, whose belief in the idea and willingness to invest allowed us to move forward with confidence. We hired a chief technology officer with a deep knowledge of Salesforce as a development platform and experience with cloud-based relationship management systems. We hired an expert from Educational Testing Services (ETS), international experts in testing and the creators of SAT, to help us establish both the curriculum and the rubric by which we assess competencies. We hired the founders of the Workforce Strategy Center to help us build a strategy to approach employers with a focus on workforce development. We also hired a director of partnerships with long experience in building business development teams in the information services business. These four hires gave us the essential competencies we needed around systems, curriculum, and assessment, and business development. We already had on the team one of the key people from SNHU's online division, an expert in student services and user experience, advising, and analytics. Since we are still a small part of SNHU, we share some services such as finance, human resources, legal, and IT where it makes sense, but at key hurdle rates we will have to decide whether to break away and develop our own infrastructure."

Focused Strategy Is Essential

When you develop a disruptive idea, inevitably it can be formed in various ways, for a spectrum of customers, each requiring a slightly different strategy. The key to winning is focusing on the strategy with the most value potential, the most loyal customers with the fewest alternatives, and the greatest barriers for your competitors to enter your space. One of Kris's key roles is to keep the team focused on their target market sweet spot while assessing and planning future paths for growth. "Today we understand that the greatest opportunity for us that provides the least cannibalization of SNHU's COCE is to focus on building the business-to-business customers, those large employers who can clearly articulate their workforce development needs, can support their employees, and are willing to pay for our offering through scholarships and tuition assistance programs," Kris said. "We see this as a huge target market, more than sufficient to bring us well past break-even and enabling us to incrementally improve our offering and build our proof points. As we develop our workforce strategy and develop new degree programs targeted at the needs of high-growth occupations, that opportunity seems even brighter. Future inflection points could occur if we shift to direct-to-consumer or in partnerships with community colleges as they look to implement new models but face internal barriers. We are also doing small pilots with high schools and an international partner. We feel that large nonprofits, such as unions or other service organizations, might be interested in offering higher education programs to their constituencies and have begun cultivating relationships in that sector. Despite all these tempting alternatives, my job for today is to keep us focused on executing on our current target market while placing bets on a few possible inflection points."

The three chapters that follow offer practical guides to developing your innovation, beginning with shaping the opportunity and mapping the business model, to testing the sustainability and resilience of your innovation, to execution strategies around when and how to pivot when conditions inevitably change.

10

Value Creation through Shaping Opportunity— The Business Model

D. R. Widder is Vice President of Innovation at Philadelphia University, where he is a catalyst for innovation in areas such as entrepreneurship, online learning, analytics, and partnership development. His 20-year career in industry has included multiple high-tech ventures and patents spanning artificial intelligence, medical imaging, and sustainable products, as well as an entrepreneur-in-residence role at IBM. D. R. is on the executive committee of the early-stage venture investment and advisory group RVI. D. R. has a master's in Engineering with a focus on Applied Mathematics, and an M.B.A. in Entrepreneurship from Babson College.

The gulf between the back-of-the-napkin sketch and achieving business success is bridged by opportunity shaping. Opportunity shaping takes an idea from theoretical greatness to real value delivery and capture. Most of the life cycle of opportunity, from idea to full-scale success, is spent in an opportunity-shaping mode. Shaping opportunity is the difference between an interesting idea and successful execution that creates value for the world.

"No plan survives contact with the enemy" and no opportunity remains unchanged by contact with its stakeholders. An idea must be forged and reshaped as it contacts more of the real-world environment. Contact and feedback from customers, advisors, suppliers, stakeholders, competitive reaction, and macroeconomics shift all test and stress assumptions and execution. The successful entrepreneurial team uses this continual feedback to hone, retool, and its ideas and plans. Teams can outright pivot in a new direction as part of this process (on which David Charron offers greater detail in Chapter 12, "Business Model Execution—Navigating with the Pivot").

As an opportunity is developed, it needs to be systematically evaluated and refined. This evaluation is composed of the value potential of realized opportunity, the fit of the opportunity internally with the team and externally with the market, the resources needed, and the risks and challenges in reaching the goal.

The evaluation serves three purposes. First, it provides a framework to objectively evaluate all the elements of an opportunity. Entrepreneurs and inventors are necessarily passionate about their ideas, and objective measures will provide an unbiased view of the opportunity and highlight possible weak points. Second, it allows the opportunity to be seen holistically, as customers and other stakeholders will, in order to build support, marshal resources and build a team. Finally, we can use the evaluation to shape the opportunity, highlighting and addressing gaps, to make it stronger.

This chapter provides frameworks and tools for evaluating and refining opportunities. To do this, you need to Map, to Screen, and to Shape (see Figure 10.1). Dimensions of assessment are described and illustrated, as are multiple frameworks that can be used to map and screen concepts. This mapping can provide measures of relative value of opportunities, as well as point to weaknesses and gaps that can be addressed to increase the potential value of an opportunity. Like many of the chapters in this book, this process is iterative.

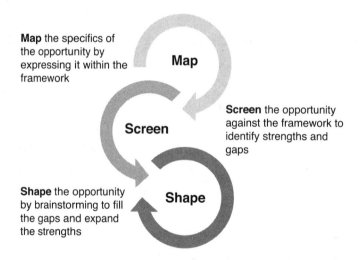

Figure 10.1 *Map-Screen-Shape opportunity development framework.*

An opportunity can be viewed through many lenses and perspectives. This chapter lays out some of the most valuable lenses as frameworks. Each can be used with the general iterative processes of Map, Screen, and Shape.

The Dimensions of Opportunity

There are four main dimensions that underlie all the opportunity evaluation frameworks:

1. Value
2. Fit (for both the team and external stakeholders)
3. Resources
4. Risk

We will work through these sequentially even though in practice they should be seamlessly intertwined, as illustrated in the interdependencies articulated in Figure 10.2. As with all the frameworks presented here, they are iterative.

Figure 10.2 *Dimensions of opportunity.*

Although it is difficult to decouple components of business model evaluation from the whole, arguably an articulation of the Value Proposition and the Sustainable Competitive Advantage are the most critical components that drive value, fit, resources, and risk.

Value

What is the value of an idea? We will define business models in terms of value creation, value delivery, and value capture. The common theme is obviously value! The first association with value is money, but value includes social value, aesthetic value, political value, and internal and psychological value. The other aspect of value relates to whom the value is provided for. Again, the quick answer is the customer, but a sustainable business model needs to provide value to all the stakeholders involved, including the founders/leaders of the model and key partners.

Strategic Fit

Fit matters both internally and externally. Internally, what is the fit of the opportunity with the founders' (individual, team, and/or organization) resources, skills, and expertise? Externally, what is the fit of the opportunity with stakeholders, including resource providers (investors, management), value chain components (suppliers, distributors, channels), and, most important, customers? (Chapters 8, "Design Process and Opportunity Development," and 9, "Navigating Spaces—Tools for Discovery," explored the process of discovery for unmet needs of users and customers.)

Within the fit-to-market needs, what is the sustainable competitive advantage of the value proposition? The value proposition is why the customer will desire the offering. The sustainable competitive advantage is how you can create it, deliver it, and renew it, in a way that others cannot. What are the aspects of the business model that competitors cannot easily duplicate or surpass?

Competitive advantages drive success if they are

- *Differentiated:* They are unique among competitors.
- *Valuable:* They provide some advantage to reaching and satisfying customers.
- *Sustainable:* They are durable over time and difficult to replicate.

By analyzing and developing competitive advantages for a wide range of businesses, I have developed this distilled inventory of possible competitive advantages in Table 10.1.

Table 10.1 Drivers of Competitive Advantage

Drivers of Competitive Advantage		Notes
Customer-Based Competitive Advantage	Market share	Leading the market, fastest growing, largest market share, protected market
	Pricing power	Market leader, premium niche
	Reach	Access to distribution channels
	Network effects	Value that increases proportionally to the number of customers
	Reputation	Brand promise backed up with a track record with customers
Organizational-Based Competitive Advantage	Nimble, rapid response to change	Leadership, organizational elements, and financial cost structures that monitor and adjust to market and technological change
	Integration	High switching costs
	Entrepreneurial culture	Willingness to take risk, continual reevaluation and reinvention
	Partnerships	Leverage of internal resources with key partners
	Access to resources	Access to capital, talent, positive cash flow
Value-Based Competitive Advantage	Breadth of offerings	Capability to satisfy broad needs of customer, one-stop-shop partner for customer
	Offering quality	Quality of products/services, delivered and ongoing support
	Advantageous cost structure	Low-cost producer, flexible capacity/ variable costs
	Technology leadership	Ongoing innovation, intellectual property protection

Resources

What is needed to make the business model work? Resources are what are required to realize the value, including team, capital, partners, and time. A subtle yet important resource is opportunity cost—if this opportunity is pursued, what others will not be? The most significant of these can be the investment of the founders' time.

Risk

Risk is about the chances of realizing the value coupled with the chances of wasting the resources. Known risks include the accuracy of the assumptions behind the model and execution risk in realizing the plan (sometimes referred to as unsystematic risk). Unknown risks are those risks associated with components of the model currently unforeseen, and externalities beyond the control of the business model, such as macroeconomic change (sometimes referred to as systemic risk).

Risk also implies what could be lost: investment capital, reputation, time, or future opportunity.

The hardest risk to evaluate can be in the biases of the founders. Because of this, the importance of using objective frameworks, such as those presented here, and having a set of candid mentors and advisors, is paramount. "Drinking your own Kool-Aid," "falling in love with your own ideas"—the expressions abound that describe our difficulty in remaining objective when we have invested our entrepreneurial passion and energy. Most ideas fail, but none fails from lack of love from their champions.

The Business Model and Frameworks

As we move from idea to execution, it is important to express an opportunity in terms of the business model it supports. We are crossing the chasm from opportunity recognition to value creation. The business model is a framework for creating value from an idea, by building the idea into a system that considers all stakeholders' needs. The business model, financial model, and business plan are closely related but distinct, and often confused and conflated. Using the car as an analogy, the business model is the engine, the financial model is the fuel or energy that makes the car go, and the business plan is the road or route on which you will drive (execute).[1] It is essential to entrepreneurship and innovation to understand how the pieces come together in the engine to drive the idea forward.

The business model as the building block of innovation and entrepreneurship is increasing in importance in the collective conscience and literature. Not long ago, an organization would craft a business model and execute on the same model for decades. In today's rapidly changing environments, the business model is viewed like a product line; it must be reviewed (and possibly reworked) frequently. This is in part driven by the diversity of possible successful business models in information-based economies, and experience-based economies. Information economies trade less tangible value, which can be packaged and delivered in ways decoupled from the restraints of the physical. This opens a wider range of possible business models. As James Gilmore and B. Joseph Pine describe in the book *The Experience Economy*, the evolution of economies has increased demand and opportunity for experienced-based and transformation-based businesses.[2]

Types of business offerings, in order of increased differentiation and the factors upon which they compete, include the following:

1. A *commodity business* charges for undifferentiated products. (Examples: oil, sugar.) Commodity businesses sell undifferentiated products and therefore must compete entirely on price.

2. A *goods business* charges for distinctive, tangible things. (Examples: shoes, televisions.) Goods businesses compete on the uniqueness of the value proposition in balance with price.

3. A *service business* charges for the activities you perform. (Examples: consulting, Internet access.) Service businesses compete on reliability and reputation of the offering.

4. An *experience business* charges for the feeling customers get by engaging it. (Examples: Starbucks, Disney theme parks.) Experience businesses compete on the brand promise of the experience.

5. A *transformation business* charges for the benefit customers (or "guests") receive by spending time there. (Examples: vacations that teach skills, restaurants that educate about cooking/health, higher education institutions.) Transformation businesses deliver value that changes the customer beyond the delivering of the experience.

The more evolved stages allow more diversity in approaches, more innovation, and more creative business models.

Thought leaders such as Steve Blank have tied business models to the essence of entrepreneurship, stating, "A startup is an organization formed to search for a repeatable and scalable business model."

Definition

There are many definitions of business models, but at the core a business model has three critical aspects: value creation, value delivery, and value capture. What value will be provided for customers and other stakeholders? How will the customer get that value? How will the business model capture that value for all the stakeholders involved? By value, we extend beyond financial gain, to include social entrepreneurship and societal, political, and organizational value.

The Business Model Canvas Framework

The Business Model Canvas (proposed by Alex Osterwalder and Yves Pigneur in their best-selling book *Business Model Generation*), depicted in Figure 10.3, has become the framework of choice for mapping out business models. Developed in an open-source format, with more than 450 experts' input, it maps the key components of any business model.[3]

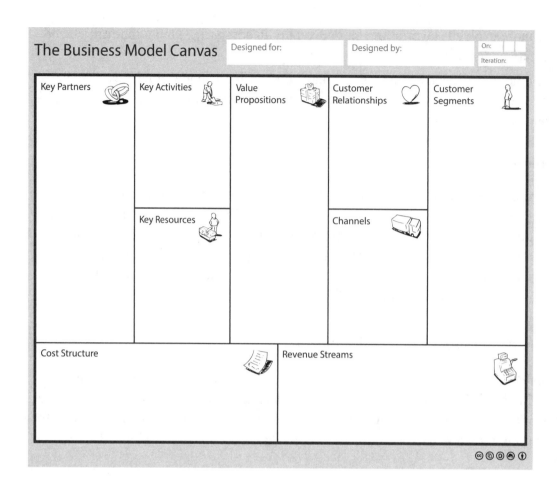

Figure 10.3 *The Business Model Canvas. Courtesy of www.businessmodelgeneration.com.*

Part of its elegance is to lay out the entire model in a single view. All the major components important to a business model are defined and visible. The canvas breaks down the business model into nine components, which we cluster into these categories:

- Value Proposition (VP) *(What you are offering)*
- Customer Components *(Who you are doing it for and with):* Customer Segments (CS), Channels (CH), Customer Relationships (CR)
- Financial Components *(What results you expect):* Cost Structure (CS), Revenue Streams (RS)
- Resource Components *(How you will do it):* Key Partners (KP), Key Activities (KA), Key Resources (KR)

We use the canvas to map the opportunity across these components. Additionally, we use the canvas as a Screen, to determine strengths and gaps. Although the Business Model Canvas is most commonly used to map out and define an opportunity, it can be extended as an evaluation tool as shown in Table 10.2. With a business model defined on the canvas, we can evaluate the potential value of an opportunity by the nature of the canvas components using the following framework. The first column ("Map") describes the components of the Business Model Canvas. "Screen" extends the canvas to evaluate the opportunity by components.

Table 10.2   Map and Screen the Business Model

MAP—Business Model Component	Screen	
	Higher Potential	Lower Potential
Value Proposition (VP)		
The core of it all; What value are we creating and delivering to the customer? What problem is being solved? What benefits does this business model provide customers, from the point of view of satisfying needs and/or solving problems? The Value Proposition is the promise of value to be delivered.	Well-articulated, based on customer's needs.	Addresses non–core customer pain point; "nice to have."
	Clear and easy to understand.	Hype-based, intangible.
	Addresses major customer pain point.	Complicated.
	Differentiated from substitutes/competitive offerings.	Not differentiated or differentiated.
	Creates tangible measurable quantifiable value for the customer.	Nuanced and not sustainable.
	Value proposition has been tested by customers.	

Continues

	Higher Potential	Lower Potential
Customer Segments (CS)		
Define who will value the value proposition and adopt the offering, and what characteristics this group possesses that are relevant to the business model. Some business models required multisided adoption, where more than one segment must adopt the offerings in order to be successful. For example, a travel website might need to attract both travelers (consumers), and travel service providers (hotels) to be able to connect the two.	Specific in definition and in the needs that the VP addresses. Focused so that needs of the segment are homogeneous, yet broad enough that total addressable market supports model and scale.	Overly broad market. Connection between the value proposition and the unique characteristics of the customer segment not clear or compelling. Generally multisided models have more inherent risk, due to the requirement to meet the needs of multiple segments.
Channels (CH)		
How will the customer segments be reached? What is the cost structure of accessing the channels? What is the value of the opportunity from the channels' perspective?	Well-defined path to customer. There is value to the channel in the offering. Scalable/low-cost structure to channel/economies of scale.	Poorly defined. "Build it and they will come" mentality. Reaching customer predicated on brand building/high marketing expenses.
Customer Relationships (CR)		
What is the nature of the relationship with the customer? How will the model service the customer? What is the customer's role in the value creation and delivery process? What current relationships are there with customers and how have they shaped the business model?	Customer role and needs in the creation, delivery, and servicing processes well understood and defined. Existing relationships with customers. Customer input into offering/model. Early adopter short list known. Offering is well defined in the context of an individual customer. Customer adoption fits with current behavior.	Customer behavior and interactions with the business model not defined. Business model requires change in behavior in customer. Overall market share perspective rather than how an individual customer is attracted and served.

MAP—Business Model Component	Screen	
	Higher Potential	**Lower Potential**
Cost Structure (CS)		
Defines the main costs and what business model components drive costs. Often these stem from costs relating to the Key Activities, Key Assets, and Key Partners in the model. A key consideration is what costs are fixed (costs incurred regardless of the number of customers or production of value) or variable (costs that are proportional to the volume of business)	Cost < Value. Costs well understood and articulated. Driven by variable costs at startup (to reduce risk) and fixed costs at scale (to increase profitability). Cost advantages at scale. Leverages resources and assets of partners.	Capital-intensive startup costs. Little economies of scale or scope. Identified costs approach value to customer; low margin of error if costs are higher than expected.
Revenue Streams (RS)		
How does the model capture the value that is created? How do customers pay? What is the pricing structure and level? If there are multiple segments (i.e., different subgroups or tiers of service), how does the pricing structure tie to value and appropriately address each segment? An important principle of revenue streams is that it must be all about the value delivered, and not about cost.	Driven by quantification of the value proposition from the customer segment's perspective. Recurring revenue from previously acquired customers. Durable. Customer acquisition cost and total lifetime value of customer well understood.	Driven by costs + markups. Low potential for recurring or add-on revenue beyond initial transaction.
Key Partners (KP)		
What partners are required to deliver the value proposition? Who are the stakeholders and how does the business model interface with them? What relationships are required across the value chain—suppliers, distributions, partners, and customers?	Partners identified and relationships established. Potential for exclusivity or first mover advantage in partner development. Redundancy in relationships, pricing power over others. Value proposition of model to partners clear and durable.	Hypothetical relationships. Dependent on a specific relationship. Unclear motivation of partners to participate in model.

Continues

	Higher Potential	Lower Potential
Key Activities (KA)		
What activities are critical to make the business model work—to create and deliver the value proposition to the customer segments? Are they production related? Delivery related? Relationship building? Creation of a network or other critical mass component? The emphasis here should be "Key," because every business model has a large inventory of activities that must occur.	Well defined and straightforward. Limited number of key activities that are critical success factors. Good match between team resources and key activities. Measurable, with key metrics defined and goals for metrics tied to overall goals.	Complicated. Involve a critical mass component, such as a network effect, viral component, or network externalities, in order to create any value.
Key Resources (KR)		
What are the key resources needed for the business model to work? These include both hard assets (including financial resources for startup and growth) and other key resources (such as intellectual property that must be acquired or maintained, key people/skill sets, or resources related to creating and maintaining a company culture required by the value proposition).	Identified and obtainable. Cost-effective and scalable. Can be secured for the long term. Revenue Streams in relation to Key Resources provides a superior return on resources commensurate with risk.	Complicated and expensive to maintain. Capital-intensive, expensive to scale. Highly dependent on unique personalities/founders.

It is important to note that this framework addresses general truths. Plenty of successful business models might have characteristics that are identified as "Lower Potential" in this framework. "Lower Potential" components can mean more risk or complexity or difficulty in execution, but are not necessarily fatal flaws. In some cases, the same components of a business model that are complex or difficult to execute are transformed into competitive advantages in retrospect, because they are barriers to entry for new entrants trying to replicate the model.

"Lower Potential" aspects are inputs for opportunity shaping. How can the business model be recast or modified to address these gaps?

Assessing Strategic Context—SWOT

SWOT analysis—Strengths, Weaknesses, Opportunity, and Threats—illustrated in Figure 10.4, is a straightforward framework for mapping opportunity. Pioneered at the Stanford Research Institute, it has been widely adopted and used for over 50 years. We have found it most useful to get specific about the major factors that influence an opportunity. Factors are categorized as originating internally or externally, and according to whether they are a positive or negative factor in evaluating the opportunity.

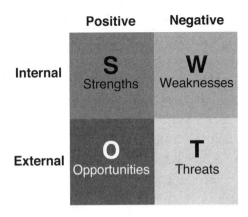

Figure 10.4 *SWOT table.*

SWOT analysis is valuable because it is straightforward and concise. It provides a specific inventory of the major influences on an opportunity. It is less useful for measuring opportunities relative to one another or otherwise quantifying or evaluating.

Assessing the Essence of the Idea—TRIZ

TRIZ stands for the Theory of Inventive Problem Solving, an acronym based on its Russian language origin. It is a methodology and framework that identifies abstract patterns around specific problems and opportunities. It is very useful in the design and development of solutions.

Problems and solutions have underlying themes that are repeated across disciplines and application. Although there is a vast diversity of innovations, there are repeating patterns behind the specific solutions that form general rules of innovation. When you look at a specific problem and evaluate it in a TRIZ framework, the pattern of the problem points to a pattern of solution. The TRIZ process is visually depicted in Figure 10.5.

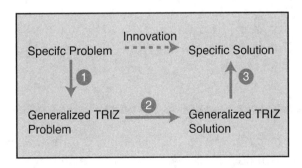

Figure 10.5 *TRIZ framework.*

You start with the specific problem to be addressed, apply TRIZ principles in a generalized problem space, and then adapt generalized solutions back to specific solutions. TRIZ includes 40 inventive principles that are recurring patterns in innovation.[4] For example, the principle of "Segmentation" is the general solution based on dividing an object into independent parts. The principle of "Universality" is the general solution of performing multiple functions with the same components (specific examples: a camera combined with a phone, or a child safety seat that converts to a stroller). An in-depth description of TRIZ is beyond the scope of this chapter, but it is a valuable framework to consider. It has the following strengths:

- It is more linear and methodical than the majority of brainstorming techniques, and can be more appealing to "left brain"-oriented thought.

- It cuts across disciplines, and is predicated on the assumption that solutions can come from other fields.

- It can stimulate new modes of thinking. With a finite number of patterns, each pattern can be considered in the context of the specific problem, in a search for solutions.

- It can be used to evaluate a specific opportunity or solution. Does the proposed opportunity follow an established TRIZ pattern? Do similar patterns offer insight into how the opportunity or solution can be refined or enhanced?

- It assumes a specific problem statement as a starting point, so it is philosophically different from problem-finding and exploratory approaches.

TRIZ is also useful in evaluating and reconciling performance trade-offs ("contradictions" in TRIZ terminology). These include technical contradictions such as engineering and business trade-offs (example: strength as beneficial, with a trade-off of added weight/cost). Also, this includes inherent contradictions such as trade-offs involving opposite requirements (example: desire for a comprehensive feature set, yet simple to use).

Assessing Internal Drivers—Organizational and Personal

How does an opportunity fit the founders and the founding organization? Ellen di Resta describes this well in Chapter 4, "Assessing Your Innovation Capability," so we will not reiterate here.

Assessing and Addressing Risk—Discovery-Driven Planning

Discovery-driven planning[5] is a way to think about and prioritize execution with scarce resources. Its elegance is in how it stages risk, and allocates resources based on risk reduction.

The key elements of the framework are to Map an opportunity in the following ways:

1. Start with the desired end state, mapping out what success would look like. Build an end-state financial statement for the business (revenue, profit, scale, etc.).

2. Make these financials flow out of a model of key assumptions; for example, the goal revenue built from assumptions about the number of customers, price points, and purchase volume.

3. Work backward through time from the end state to how to get there. If the end state is projected five years out, what assumptions are required to ramp to achieve those goals? The result at this point is a financial model of the business, and a set of the assumptions that drive the model.

4. Evaluate the reasonableness of assumptions against prior experience, business intelligence, and expert opinions. Tune the assumptions and model accordingly.

5. Now, look at the sensitivity of the model to the various assumptions. Do small changes in some assumptions have big impact on the end-state financials? What assumptions drive the model, and what is the risk associated with the accuracy of those assumptions? Are the key assumptions conservative or aggressive against benchmarks?

6. Based on this, develop a startup plan that spends time and resources to reduce uncertainty about those key assumptions. For example, if the most important driver that is least supported by data is product pricing, what early activities will increase confidence in pricing assumptions?

The shift in thinking in a discovery-driven way is subtle but the impact is profound. It has an inherent bias toward beginning with the end in mind, putting the goals and path to get there at the forefront. It also formally ties operations and operating assumptions directly to financial outcomes.

It is a road map for how to invest time and capital that optimize risk reduction, and therefore optimize return versus risk. Traditional approaches will allocate resources to sequentially build the business. In contrast, discovery-driven planning builds value by reducing uncertainty.

The model also provides ready feedback for progress. Revisiting assumptions as more information is learned directly ties to impact on the big picture.

Assessing Financials

Financial tools and evaluation is a field in itself, and detail is beyond the scope of the book. Briefly, expressing the business model in financial terms links the model, operating metrics, and financial outcomes together. Two critical measures flow out of the financial model:

1. **Capital Requirements:** Projections will show cash reserves/deficits over time. All startups will show a resource drain until a point where there is enough traction to generate positive cash flow (where sales exceeds costs). This point drives how much investment is needed, after which the business can pay its bills directly out of operations. More colorfully put, "Happiness is a positive cash flow."

2. **Valuation:** Projections can also be used to estimate what the venture is worth now and in the future. Comparing financials measures (for example, revenue, profit, growth) to comparable established businesses provides a view on future value. Net Present Value and similar analyses can provide a view on the current value of the idea, factoring in future sales projections, the resources required to get there, and the risk along the way.

Investopedia (www.investopedia.com) is a great starting point for financial terms and tools.

Assessing Innovation—The Innovation Bull's-Eye

For innovation to be realized, three core elements must come together. An idea must be desirable, feasible, and valuable: desirable in that it fulfills a need and fits into a person's life; feasible in that the solution can be realized from a practical and technical standpoint; valuable in that there is a business model and path to adoption. These come together at the Innovation Bull's-Eye.

These characteristics are derived from the major disciplines in the Kanbar College DEC curriculum—Design, Engineering and Commerce (Business)—a curriculum built around innovation. Design can improve the world by helping find problems and model solutions that improve the ways specific groups of people interact with each other and the world around them. Engineering can improve the world by using the rigors of mathematics, science, and simulation to solve the complex problems that occur when these solutions are integrated into actual products and processes. Business can improve the world through strategies for capturing the economic, social, or environmental value generated by interactions between these solutions and the people who benefit from them.

Design is where innovation intersects with people and identifies what is usable and desirable. The scope of design has evolved beyond objects and products to more broadly include the process of conceiving, planning, and modeling what might be possible.

What design and the design process bring to innovation:

- The ability to find opportunities for positive change
- The process of evaluating and responding to context and imagining something different

- A way to be empathetic, to view the world through the eyes of others, and to thoughtfully analyze what they see
- The role of inquiry in problem finding and framing

Design is a means of not only solving problems, but also finding opportunities to solve the right problems for particular groups of people.

Engineering is where innovation intersects with technology and identifies what is feasible and attainable. At the highest level, engineering can be viewed as the overlap of scientific knowledge with societal need.

What engineering brings to innovation:

- Rigorous problem-solving and troubleshooting skills
- An understanding of systems dynamics and rigor in systems thinking
- The ability to identify what can be developed and how
- An ability to evaluate trade-offs of benefits versus cost and form versus function

The engineering perspective not only is a means of solving problems with technology, but also is about the possible, and finding new opportunities that are enabled by new technologies.

Business is where innovation intersects business to create value and identify what is valuable. It is the process that connects the needs of people to the systems, objects, products, or services to fulfill these needs.

What business contributes to innovation:

- A way to identify and frame new business opportunity
- A way to understand how an innovation can scale to have broad reach and impact
- The ability to plan and marshal resources to execute a project/business/innovation
- A way to understand the delivery of innovation in terms of the fit with existing social systems, delivery mechanisms, and channels
- The perspective of value creation and its qualitative and quantitative impacts

The business perspective is not only a means of commercializing innovations, but also a means for finding new opportunities to create value.

We can use this innovation framework as a lens to evaluate and shape specific opportunity. To this end, we take the innovation ideal of the intersection of all of these dimensions as the Innovation Bull's-Eye, and deconstruct each element as depicted in Figure 10.6 and Table 10.3.

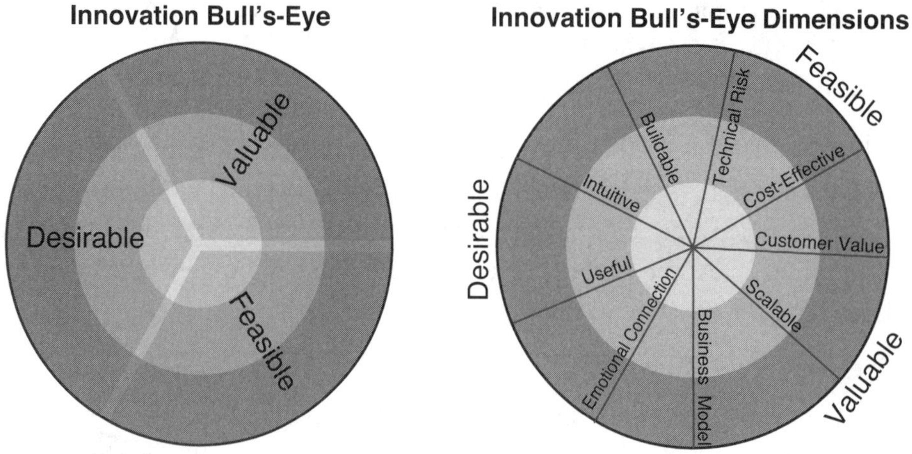

Figure 10.6 *The Innovation Bull's-Eye.*

Table 10.3 Innovation Targets and Potential

Innovation Target		High Innovation Potential
Desirable	Useful	Fulfills an unmet need, either expressed or inherent.
	Intuitive	Elegant, easy to adopt and use.
	Emotional Connection	Fits lives and motivations; aesthetic appeal invokes emotional connection in users. Customer experience is meaningful; fun.
Feasible	Buildable	Benefits can be created within limits of physics and logistics.
	Cost-effective	Utility can be realized and delivered to customer at a cost below its value.
	Technical Risk	Limited technical risk, limited technical unknowns, to create and deliver value.
Valuable	Customer	Creates tangible value that can be communicated.
	Scalable	Market perspective.
	Business Model	Specific and realizable model for value creation, delivery, and capture.

Ideas with high innovation potential will simultaneously be desirable to users, feasible to create and deliver, and valuable to all.

Screening Matrix Frameworks

These frameworks can be viewed as screening matrices. We map the opportunity against each framework components, and how well an opportunity stacks up against those factors. We evaluate a specific opportunity against an ideal, and also to screen a portfolio of ideas to rank those that should get more resources. We use them to screen results of brainstorming, and as parts of a stage gate process for development pipelines. Different screening matrices serve different stakeholders. As entrepreneurs, we can use a screen that fits our personal criteria to evaluate where to put our energy. As inventors, we can use a screen that matches ideas against customers' needs and pain points to evaluate their merit. As investors, we use screens that match investment criteria against companies seeking capital.

Scoring with Matrices

For those who seek more quantitative approaches (guilty by confession), matrixes can be extended to score an opportunity against an ideal, or rank it against others. For each component of the matrix, a score can be assigned for that component based on how well the specific opportunity fits the criteria of that component. Adding up all the component scores provides a numerical measure of the opportunity against the ideal, and provides a holistic summation of the idea.

Shaping: Rinse, Lather, Repeat

Recommendations: A recurring theme of this book is iteration. Although many of these frameworks are meant to evaluate opportunity, that is the beginning not the end. Use the gaps—the areas where an opportunity does not measure well against a criteria—as stimulus for iteration, refinement, and new ideas built on the old. Although the frameworks highlight why a particular solution might fall short, they are also guideposts that say if these gaps can be addressed, there is real opportunity to be realized and value created.

Endnotes

1. Credit my colleague Heather McGowan for this helpful analogy.
2. For more information refer to *The Experience Economy,* Pine and Gilmore (1999).
3. Business Model Canvas, www.BusinessModelGeneration.com.
4. Tate and Domb, "40 Inventive Principles with Examples," *TRIZ Journal*, 1997.
5. Discovery-driven planning was developed by Rita Gunther McGrath and Ian C. MacMillan.

11

Developing Sustainable Business Models

Nabil Harfoush is the Director of Strategic Innovation Lab at OCAD University in Toronto and Assistant Professor in the Strategic Foresight & Innovation Masters Program. He leads a research group on Strongly Sustainable Business Models. He is a Fellow at Philadelphia University, where he teaches Business Model Innovation. Nabil has over 40 years of experience as engineer, executive, entrepreneur, and educator. He has consulted for enterprises, governments, the World Bank, W.H.O., UNESCO, and IDRC and has served as CIO of several technology companies. Nabil has a master's in computer engineering and a Ph.D. *summa cum laude* in digital data communications from Germany.

What Is a Business Model?

Much has been written about business models in recent years, but the term "business model" is relatively recent in business language. It hardly appeared in print before the late 1990s.[1] Since then, it has moved from being a novel, intangible concept to something more concrete and has rapidly occupied a place in management language that is at least as prominent as the traditional terms of business plan and business strategy.

So what is a business model? As to be expected, there are many definitions of what a business model is, and they tend to vary depending on the line of business discussing it: sales, marketing, operations, research and development (R&D), and so on. But when the various lines of business have to collaborate on creating new business models or even to discuss the current business model of their organization, these many definitions and frameworks collide. The result is an inefficient process for business model innovation in an era when speed of innovation is key to the survival of the enterprise.

In the previous chapter D. R. Widder introduced the definition prevalent in business model professionals' circles: A business model is a description of how an organization creates, delivers, and captures value. Let's consider the case of an invention that is patentable. Registering the patent creates value, but as long as the patent is not converted into real applications it does not deliver value; and only when the patent generates revenues for the organization does it capture the value created and delivered. A charitable organization, on the other hand, creates value (social or financial) and delivers it to people who need it, but does not capture that value for itself and therefore usually remains dependent on external donations and hence financially is not sustainable.

The Business Model Canvas

Chapter 10, "Value Creation through Shaping Opportunity—The Business Model," also introduced the Business Model Canvas framework proposed by Alex Osterwalder and Yves Pigneur in their best-selling book *Business Model Generation.*[2] The Canvas provides a simple visual tool that captures the nine essential elements describing any business model:

1. The *value propositions* at the core of the business model
2. The *customer segments* targeted by these value propositions
3. The *channels* through which the value proposition is delivered to customers
4. The type of *customer relationships* necessary to successfully deliver the value proposition
5. The *revenue streams* resulting from the delivery of the value propositions
6. *Key activities* necessary for the business model
7. *Key resources* needed for the key activities to occur
8. *Key alliances and partnerships* enabling the organization to deliver its value proposition more efficiently
9. The *cost structure* resulting from elements 6–8

The first five elements form the right side of the Canvas (see Figure 10.3) and describe the essence of the business model in terms of value proposition and desired delivery. The left side consists of all the cost elements needed to deliver the proposed business model.

The visual aspect of the Business Model Canvas has an importance that is frequently underestimated. The visual nature of the Canvas and its nine elements presents a common framework to the various lines of business simultaneously. It has proven in practice to be an excellent tool for overcoming the different frameworks and vocabularies used by the various lines of business when considering business models and for emerging a common vocabulary and mental model about the enterprise's business model among the lines of business involved. It thus leads rapidly to a shared understanding of the organization's current business model and potential alternatives and thus improves the efficiency of the enterprise's innovation processes not only in the business model area but also across the lines of business of the organization.

Incidentally, a similar challenge arises in multidisciplinary teams working on solving a complex problem. Here, too, the visual aspect of the Canvas can provide an effective tool to accelerate the common understanding by team members of the different aspects of the problem at hand as well as on the perspectives, methods, and tools available from the various disciplines to address that complex challenge.

Better business modeling tools also play an important role in the overall efficiency of investments made in the company's innovation activities. Developing a detailed business plan is usually a labor-intensive and time-consuming process. Consequently, business plans tended traditionally to be developed for one set of value propositions and customer segments, usually not straying too far from the previous set. Developing and evaluating several business models, on the other hand, enables the exploration of multiple alternative models, each investigating a different set of the nine elements and identifying the few promising combinations, for which then the substantial time and effort needed for developing a detailed business plan can be invested with higher chances of successful return on that investment. In essence, exploring multiple business models before committing to a business plan opens wider options for the strategy of the organization. Figure 11.1 shows the phases of business design evolution and the types of iteration that are appropriate at each phase.

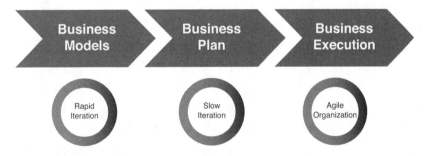

Figure 11.1   *From business model to business plan to execution.*

Exploring Alternative Business Models

Osterwalder and Pigneur introduced business model patterns, which are generic representations of business models with similar properties, for example, the Long Tail or the Multi-Sided Platform. They are similar to templates in word processing. Overlaying various business model patterns onto the Canvas of the current business model and considering the result enables the exploration of alternative business models. It is a what-if type of approach that helps rapidly define candidate alternative models for the organization as a whole or for a specific product or service. The next step is to evaluate these candidate models and to fine-tune promising ones.

After a business model has been deemed interesting for further consideration, it must be validated. The validation usually has two major components: Customer Validation and Model Viability.

Customer Validation is part of the Customer Development Model proposed by Steve Blank.[3] It aims at validating that there is actually a customer segment willing to pay for a specific value proposition. The concept of customer validation uses teachings of Design Thinking, which revolve around the idea of small iterations for rapid learning in the process of solving a problem. In business models lingo these iterations are called pivots. In the next chapter David Charron introduces in more detail the concepts of Customer Development Model and the techniques of pivoting.

Model Viability has a qualitative aspect and a quantitative aspect. The qualitative part aims at understanding the risks and opportunities of the proposed business model and the quantitative part focuses on validating its financial viability. The former applies evaluation techniques familiar from management science such as SWOT analysis and the Four Actions framework to assess the business model. If you are familiar with the Blue Ocean strategy framework, you can also blend it with the Business Model Canvas to assess the model from yet another perspective.

The validation of financial viability of the business model verifies that the value proposition that a customer segment is willing to pay for can actually be delivered while making a profit. At this stage this validation is usually done with a summary quantification of all operational costs and revenues related to the model (Canvas elements 6–8 and 1–4, respectively) and comparison of the total revenues and costs (Canvas elements 5 and 9) to establish whether the difference is positive (profit) or negative (loss).

The purpose of Model Viability is to support a decision as to whether this model should be further pursued and developed or would be better dropped. Only models with validated customers and viability would be further developed through a detailed business plan. Note also that the three elements of business model validation (customer, risk, and financial viability) are interrelated. Consequently, the validation process is not necessarily a linear process but rather an iterative process not unlike the pivoting concept. For example, if the customer side cannot be validated, it would cause changes in the value proposition or customer segments. If the risks and threats related to a business model prove beyond the tolerance of the company's governance, it might cause changes to multiple elements in the model to mitigate these risks and threats or lead to disregarding that model altogether. If the financial viability cannot be validated, it can cause the company to reconsider pricing points, customer segments, and/or cost elements. The point is that through rapid small iterations of business modeling, you are able to explore a larger number of possible models, rapidly evaluate the alternatives, and support evidence-based decision making in the selection of the most promising business model for further development and implementation.

It is important to understand that business modeling allows innovation across all categories of innovation, not only in the business model itself. Table 11.1 roughly maps Doblin's ten categories of innovation[4] to the nine elements of the Business Model Canvas.

Table 11.1 Mapping of Doblin's Ten Types of Innovation to the Nine Elements of BMC

Doblin 10 Innovation Types		Business Model Canvas
FINANCE	Business model	Revenues
		Cost Structure
	Networking	Partner Network
PROCESS	Enabling process	Key Activities
	Core process	Key Resources
OFFERING	Product performance	Value Propositions
	Product system	Customer Segments
	Service	
DELIVERY	Channel	Distribution Channels
	Brand	
	Customer experience	Customer Relationships

The Canvas allows an integrated view and consideration of innovations across the multiple categories by enabling a visual overview of the interdependencies among them. Whereas the Doblin chart reminds us of all the areas available for innovation outside of the traditional product/service innovation, the Canvas forces us to consider the mutual interdependencies of these potential innovations.

Limitations of the Canvas

With all its qualities and advantages, the Business Model Canvas does have certain limitations. These come primarily from the context in which it is applied and secondarily from the design of certain Canvas fields.

To understand the context limitations, consider the external environment that Osterwalder and Pigneur present for their Business Model Canvas.[5] It includes four broad categories that translate to about 20 more detailed external influencers of the business model, all of which are relatively complex and interdependent. The challenge of considering such a large set of factors influencing the model often leads in practice to examining only the current or near-term status of these factors and frequently only a subset of them. And yet unanticipated change in any of these external factors would have significant impact on multiple elements of the business model, if not all of them.

In addition, near-term projections of the future of a certain factor tend to be a linear extrapolation of its present state. There is ample evidence that complex systems such as micro- and macro-economy, markets, and climate develop in a nonlinear fashion. The gap between the linear projection traditionally used for evaluating a business model and the nonlinear development that is likely to occur introduces a significant element of risk that is not accounted for in the traditional validation of business models.

To mitigate such a risk, it is necessary to explore the future a little further than is the current practice of most organizations. Such explorations fall in the domain of foresight, which builds on the collection of signals of change, even presently weak ones; analysis of trends emerging from these signals; understanding the deeper drivers of the trends; identifying the most critical drivers and uncertainties for a specific organization; and building comprehensive projections of the future, usually in the form of multiple plausible future scenarios. These scenarios are then used to explore potential implications for the business plan and the organization's strategy in order to determine what actions and decisions in the present are needed to make both more resilient to any of these scenarios.

Discussing foresight applications is beyond the scope of this book; more information is available in the "Glossary and Resources" section. Suffice it to say that using foresight extends the time horizon of the risk assessment and can uncover substantial threats but also great opportunities for innovative business models.

Another limitation when evaluating business models is that the Canvas is focused primarily on risks and rewards in financial terms. It is widely accepted today that there are multiple other types of capital (natural, human, social, and intellectual) that are essential for the success and sustainability of any organization and therefore need to be considered when assessing business models or developing business strategies.

The recognition of the critical role of these other types of capital and their increasing volatility has raised awareness that there are invisible but potentially substantial risks for business related to the company's interaction with social and natural capital. These risks are not limited to the business model but extend to the viability and valuation of the organization. What is the viability of a business whose majority of assets is in a location threatened by frequent severe weather events? What is its valuation if it is in an area with frequent disruptive civil unrest or running out of water resources?

Toward More Sustainable Business Models

The need to mitigate the newly uncovered risks generated interest in new measures and tools to assess the viability of a business model when additional types of capital other than financial are included in the risk considerations. There is today a large body of literature and practitioners that advocates the use of the Triple Bottom-line approach, which takes into account costs and revenues in all three major capital categories: financial, social, and natural.

It was only logical that the first attempts to create new tools capable of accommodating the Triple Bottom-line approach were to adapt the widely used Business Model Canvas for that purpose. Osterwalder himself started the quest in a 2009 lecture in Bremen, Germany, where he presented suggestions on "how to systematically build business models beyond profit." Most practitioners of the Canvas, who are interested in sustainable business models, chose initially to add two new elements below Canvas element 5 (Revenues) that would capture social and ecological revenues and another two elements below Canvas element 9 (Cost Structure) that would capture social and ecological costs. An example of such adaptation is the Extended Business Model Canvas by Vastbinder et al.,[6] shown in Figure 11.2.

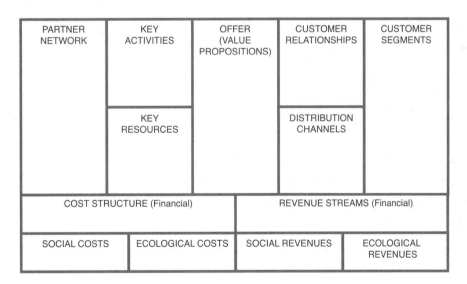

Figure 11.2 *Extended Business Model Canvas (adapted from B. Vastbinder et al.).*

Although such additions proved useful in uncovering business model patterns, particularly in the context of low-income economies, the main challenge remained generally the measurement of social capital and its quantification in economic terms. These challenges are being addressed by advances in the Social Return on Investment (SROI) theory, as well as through emerging methods and systems for measuring and tracking social assets that are rapidly accumulating experience in selecting appropriate measures for social assets and developing financial proxies for their economic valuation.

Frameworks for Sustainable Business

In parallel to the efforts of adapting the Canvas, several frameworks emerged for the "greening" of the business model. In Table 11.2, one such framework is proposed.

The Forum for the Future is developing a framework for sustainable business that integrates the various maturity stages as shown in Table 11.2: Beginner, Performer, Leader, and Pioneer.

Table 11.2 Sustainability Maturity Stages (Materials Made Available Courtesy of the Forum for the Future)

Beginner		Performer	Leader	Pioneer
• Understanding of key CR issues	• Senior-level buy-in	• CR a strategic opportunity	• Business model refocused to profit from sustainable value creation	
• Compliance systems in place	• Vision of sustainable future	• Sustainable innovations across the company		
	• Systems in place to deliver			

As shown in Table 11.3, the framework also identifies the characteristics of each of these stages as they relate to intention, business models, strategy, organizational qualities, and performance. A link to the Forum for the Future is provided in the "Glossary and Resources" section of this book.

Table 11.3 Sustainable Business Framework (Materials Made Available Courtesy of the Forum for the Future)

	Beginner	Performer	Leader	Pioneer
Intention	Keep permission to play	Useful to our existing strategy	Long-term sustainable value	Creating a sustainable future
Business Model(s)	Not considered	Taken rough edges off existing business model	Making the most of existing business model	Vast majority of business achieves commercial success by actively contributing to a sustainable economy
Strategy	• Compliance	• Cost Savings	• Strategic opportunities: product, service, and some business model experimentation	• Shaping a sustainable future to be successful in
	• Philanthropy	• Incremental innovation	• Some shaping of context • Targets are stretching	• Innovating SBMs and scaling them up for success • Targets rely on external collaboration
Organizational Qualities	People, networks, procedures incoherent on sustainability	People, networks, procedures equipped to pursue sustainability within existing business strategy	People, networks, procedures aligned with long-term articulated purpose	People, networks, procedures aligned and set up for disruptive innovation
Performance	Incoherent	• Contribution to bottom line • Improving impact, rarely in top quartile of peers	• Meet stretching targets for own operations, supply chain and use-phase	• Meet stretching targets on shaping the context

There are several other frameworks all intended to provide guidance for companies that want to begin the transformation toward a sustainable organization, for example, the five levels of sustainable activities proposed by The Natural Step[7] or the Gearing Up Framework proposed by Avastone Consulting, headquartered in Atlanta, Georgia.[8]

At the leading edge of this broad spectrum of frameworks and approaches to sustainable business is the Strongly Sustainable Business Model Group (SSBMG), based at OCAD University's Strategic Innovation Lab in Toronto, Canada. Strong sustainability is a term coined by ecological economists and is centered on the axiom that it is impossible to replace natural capital with any other type: human, social, or intellectual. SSBMG is taking a design science approach to developing tools and methods helping small and medium-sized enterprises to shift toward a strongly sustainable mode. Starting from Osterwalder business ontology and Canvas, Antony Upward, co-founder of SSBMG, has developed SSBM Ontology and SSBM Canvas, which in mid-2013 were being tested with several organizations.

The Business Case for Sustainability

In the past decade since the sustainability question entered mainstream thinking, the general assumption among business leaders has been that "sustainability" implied a trade-off between financial performance and so-called ESG (Environmental, Social, and Governance) performance. Many business leaders saw it as a necessary action at the cost of their organization's performance. In the past few years research has uncovered a direct linkage between sustainability and corporate risk management, as well as links related to access to capital. More recently, evidence has emerged that applying sustainability principles actually improves the company's bottom-line performance. In his most recent book, *The New Sustainability Advantage,*[9] Bob Willard has compiled business cases covering a large manufacturing company as well as a small service company. His business cases demonstrate seven benefits that make sustainability strategies smart business strategies:

1. Increased revenues and market share
2. Reduced energy expenses
3. Reduced waste expenses
4. Reduced water and materials expenses
5. Increased employee productivity
6. Reduced hiring and attrition expenses
7. Reduced risks

Willard offers free online access to the same calculator he used for the business cases in his book, so you can enter the data of your own organization and figure out how to optimize sustainability's impact on the bottom line. A link to this calculator is offered in the "Glossary and Resources" section of this book.

Where to Go from Here

It is obvious that developing a sustainable business model is a process, whose scope and complexity depend on many factors including the maturity of the company in its understanding of the imperative for this broader sustainability approach. Developing sustainable business models requires managing risks in the new arenas of natural and social capital. It also usually requires broader participation across the organization and attention to the culture and structure of the organization and its learning capacity. Implementing sustainable business models encompasses a wider range of change within the organization, as well as in its external network, than traditional business models.

A good starting point might be assessing your organization's position on the maturity scale using one of the frameworks presented earlier. Next, review the business cases presented by Bob Willard and explore how you can apply these principles in your organization to improve your bottom line. Now chart a path moving your organization to a higher level of maturity. A checklist of actions to do so is offered by the eight steps recommended by the Green Business Model Innovation,[10] a collaborative research project of Nordic Innovation. The eight steps are best practices toward green business model innovation:

1. Develop company culture toward sustainability.
2. Frame company values and translate them into principles or business practices.
3. Implement green strategy: a vision and mission linked to all activities of the organization.
4. Acquire appropriate skills and knowledge across the value chain through external resources and internal training.
5. Create green business cases: Green business models must be financially sustainable.
6. Involve customers to better understand their needs and expectations of a sustainable company.
7. Start small to experiment and learn before scaling up.
8. Train sales staff to communicate the company's values, products, and services in a credible way to customers.

With that foundation you can then explore new and alternative business models, taking into consideration the Triple Bottom-line approach using tools such as the Extended Business Model Canvas or the soon-to-be-available Strongly Sustainable Business Model Canvas and its tool kit.

Endnotes

1. A. Codrea-Rado, "Until the 1990s, Companies Didn't Have 'Business Models,'" April 17, 2013, accessed July 25, 2013, http://qz.com/71489/until-the-nineties-business-models-werent-a-thing/.
2. A. Osterwalder and Y. Pigneur, *Business Model Generation* (self-published, 2010).

3. S. G. Blank, *The Four Steps to the Epiphany: Successful Strategies for Products That Win* (2007).

4. L. Keeley et al., *Ten Types of Innovation: The Discipline of Building Breakthroughs* (John Wiley & Sons, 2013).

5. A. Osterwalder and Y. Pigneur, *Business Model Generation.*

6. B. Vastbinder et al., "Business but Not As Usual: Entrepreneurship and Sustainable Development in Low-Income Economies," in *Entrepreneurship, Innovation and Sustainability,* ed. Marcus Wagner (Greenleaf Publishing, 2012).

7. "A Strategic Framework," The Natural Step, accessed July 25, 2013, www.naturalstep.org/en/our-approach.

8. C. A. McEwen and J. D. Smith, *Mindsets in Action: Leadership and the Corporate Sustainability Challenge* (Atlanta, GA: Avastone Consulting, 2007).

9. B. Willard, *The New Sustainability Advantage* (New Society Publishers, 2012).

10. T. Bisgaard et al., *Short Guide to Green Business Model Innovation* (2012), available from www.nordicinnovation.org/Publications/short-guide-to-green-business-model-innovation/.

12

Business Model Execution—
Navigating with the Pivot

David Charron is currently a Senior Fellow and Lecturer in Entrepreneurship at the Haas School of Business, teaching courses in the MBA, EWMBA, and executive programs. He is Berkeley's faculty lead on the NSF ICorps program. He has served as Executive Director of Lester Center for Entrepreneurship and Innovation and the Berkeley Innovative Leader Development effort. He is an entrepreneur, an investor, a mentor, and a consultant in the Silicon Valley and has 25 years of focus on technology commercialization and entrepreneurship with Stanford, MIT, and Xerox PARC, among others. He frequently travels internationally as a professional educator and business consultant. He holds a B.S. in Mechanical Engineering from Stanford and an M.B.A. from Berkeley.

If you've ever made a significant change in a business, you have a gut understanding for the word pivot. Pivoting is a term widely used in the entrepreneurial community to describe changes in the assumptions underlying a business model (proposed or established). Managers at all levels need to understand why and when pivots happen, and how they can better lead the pivoting process. Effective management of a business pivot requires skills in both design and learning that are often overlooked in the early phases of a business.

New ventures often enter markets without established business models and use techniques to find opportunities where enough customers are willing to pay for the solutions the company will create to "build a business." These processes have been popularized through the work of Osterwalder and Pigneur's Business Model Canvas, Steven Blank's

Customer Development process, and Manifesto and Eric Ries's Lean Startup movement. These works represent a business description framework, a process for defining opportunities, and an ethic around efficient use of capital that have substantially shifted the entrepreneurial value creation process.

Pivots have come to represent the mythic capability of entrepreneurs to apply science to the entrepreneurial process. Rigorous testing guides them to alter their business models to exploit the largest and most profitable models quicker than their competitor. I view pivots as a management capability to combine learning and design to flexibly and nimbly adapt to the changing landscape that any organization encounters as it moves through a market landscape. Stories of pivots are told often in hindsight and in a manner that makes the pivot appear seamless and planned when they likely were not.

Different but Dependent Processes: Entrepreneurship and Innovation

Disrupt Together brings together two different disciplines, innovation and entrepreneurship, in recognition that disruption is based in both the new ideas and the capability of those ideas to scale repeatedly in markets. The disciplines are linked, but different in several fundamental ways. One important way to describe the differences in the disciplines is to view them as temporal cycles. Innovation cycles tend to be within a short time frame (hours, days, or weeks of effort), whereas entrepreneurial processes tend to be longer (years to many years) efforts.

Innovation processes typically use a framework that starts with problem finding followed by problem solving. The process continues cycling iteratively, testing potential solutions against a framed understanding of need until a match between the solution and an express need is found. The innovation process is a highly general process that can be used to systematically approach just about any problem.

Entrepreneurship is about using innovation processes to find a business model that can achieve economies of scale and scope. The entrepreneurial team uses innovation processes across all the elements of a hypothetical business model canvas—finding specific problems and then looking for specific solutions. Customer Discovery techniques put the customer and value proposition first in line to be solved before the other elements in the business model can be resolved. This is called the search phase, when the entrepreneur seeks to validate the business model before executing against it. The execution phase in entrepreneurship follows the search phase and is operational in nature, exploiting the found business model.

Whereas the innovation process is applicable across many situations, the entrepreneurial process is a highly specific technique used in business to create and grow successful organizations that create value through scale and scope.

These processes are different but dependent. Entrepreneurship needs innovation both as the seed of its effort and as a business process that constantly drives new inputs as the company grows toward greater scalability and repeatability. These innovations often cause a company to pivot, or alter its business model.

What Is a Pivot?

This chapter recognizes two distinct phases in an effort to bring an innovation to market through either a new venture or a corporate effort: the search phase and the execution phase. All efforts start with a search phase in which the new venture seeks to establish a business model and transition to the execution phase. In the search phase, pivots occur when a hypothesis regarding an element of a business model either is invalidated and replaced with a new hypothesis, or is proven to be true. During the search phase, pivots can occur rapidly. Investment in a particular model has not yet occurred and the cost of pivoting is very low.

The Business Model Canvas is the commonly used framework for exploring new business opportunities regardless of phase (see Figure 12.1). In the search phase, entrepreneurs populate the canvas with hypotheses about how each element could work.

They start on the right-hand section of the Business Model Canvas called Customer Segments. These segments or target customers are easy to define and validate through testing. Although they're seemingly easy to define, many search-phase companies pivot quickly around their customer segments. In practice it seems that this is the most difficult section for new entrants to define and evaluate. This difficulty might stem from the entrant having limited knowledge of the opportunity chosen. Entrepreneurs are limited by their direct experience and can make mistakes in interpreting the signals from the customer. They are forced into a learning mode to better understand the critical aspects of their customers and markets.

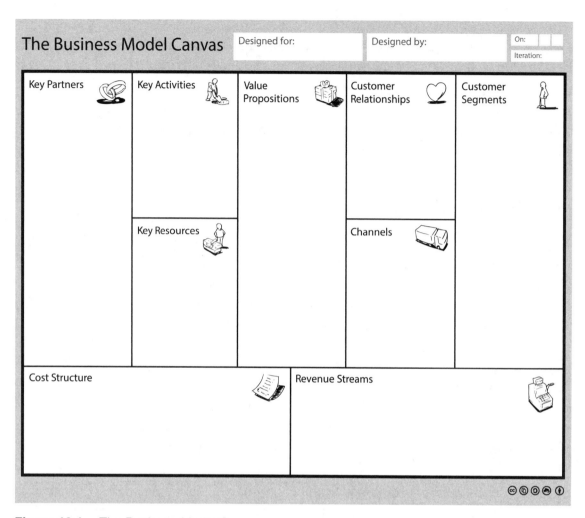

Figure 12.1 *The Business Model Canvas.*

Many search-phase companies fail to define a target market of a reasonably homogenous set of customers who will express loyalty to the product idea. Loyalty in its first set of customers allows a company to more favorably set its pricing, value creation processes, and resource acquisition plans.

After the target market is set, the company must turn its attention to its product configuration. The goal here is to obtain product-market fit, a concept measured by steep reductions in the customer acquisition cost and increasing demand. The company is still in search phase here, validating its value propositions, relationships, distribution, and possible revenue models. Hypotheses are generated and tested quickly, with as little capital consumed as possible. The hypothesis generation and testing begins to extend to the left side of the canvas and to costs also in anticipation of possible product-market-fit.

If the members of management of the search-phase company bring anything with them into the execution phase of the business, it is the flexibility of mind that comes from making multiple, albeit inexpensive, pivots. It is often the lack of ability to pivot, not the pivot count, that indicates the potential decline of a company. Management should have learned the process of pivoting and accumulated the know-how about why the opportunity does or doesn't work.

The transition from search to execution phase as depicted in Figure 12.2 happens as demand for its product increases and the company begins to scale its internal processes. The business model has become established (it doesn't have to be correct) and the company begins to execute against the model. For such an execution phase company, a pivot now becomes any intentional and significant change in the operational business model of the organization. Significant means a reconfiguration or redirection of the assets and operations of the company. Pivots are designed to improve the performance and expected outcome of the company.

For the majority of this chapter, I will focus on pivoting in execution phase companies.

Figure 12.2 *The transition from search to execution phase.*

Magoosh: Changing the Content Model

Magoosh (www.magoosh.com) was formed by three M.B.A.s from the Haas School of Business at UC Berkeley and is focused on providing effective test preparation for the GMAT, SAT, and other standardized tests. The company is still pursuing the original idea and has found a reasonably scalable business model. When the team originally formed, the decisions at hand became "how to source content" and "how to source customers."

The company successfully negotiated both of these activities by forming content partnerships with successful tutors and teachers who were typically in one-to-one settings with students. This content got the company moving quickly and into a distribution partnership with a highly targeted website focused on reviewing test preparation systems. They were off to the races.

As the company progressed, they began to realize that they were creating a highly defined learning experience for their users and that experience was going to be at the core of their brand. Having outsourced content was a great way to start the company, but controlling the content and its consistency became a higher level priority in the value proposition. They needed to change their content model away from licensing to content creation.

Original Hypothesis: Building strong partnerships with content developers would allow Magoosh to avoid development costs, find and deliver the best content to its users, and command a premium price.

The Pivot: Build an internal content development capability and reduce the company's exposure to third-party content. This would allow a more consistent customer experience and would also allow Magoosh to minimize royalties to third-party content owners.

Why Pivot: Magoosh had instrumented its product for customer feedback on content: what was working, what wasn't. What the heads of the company learned was that content, though it appeared static, needed to be dynamic. Updating the lesser-effective content improved the product. They also realized that they needed to control that innovation process to ensure quality and timely updates. Their prior content model was not effective at producing timely updates. Customer feedback and data drove the decision to modify the partnership structure and invest in building a Key Activity around content development.

In either the search or the execution phase, pivoting can be thought of as a form of innovation process. When it's done correctly, management tests assumptions, learns about requirements, finds problems, and then experiments with new solutions. Those solutions that work survive and are implemented.

Why Pivot?

Each day the management of a new venture must decide to continue to rely on hypotheses underlying the business or to refocus on a new set of hypotheses. The Persevere, pivot, or perish decision frame is front and center daily for start-ups.

The decision to persevere, or continue the operations of the company as they were the day or week before, is often the default for management and is based on hypotheses created when the operating model of the company was chosen. Those hypotheses span the business model from revenue and costs to partnerships and asset creation. New information generated by the activities of the company should be used to continuously test those underlying hypotheses. Does the information generated invalidate a hypothesis and cause a need to improve the business model? Does it generate a need to pivot?

If an operating assumption is disproved, an alternative must be chosen to replace the now-defunct part of the model. At the heart of creating the new model is a problem-solving innovation process in which management creates several alternatives that can substitute for the disproven hypothesis and then tests them in the market and against one another. Only when the best alternative is discovered does the company pivot its business model.

If the company discovers a better opportunity than the one currently pursued by the company, a pivot should also be considered. Management considers the risk/reward trade-off of persevering compared to pivoting to the new model. Only when the risk is small and the reward large in comparison to risk/reward of persevering is the pivoting warranted.

Even a casual reconsideration of a business model can create many opportunities to pivot. Pivoting based on data that is not relevant to the current business or that is of low quality or quantity can lead to mistakes and wandering through business models. Pivoting based on the creation of a single alternative to the current business model generates the potential of jumping from one model to another, wandering through a series of costly pivots.

The best pivots occur when the team creates an open learning environment and carefully considers the quality and quantity of new information driving their design process. The team is allowed to define several alternative hypotheses and business models that can be compared to each other in their ability to solve problems and generate larger opportunities. They can filter through opportunities quickly looking for advantages in both market entry and long-term sustainability.

Uber: Entering New Market Segments

Uber is a car service that fundamentally changed the relationship between a rider and the driver. Founded in 2009, the company has stayed true to its basic value proposition, which was to provide users with extraordinary transportation service for a premium price. The rider uses a GPS-enabled device, a cellphone, to request a ride from an Uber driver. The service connects the rider and driver, and handles logistics, payments and ratings, ensuring a predictable and superior experience.

The Uber software technology can be thought of as sophisticated dispatch service. It doesn't own or license the drivers or cars. It optimizes the market making between riders and drivers. Uber's initial target market, black-car limousine rides in San Francisco, created a profitable business.

The Pivot: The original target customer segment was consumers willing to pay for a premium black car service experience created by bundling several products together. Uber pivoted to providing vehicles other than limousines, namely cabs, specialty vehicles and other rideshare modes. That pivot took its focus to a customer who had lower willingness-to-pay and lower service requirements.

Why Pivot? Uber pursued this change in customer focus for several reasons. I'd like to highlight two here:

1. **Regulation.** As the company entered other markets it found that the local governments and entrenched incumbents were using regulations to hinder the company from expanding. This occurred in New York City and other locations.

2. **Competition.** At the same time, competitors were springing up quickly across all the market segments. While the Uber service has an incredible set of algorithms driving superior service, others soon copied some of the service attributes or entered the low-end of the market (Lyft) and captured market share.

Ultimately, Uber's pivot was strategic but driven by external forces. It pivoted to improve its long-term business outcome and to protect its service from being disrupted by low-end competitors.

Companies pivot in response to opportunities to make the business perform better.

How to Pivot

When management decides that the business must change its business model, speedy but careful modification must occur. Changes in the model have impact on the market's perceived position of the company and the company's employees. Leadership should be able to integrate its understanding of the market environment (learning) and its value-creation strategy (design) and clearly bring its employees, managers, and board into alignment around any pivot.

> ## *How to Pivot?*
>
> *Magoosh:* The pivot executed by Magoosh changed its content creation and maintenance model. Management entered into a series of concerted experiments to validate each step in the pivot and its impact on the business outcome. Through low-cost experimentation, they first understood how to execute the pivot and discovered how to maximize value creation in the process. As the experiments proved fruitful, management turned each experiment into embedded business processes that created a successful pivot. The company reduced its capital risk by breaking the pivot into several efficient and reversible experiments that drove the final outcome.
>
> *Uber:* Uber altered its market focus to include different sets of drivers and passengers. Provisioning the new markets with their software was reasonably straightforward. With their extensive experience developing relationships with limo drivers, the company simply expanded its driver-acquisition apparatus to other types of cars. Distribution of the new services was done through the same Uber mobile application, giving their large customer base immediate access to the new products. The challenge was deciding to implement these changes and to suffer any negative consequences that might arise, such as channel conflict. Uber management can be described as aggressive about market entry and this pivot is in keeping with that style. Uber's experiments with distributing other transportation services is occurring in 2013 and the results should be known soon. Will the company be as aggressive at removing services that aren't working?

Table 12.1 is a guide for execution phase companies to help them determine how to approach pivoting the company.

Table 12.1   How and When to Pivot

For Execution Phase Companies		Information Quality behind the Pivot's Cause and the Opportunity Size It Represents	
		Low or Medium	**High**
Cost to Pivot in Terms of Capital Risk	Low	Run customer development experiments.	*Go*—proceed with pivot until more information gives different insight.
	High	Explore how to reduce capital risk.	Proceed but reduce capital risk by staging pivot and securing capital resources.

There is one other type of pivot: the bet the company pivot. This kind of pivot arises when the company is doing so poorly in its execution that it must redefine itself. These pivots tend to be more like a company restart, when the entire business model is changed in an attempt to save the company.

If your company is in the search phase, your business model is filled with untested hypotheses and the operations of the company are focused on finding information to validate or invalidate the hypotheses. Your goal is to move from search to the execution phase by filling in your business model with assertions supported by field data gathered through customer development and validation. If an assumption behind the proposed business model is wrong, it is replaced with a new hypothesis, and the testing continues. The cost of a pivot is very low and is primarily the time invested to develop quality data.

Resource acquisition is a critical step in the pivoting process. Ample funding and key resources are critical before, during, and after the pivot. The Lean Startup movement teaches a mechanism that is applicable to all companies: Do not overspend on activities for which the outcome is based on risky hypothetical outcomes. In the case of both Magoosh and Uber, cash resources were available from sales and from investors. Deploying that capital for the purposes of the pivot was the responsibility of the CEO. Both acquired the key resources and shifted operations appropriately to the new models given their appetite for risk. Magoosh did the pivot more concertedly and Uber more aggressively.

When Pivots Don't Happen

Failure is a high-percentage bet for most efforts to bring new products and services to the market. If pivoting is a skill or technique that can be taught, why don't most efforts work themselves into a position of success through pivoting? Is the lack of pivoting the cause of failure?

Pivoting is about having options and the ability to pursue those options. Certainly an energy production company pivoting to become a software producer might be nearly impossible. But a company of talented individuals moving from one market focus to a better market seems easy—except that the cognitive struggles of the entrepreneur, their advisors, and the board often get in the way. The Hypothesis-driven entrepreneurship movement is an attempt to bring rationality to start-up decision making. If only it were that easy.

Those who take on risk often suffer from one or more cognitive biases that skew the decision-making process:

- **Overconfidence:** Entrepreneurs enter into a new venture confident of their own skills, product vision, and customer understanding. Overconfidence is a cognitive bias in which the individual holds strong beliefs without regard to information that is available or that could be developed that might disprove the original assumption or the cause of the belief.

- **Escalation of commitment:** This is related to overconfidence because overconfidence can drive an escalation of commitment, but there is another more insidious part. Loss aversion is a cognitive bias in which people strongly prefer avoiding losses in favor of gains. This causes innovators, when faced with a pivot, to ascribe undue risk of loss in pivoting and undue gain to staying the course.

- **Inability to see new opportunity:** This is a framing effect bias in which information about a new opportunity is readily available but the individual cannot reach a conclusion to pivot. We all bring our own specific experience to new information, and our experience limits and shapes our ability to see and comprehend new data and scenarios. Investors know this bias well—they see it in their CEOs quite frequently. When they see it, the question turns to pivoting the CEO either by strength of argument or by positional authority.

- **Inability to pursue the pivot:** Pivoting costs money and can create dislocations in the operations of the company. Employees might be let go and new employees hired with different skills. Investment capital might be required to acquire new customers, create new product lines, and scale the business. Even though the new pivot might save the company, exploit a larger opportunity, or provide a greater financial return, there is no guarantee that the quality and quantity of resources required will be available to successfully pivot.

We all carry those cognitive biases, along with many others, and they inform and shape our behaviors. Pivoting a business is the responsibility of the CEO—the one person the team and board has trusted with decision-making authority. But even in the case in which the CEO chooses to pivot the company, the company must follow to ensure the success of the pivot. So lastly, the CEO must have significant leadership skills to motivate and convince others that the new direction, at least at the moment, is the best opportunity and should be pursued with alacrity.

Summary

Pivoting a company requires the confluence of an opportunity and the skill and resources to execute. An innovator's ability to pivot, their flexibility of mind and skill, is a key success factor in today's world of market entry. No markets remain constant over time, and opportunities that appear today might fall out of favor over time. Innovators must embrace the concept of pivoting, and must understand why pivots occur, how to change an organization to execute a pivot, and finally the challenges we all have that limit our ability to realize value when a potential pivot arises.

Pivoting is also an innovation process that requires a disciplined process to avoid being misled and executing well against newfound opportunities. Innovation processes have costs that can be modeled and applied to return-on-investment metrics. Innovation and pivoting are management techniques that organizations should embrace and embed into their culture to foster agility and openness.

Section 5

Disruptive Innovation in Action— Stories from the Field

In this section you will learn from a diverse array of practitioners about their experiences in launching disruptive innovation efforts. Our authors share stories here, from the importance of interdisciplinary engagement in building brand to the challenges of disrupting yourself through launching new, often cannibalizing, business models from within established enterprises to how deep customer empathy in cross-disciplinary teams can lead to unique customer relationships.

For additional perspective we spoke with Ryan Armbruster, Vice President of Innovation Competency for UnitedHealth Group. Ryan has led disruptive innovation efforts with a focus on service design in various healthcare settings. Previously, Ryan was the founding director of the Innovation Center (SPARC Lab) at the Mayo Clinic, the United States' largest healthcare delivery innovation group working within a major academic medical center. At United, Ryan reports collectively to a group of C-level executives and is charged with identifying, incubating, and launching innovation capabilities across more than 110,000 employees. We spoke with Ryan about his experiences in launching innovation efforts in these very different settings.

Understand Your Culture First

As both Dr. Cromarty highlighted in Chapter 2, "Becoming a Strategic Organization," and Ellen di Resta further explores in Chapter 4, "Assessing Your Innovation Capability," the importance of understanding your organization's personality and its collective capabilities cannot be underestimated. As Ryan emphasized, "You need to first understand the personality of the enterprise because if you don't get it right internally first, it isn't going to work. For example, at Mayo Clinic, as a provider of healthcare services, there is a long legacy and passion around empathy. While United is also in the healthcare space, it is a large payer and has a significant responsibility for high performance and achieving the metrics to monitor that performance. Additionally, United is a public company with obligations to serve shareholders, which adds to the emphasis on performance metrics. Understanding the raw materials you have to work with is essential. Successful innovation is built on the unique characteristics and assets of an organization." Maryann Finiw's chapter on branding offers tangible examples of the importance of understanding the collective capabilities of the organization, as well as its customers, embodied in the brand. Brandy Fowler's chapter on disruptive business models explores leveraging capabilities in new markets or for new users.

Innovation Is a Contact Sport

As our book title suggests, innovation is a team sport and contact is key. In the assessment chapter Dr. Beckman shared her research on learning styles and team design with an emphasis on understanding type, composition, and integration. In this upcoming section, Yvonne Lin of Smart Design offers a look at how those interactions can bear fruit when deeply engaging with customers as part of the integrated team. In the Mayo environment, Ryan noticed that geographic proximity of the employees was key to their success. Upon reflection he said, "You will notice you don't hear of many successful start-ups that were spawned from teleconferencing. They often start in a "garage" for a reason. The close contact and personal interactions are essential in the early stages of discovery. We are a bit more challenged to leverage proximity at United given our diversity of offerings and the geographic distribution of our 110,000 employees. I have discovered that although we can communicate effectively through telepresence, to really engage teams to collaborate on interdisciplinary teams, we need to create geographic hubs for face-to-face collaboration."

Discovery Space Is Important

As most businesses are focused on developing and optimizing solutions that leverage their core competencies, the notion of creating space, time, and resources to discover new opportunity can be a challenge. In Chapter 14, "Interdisciplinarity, Innovation, and Transforming Healthcare," Dr. Stahl describes the challenge in creating the operating room of the future, which required taking two operating rooms offline in order to identify, test, and prototype solutions in a real-world simulation. In Chapter 16, "Opportunities in Branding—Benefits of Cross-Functional Collaboration in Driving Identity," Maryann Finiw describes the importance of creating a war room as a discipline-neutral space for exploring brand artifacts. Ryan described this challenge as well: "You need to carve out the space and time to probe the problem. That is often difficult for senior management to appreciate as we all live in a culture that rewards results, oftentimes even if it solves the wrong problem. I often feel I need to translate the power of problem exploration and definition; the power of using design thinking and empathy work to more deeply understand opportunities. They often don't understand it until they see what it can do for them."

Evidence Is Key

Because the process of discovery and formulation in opportunity recognition for disruptive innovation is inherently ambiguous and nonlinear, it is key to develop milestones that provide insights or evidence to the broader team of stakeholders. Dr. Stahl notes in his chapter that evidence is key for engagement with healthcare decision makers. Evidence can be quantitative but more often at these early stages it is qualitative as long as it is in some way validated. When constructing his innovation efforts, Ryan has learned a great deal of balancing this science and art: "I strive to keep all innovation projects under a year. When you are committing resources to exploration where the outcomes can't be predicted, it is key to offer tangible insights or evidence of progress at a minimum of every 90 days. I have also found that projects that go on longer than a year, for the most part, run into challenges as research becomes less relevant and factors upon which you built your hypothesis have undoubtedly shifted."

The Balancing Art of Transition to Implementation

Moving the innovation effort from exploration to implementation requires skilled leadership coordination. In Brandy Fowler's chapter on disruptive business models, she details the challenges of managing these efforts internally, externally, or through hybrid models. Ryan's perspective was this: "It is very important to have senior leadership that understands the difference between innovation work and operational work. These efforts must be kept separate without crossing paths as often the innovation team may be working on an effort that could threaten the current operations. A skilled senior leader will keep both running independently until the key moments of integration, when the innovation effort has matured enough for management by a development and integration team."

The four chapters that follow offer real-world case studies, from branding to technology adoption in healthcare to launching disruptive business models from within to designing new product, service, and brand solutions by deeply engaging with customers.

13

Broad Thinking—Connecting Design and Innovation with What Women Want

Yvonne Lin is an expert at considering gender in developing compelling and functional solutions to complex design problems. She is one of the founding members of 4B and the Femme Den. She was a named a Master of Design by Fast Company. Previously, she was an Associate Director at Smart Design. She has a B.A. in Visual Art and a B.A. in Engineering from Brown University. She is the inventor on more than 20 patents and has designed products and experiences for companies like Nike, Johnson & Johnson, Hewlett-Packard, American Express, LEGO, Pyrex, Nissan, and Under Armour. She also spends a lot of time skiing, rock climbing, and putzing around her apartment making small art projects.

On writing projects, Yvonne frequently collaborates with Boris Itin, whom she would like to thank for his contributions to this chapter.

Every year, thousands of corporations invest billions of dollars into designing and making toothbrushes, flowerpots, cars, remote controls, and all the thousands of products that we interact with every day. As illustrated throughout this book, innovation is a complex process involving people with a wide range of skills. Designers, engineers, sales and marketing teams, advertisers, business strategists, and many other talented and hardworking people strive at the best of their abilities to satisfy the customers, male and female alike. And yet I know so many women who wonder:

"Do they have a clue about who I am?"

Women buy or influence 85% of all consumer purchases. Yet they feel that the majority of products are not meeting their needs. This is true across the vast majority of industries. Despite buying or influencing the purchase of 90% of all consumer electronics, only 15% of American women think that computing and mobile products are designed to be appealing. Despite making 69% of the household health decisions, 66% of American women feel misunderstood by healthcare marketers. Despite controlling 73% of household spending, 84% of American women feel let down by the level of quality and service they get from financial companies. Despite purchasing 60% of cars and heavily influencing the purchase of an additional 30%, 74% of American women feel like they are misunderstood by the automotive industry.

Most companies are aware of how important the women's market is. They try very hard to appeal to women on all levels, from marketing to design to customer service. Yet they often admit that they fail. This is not a failure of intent or of lack of effort; this is a failure of understanding. Driven by misconceptions and adherence to stereotypes, many companies resort to a "pink it and shrink it" design strategy. Instead of appealing to women, they ended up insulting their customers.

To create a good product, a designer has to understand the user. This is also true if a user is a woman. Here comes the great challenge of design: While the majority of consumers are women, 85% of product designers and engineers are men (see Figure 13.1).

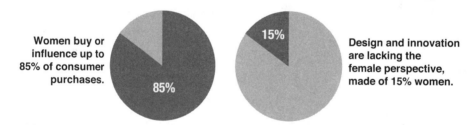

Figure 13.1 *Disparity between the percentage of women designers and purchasing power.*

There are few things that men find as difficult to understand as women. The lack of understanding spills over into the design and innovation industry.

Five years ago, three of my female colleagues and I noticed this opportunity and we launched an experiment within Smart Design called the Femme Den. Today, we continue to design for the 4 billion women in the world with the design collective, 4B. We represent educational and professional expertise in industrial design, design engineering, design strategy, design research, and architecture. Between us we have over 35 years of professional design experience. The Femme Den achieved deep traction with early clients including major corporations in medical, consumer electronics, housewares, automotive, and sporting-goods industries, such as Johnson & Johnson, GE Medical,

Hewlett-Packard, Proctor & Gamble, LEGO, Nissan, and Nike. Press coverage on this approach was given in *Fast Company, ID Magazine, New York Times,* and more. Our designs have won multiple awards, have become bestsellers, and have made women happy.

Four Key Insights into "Broad Thinking"

We take a holistic and interdisciplinary approach to understanding how women think and make decisions. Our path to understanding women has been long and full of unexpected discoveries. Like anthropologists, we studied women in their natural habitat. We followed them when they were driving, shopping, cooking, cleaning, talking, and playing. We observed them at their jobs, in their homes, and with their families. We studied trendsetters and more mainstream women. We analyzed how women interact with products and services at every stage. We listened carefully to what women said and, even more carefully, to what they didn't say. We learned many things not mentioned in design literature or discussed at design conferences. Based on many years of design and research, we developed strategies and tools to analyze women's needs and to make products and services that they appreciate. In particular, we have identified four issues that are important for women but are often ignored in the current world of innovation and design. We call our approach Broad Thinking. Understanding women and gender issues will enable designers to deliver better products and services. Gender can be and should be a part of any design project just as ergonomics, function, or aesthetics are. Following are four key broad thinking areas and some examples of how they work.

Women Think About "We," Not "Me"

To design a successful product, a designer should first ask himself or herself the following questions: "Who is the user?" and "What does this person want and need?"

A product doesn't become successful just because it has high performance. It becomes successful because it fulfills people's needs. Men and women might have different sets of needs from the same product. A source of these different needs comes from how the two genders define themselves differently. Men tend to think in terms of "I." A man buys a product because he likes it and he is going to use it. Women tend to think about "we." A woman buys a product because she likes it and she wants to use it; but she also wants her partner to enjoy it, her kids to understand it, and her parents to approve of it. She also wants the product to fit her lifestyle and her home.

When designers try to make a successful product for women, they should be very well aware of this difference. Our team didn't recognize this immediately. It took years of design experience to fully appreciate how impactful this distinction is. We always start design projects with an in-depth qualitative research. One of the tools we use is a "chat." A chat is a small informal single-gender conversation generously lubricated by wine, beer, and food. We couldn't help but notice this mind-set difference between the groups of men and women. The women quickly introduce themselves, as well as their children, husbands, parents, and pets. They use the pronoun "we" throughout the chat. They are constantly referring to something their kids did or didn't do, to what their husbands like or hate. They talk about their relatives and friends. They define themselves as a result of a social interaction matrix. They describe their homes and how much effort they invest in having their homes harmonious and happy. When the men describe themselves, they specify their age, work, and interests. They use the pronoun "I." Often, it's not until the second hour of the chat, when prompted directly, that they succinctly describe their families.

The problem is that numerous products are designed to please a single person. Designers consider the user an "I," not a "we." This approach does not reflect their female customer's perspective. Women do 85% of the shopping and they judge products through the lens of "we," not "I." A woman buys for herself, her family, and her home. Her list of user requirements is much longer. This means that when the product is being judged through her eyes, it often falls short of her standards. To please her, designers need to think about "we." They need to consider the complex web of user requirements from multiple viewpoints. Let us look at some examples.

A man needs a thermometer. He walks into a drugstore, walks to the corresponding section, and takes a look at the thermometers. His eyes fall on a classic stick thermometer. He sees that the temperature gauge looks easy to read. "I can use it," the man thinks as he buys it.

A woman walks into a drugstore and she looks around. "I can use it," she thinks about the classic stick thermometer, "but what about my kids? No, they are going to hate it." The thermometer is pointy and it looks like a long, scary needle. Her six-year-old son hates needles and he will be upset.

Nearby are various Vicks thermometers. They look safe and comfortable—not intimidating at all (see Figure 13.2). They are interactive—her son can see how the temperature indicator changes as he keeps it under his armpit. "Wonderful," his wife thinks, "we can all use it."

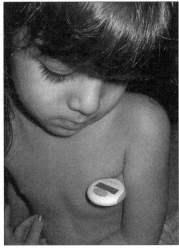

Figure 13.2 *Vicks thermometer.*

A man buys a video game console to shoot monsters from outer space and drive tanks through the enemy's defense lines. "I like playing these games," a man thinks as he buys it. Naturally, most video game consoles were designed for young to middle-aged men. Except for one.

When the Wii came out, the female market literally exploded. The consoles were immediately sold out and it took months of patient waiting to get your hands on one. Why did women like the Wii so much? Amazon user reviews answer this question quite clearly:

> "We had more fun, and more laughs, playing those games together than we did playing our individual games."
>
> "The Wii is the best way to go because there are more multiplayer games that are age-friendly from parent to child."
>
> "My father, who hates video games as a way of spending time and money, thinks that the Wii is great, and was like a little boy playing it. (He's 55.)"

Numerous high-ranking reviews by women stress the same point. They think in terms of "we," not "me"; they are looking for a product that everybody in the family can enjoy and play together. They are excited that all three generations—grandparents, parents, and children—and both genders can use it. The Wii console offered universality and a joint gaming experience.

To summarize this point, a man looks for a product that would make him happy whereas a woman looks for a product that would make her whole family, including men, happy. A man's requirements for a product are a subset of a woman's longer list of requirements. If a man is satisfied with a product, that doesn't mean that a woman will be satisfied. But if a woman is satisfied with a product, a man is likely to also be satisfied.

Women Pay Attention to the Whole Experience, Not Just the Product

A whole user experience consists of many complex parts. It includes messaging and advertising, online experience, retail, packaging, first product use, storage, hundredth product use, customer service, and disposal. For women, all of these parts matter; they tend to judge the experience holistically. A product is only a fraction of the overall experience. To please women, companies need to consider and design the whole experience. However, this rarely happens. The root cause of this is that men tend to judge the product, not the whole user experience. They are more likely to overlook or forgive the bad parts of the whole experience and focus primarily on the quality of the product itself. In the male-dominated world of innovation, many companies reflect this mind-set and pour a disproportional part of their efforts into improving the product while paying less attention to the whole experience.

This approach frustrates women. If a woman has to spend several hours browsing a confusing company website, she will walk away before she has a chance to find out how good the product is. If she had an unpleasant warrantee experience, her overall feelings about the company will be negative, however outstanding the product might be. To make women happy, companies need to deliver a high-quality and cohesive whole experience. A good whole experience will also please men. Although men do prioritize, they still don't like meaningless advertising, baffling websites, unopenable packaging, churlish salespeople, and indifferent service departments.

As designers, we often get project briefs from companies asking us to redesign a product. Quite often, we realize that this is not where the problem lies. We work with the client to redefine the project brief to include the design of the product and the design of whole experience. Our interdisciplinary team integrates needs from product to customer service to retail to brand; we design the whole customer experience.

For example, recently we were approached by a major car company—they were looking for ways to redesign their cars, making them more attractive for women. We found that although women had certain issues with the car design per se, the biggest challenges lay with the whole experience.

One of the primary questions we ended up with asking ourselves was, "Why is buying a $4 coffee in Starbucks a far better experience than buying a $30,000 car?"

First, it is difficult to research cars. Car company websites tend to describe the cars in terms best appreciated by car engineers and aficionados. Three out of the first five features describing the Nissan Versa are "Xtronic CVT," "active grille shutter," and "1.6L DOHC 4-cylinder engine." To persuade consumers to buy the Chevy Cruze, the company has a large picture of "2.0L Turbocharged clean diesel engine" on the vehicle's front page. The first thing that a prospective buyer learns about the Honda Crosstour is that its "new 3.5-liter i-VTEC V-6 engine delivers 278 hp and 252 lb-ft of torque." What percentage of people will find this information relevant to their needs? Suppose that, in spite of this unwelcoming start, a woman learned from other sources that a Nissan Versa or Honda Crosstour or Chevy Cruze is a good car and decides to buy one. Then comes arguably the worst part of a woman's experience. One of our users called it "car stealerships." The overwhelming majority of women have very negative experiences with car dealerships. They can't figure out what a fair price is for a car—Internet sources offer half a dozen different prices varying by as much as 10% to 15%. Women don't like haggling; they feel cheated and ignored by car dealers. It's so bad that most women try to bring a male friend or relative with them when they buy a car—they know that a man will get a better deal. After she passes the ordeal of buying a car, she drives it, she might have some issues with it, but generally she is not terribly unhappy. This is the high point of the whole experience. Then, the car breaks and she has to get it repaired. When the warranty runs out, the woman has to go to a repair shop. This experience is so frustrating that most women would rather delegate this unpleasant task to their male significant others. However, single women head 30% of American households and delegating is not an option for many of them.

If car companies are having such a hard time, why not innovate on the whole experience and improve women's attitude toward them? If a car company made learning about and buying cars fun and interesting, instead of confusing and stressful, women would buy their cars. If a car company made it easy to take care of their cars, women would know that the company cares about them and would loyally return for their next car. Instead, many women use words "sleazy" and "disgusting" in describing their experience with the car industry.

It does not have to be this way, in the car industry or anywhere else. Recently a small company has been able to remove the "sleazy and disgusting" stigma from a much more questionable industry: the adult store. This small company's adult stores deliver a satisfying whole experience. Ask anybody to imagine a typical adult store—it will be a small dirty place with a few creepy guys lurking around. In fact, it's hard to imagine a place most women would less like to visit. At the same time, women and couples make up a large consumer segment of the adult toy industry. Enter Babeland (see Figure 13.3).

Screen comps © Aislinn Race/Website design © Babeland

Figure 13.3 *Babeland website and marketing strategy.*

If you visit their website, you will see a tasteful and well-organized space. The website aims to create a sense of community rather than just to sell products. Learning is fun through the blogs, videos, reviews by real people, and workshops. The message is clear: Here a woman can find a fun experience. The Babeland retail stores deliver the same message as the online space. They are clean, brightly colored, well lit, and spacious; they feel pleasant and safe. A woman can visit this store by herself, with friends, or with a partner and enjoy it. Each purchase comes with fun-to-read and informative care instructions written by Babeland. To sum it up, Babeland delivers a cohesive friendly and fun whole experience. The power of a great whole experience is that it's able to transform an awkward product category into a shamelessly positive experience.

Women Want Real-Life Benefits, Not Potential Ones

Men and women perceive the relative value of potential and reality in products quite differently. Men tend to prioritize product potential—what a product is capable of—whereas women prioritize product reality—what they are going to do with a product. Potentially, a car can accelerate from 0 to 100 mph in four seconds; a camera can take 30MB picture for a wall-sized print; a TV can have facial recognition, voice control, and an Internet link to the refrigerator. But how relevant are these features in real life? What if a woman cares more that a car fits her two children, dog, and a cartload of groceries?

What if she wants a camera that operates intuitively and does not need extra accessories to connect to a computer? What if she would rather have a TV that does not clash with her living room?

Often, companies, particularly in the consumer electronics and automotive industries, concentrate on potential—they find it more valuable and exciting. This approach drives technological innovation. Designers, engineers, and other technology fans constantly aim to improve product performance, particularly with respect to quantifiable specifications, like dpi, megabytes, gradation steps, and horsepower.

One of the reasons many women are unhappy with consumer electronics and cars is that they value reality more than potential. In the best-case scenario, both real-life and potential benefits should coexist in the product. However, if one needs to be sacrificed, women would rather see the potential benefits go. Since they don't actually use it, the potential is less valuable to them. They choose simplicity, ease of operation, and other practical considerations over the ultimate potential.

Consumer electronics generously provides us with numerous examples that demonstrate the difference between potential and reality. Let us take a look at TVs and cameras.

If you walk into a Best Buy, you will see a long wall that carries several dozen TV sets that look identical, except for their size. To differentiate, the electronics companies invest an incredible amount of talent and effort to improve performance by a few percent. They are competing very hard on a narrow spectrum of easily quantifiable specifications. What if, instead, they took a closer look at what people, particularly women, want from a TV?

A major consumer electronics company asked us to find out what people wanted from a TV. We conducted ethnographic research on design-savvy women and couples. Our findings surprised the client quite a bit. Most women, and a large chunk of men, were less enticed by the electronic dream and more by the living reality. They didn't care that a TV had 1% more resolution or that it was one-tenth of an inch thinner than its competitors. Instead, they cared about how it fit into their living rooms, how easy it was to install and operate, and how much effort it took to integrate the TV with their other devices.

A woman doesn't just buy a TV; she creates her home as a unique environment to reflect her taste and desires. The visual disconnect is depicted in Figure 13.4. Everything from a couch to a rug to the paint color should work together. A very large shiny black plastic box aesthetically fits perfectly into a Best Buy, but it doesn't fit most home environments. One desperate woman painted a whole wall in her living room black in an attempt to make it work aesthetically. Another opted for all black furniture. Many just convince their husbands to buy smaller TVs so that they don't stand out so much.

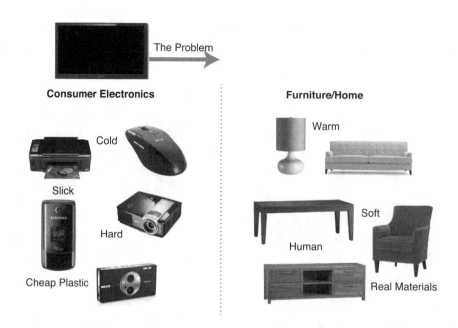

Figure 13.4 *Disconnect between consumer electronic aesthetics and home aesthetics.*

Mounting a TV is another major headache. Interior design magazines are full of photographs showing thin, flat TVs mounted on the walls and seamlessly integrated into the living space. People buy a flat TV only to discover that it's either impossible or prohibitively expensive to mount it and to hide half a dozen cables in a wall.

The women complained about integrating the TVs with the other devices such as computers, cable boxes, speakers, DVD players, and other units. Interfacing these devices requires numerous cables and plug-ins that are often poorly marked. Each device is designed by a separate subdivision in a consumer electronics company. Each remote control to each device is designed by yet another subdivision. The engineers from the different groups often don't interact and neither do their devices. This means that each remote control is unnecessarily complicated. A user has to invest significant time and effort into mastering interfaces that are not very intuitive. Men tend to fight their way through the process; some even enjoy the challenge. Women don't see it as a challenge; rather, it is an annoyance and a distraction from other things that are important to them. All of it causes women to feel that the TV industry does not understand them and it does not address their real-life needs.

Video cameras tell a similar story. To understand how people decide which camera to buy, we spent a few hours observing shoppers in a Best Buy. Here, a couple of dozen of video cameras were attached with long cords to a table. A white card with specifications was attached next to each camera. Some people would start by reading the cards. The majority of people, particularly women, would pick up the cameras and start playing with them. A woman would turn on the camera, try to take pictures or videos, and play them back on the little screens. If she couldn't figure out how to operate a camera in a few seconds, she would put it back on the stand and move to the next one. Our key conclusion is that despite whatever amazing technical performance a camera has to offer, a woman won't buy it unless she can figure out how to use it in less than 30 seconds. And yet so many companies invest huge efforts in boosting performance while sacrificing this first interaction. A common innovation pitfall is getting excited about a "cool" new technological feature and deciding to highlight it. The problem is that most of the time these "cool" features are potential benefits, not real-life ones. The digital interfaces become needlessly cluttered, frustrating, and difficult to operate, exasperating users away.

GoPro chose an opposite approach. Instead of coming with more "cool features," they identified an important real-life need that was not addressed by the video world. Then, they created a device precisely to fill this niche, to make action videos of extreme sports. They concentrated on delivering real-life benefits—how to enable users to take good-quality videos under real conditions from underwater to a snowstorm. They built a small rugged camera with a very simple interface that can be operated blindly in winter gloves. They designed a variety of reliable and practical attachments that enable users to fix the camera to a head, a helmet, a snowboard, a kayak, or a car. Interestingly, by offering real-life benefits instead of potential ones, GoPro conquered a young and mostly male customer base—extreme sport fans. But, as the general public realized the advantages of the cameras, the GoPro camcorders flooded the market; everybody wanted to easily record exciting moments in their lives. Now, the ubiquitous little boxes are everywhere and they are used by children, men, and women alike. The GoPro website also shows a shift in their consumer base—their large collection of videos starts with extreme sports and ends with a mother recording her 6-year-old son's first ski turns. Even under the guise of extreme sports, women recognize and are happy to adopt the real-life benefits of the GoPro.

Women Appreciate Human Traits in Objects

This broad-thinking topic is the most difficult to describe, quantify, or measure. Many designers either are not aware of it or underestimate its significance. Based on many years of successfully designing products for women, we've learned that a woman can connect to products on an emotional level and that she is more likely to connect when the product possesses human traits and has an attractive personality.

Scientific studies (and our own design experience) demonstrate that women are better at observing, understanding, and relating to other people, whereas men are more comfortable with machines.

In one experiment, Diane McGuinness and John Symonds showed pairs of images of humans and mechanical objects, using a stereoscope, to men and women. The two images fall on the same part of the visual field and compete for attention. The women reported seeing more people and the men saw more machines. The Profile of Nonverbal Sensitivity (PONS) Test was developed in 1979 and has been studied in multiple experiments in the decades since. These studies have shown that women are significantly more sensitive to facial expressions than men. This gender difference holds up in areas as varied as New Guinea, Israel, Australia, and North America. Ruben and Raquel Gur, neuroscientists from the University of Pennsylvania, conducted experiments with Brain MRIs and found that women are capable of recognizing a facial expression before men even recognize it to be a face. Jennifer Connellan and Anna Ba'tki from the Autism Research Centre at Cambridge University ran an experiment in which they found one-day-old girls spend more time looking at faces whereas one-day-old boys spent more time looking at mobiles. And it doesn't stop at humans. Melissa Hines of City University of London and Gerianne Alexander of Texas A&M University gave a large variety of toys to a group of baby velvet monkeys; girls preferred dolls, boys preferred cars and balls, and everybody equally liked stuffed dogs and picture books.

As designers, we have regularly observed similar preferences in our field. Women are instantly drawn toward products that project human traits, something they can relate to. They often see distinct personalities in products. At a first glance, a woman will see that a car is aggressive, a TV is boring, and a chair is cute. If a woman thinks that a product has a boring or unpleasant personality, she is far less likely to want it in her life.

Designers are very well aware that any product projects an image. They work hard on object aesthetics and they might aim to make their product look sleek, expensive, powerful, or rugged. They try to design products that project an image of a desirable product. But this is not enough. A woman might notice when a product looks sleek, expensive, powerful, or rugged. But she might not emotionally connect with it. To win her heart, the product needs desirable human traits.

One of the tools that we use to identify human traits is this set of questions: "What type of person would this object be? What gender would they be? What would be their hobbies and work? What car would they drive? Who would their friends be?"

Women pick up this game immediately and enthusiastically. It is surprising how similarly women describe an object. If a woman says that the person inside the object is boring and doesn't have much personality, it's like a kiss of death. If a woman finds that an object has an attractive personality, she immediately gets excited; she is likely to like the product more and to be more forgiving of any technical faults.

Breakup and love letters are another tool that we commonly use. This tool demonstrates how this personalization extends beyond the product to the whole experience. We ask women to write a breakup or love letter to a product as if it were a real person. They write touching and funny personal letters to TVs, cellphones, bras, and cars. They use such words and expressions as "cheat," "love of my life," "I've been having an affair," "disappointed," and "love at first glance." We have found two points particularly important: It is a natural thing to do for all women, and everybody goes past the purely product experience and includes the whole experience.

This exercise has been integrated into the Philadelphia University core curriculum. In the "Glossary and Resources," we offer links to one of the more amusing videos of this.

Advantageously for designers, human and object traits are not mutually exclusive in any way. A truly successful design is able to combine both object and human traits in a harmonious way. Then, both men and women can easily connect to the product. The most successful products manage to project different but equally positive images to both men and women.

Men describe the Mini Cooper as a former stunt car, with a large engine and a prominent air intake, and women describe the same car as their "friendly little sidekick." The Mini Cooper, Fiat 500, HP Photosmart printer, Flip videocamera, and Method soap are very different products that are united by one design consideration: They have distinct personalities. On the other hand, the Toyota Corolla (see Figure 13.5), Panasonic TX-37LX75M 37-inch TV, and HP LaserJet Pro P1102w laser printer need a personality infusion.

Figure 13.5 *The Mini Cooper versus the Toyota Corolla.*

Human traits are what make women look at this product and smile. This smile-generating capability might be difficult to measure and quantify. Nevertheless, it is key to designing for women.

Conclusions and Recommendations

In this chapter, we demonstrated how to design for women. Creating products and services for women is a challenging task that has confounded many talented designers. It has been a source of hard work and great satisfaction for my colleagues and me. Eventually, we found that truly interdisciplinary broad thinking is necessary to successfully identify, address, and solve the challenge. The main difference between men and women is that women have more angles, needs, and requirements than men do. A great solution has to address it all.

A good design will consider the needs of "we." A successful product will be only a part of the enjoyable whole experience. Every stage of the experience—from marketing to retail to packaging to use to customer service to storage to disposal—needs to be considered by an interdisciplinary design team. The design team must addresses a woman's real-life needs and design a product with a personality that she likes and relates to; then, a woman will be truly satisfied with not only the product but also the brand. She will know that the company likes her, understands her, and addresses her needs. A woman will forge a personal relationship with the brand and she will become loyal to it. Here comes the good news for the company: It will be a faithful, long-term relationship.

14

Interdisciplinarity, Innovation, and Transforming Healthcare

James E. Stahl, M.D., C.M., M.P.H., is a practicing board-certified internist at Massachusetts General Hospital, Senior scientist at the MGH-Institute for Technology Assessment, Research Director for the MGH Outpatient RFID project, and Adjunct Professor in Mechanical and Industrial Engineering at Northeastern University. He is an outcomes researcher with expertise in decision science, health technology assessment, and simulation modeling. His current research focuses on clinical process redesign, the application of new technologies in the clinical environment, technology implementation, interdisciplinary collaboration, and ethics.

What Challenges Are We Trying to Solve?

Healthcare faces many challenges. The delivery of healthcare has become increasingly complex as medical science and technology advance at an ever-increasing pace. The system is fractured among multiple competing providers and stakeholders whose incentives don't always align for the greater social good. Our mixed market economy has been relatively indifferent to quality and productivity in healthcare (Medicare 2006). Our population is aging and with age comes an increasing number of people with comorbidities and health problems. With increasing system complexity, system safety errors are rising. Recent reports indicate more than 100,000 drug-related, infection-related, or procedural errors in our hospitals (Care 2003; Century 2001; Series 2006; System 1999). This is why the Institute of Medicine (IOM) and National Academy of Engineering (NAE) have made a national call to arms to work for a healthcare system that is safe, effective, patient-centered, efficient, and equitable (Wilson and Howcroft 2005).

If these problems were simple, they would have been solved long ago. A common error when attempting to solve complex problems is to approach them from a single domain or perspective. We assume that the most salient feature of the problem is the cause, and if only we had a better scanner, antibiotic, procedure, or policy, the problem would go away.

Many problems in healthcare are complex and resist solutions via traditional single-domain approaches and are better addressed using an interdisciplinary, system-level perspective. There has been a growing recognition outside of healthcare that many major advances in science emerge out of interdisciplinary approaches (Klein 2000), and it is time this was applied more in healthcare.

However, there are also reasons why interdisciplinarity has not been widespread in healthcare. Simply, it is hard to do. Although interdisciplinarity offers opportunities for new insights and solving previous intractable problems (for example, hand hygiene), it also challenges comfortable work patterns and patterns of thought, as well as the organizational status quo.

What Is Interdisciplinarity?

Interdisciplinarity or transdisciplinary is a term increasingly used in health services but its definition is often unclear. In healthcare, interdisciplinarity can mean different things to different people and is often confused with multidisciplinarity. In clinical care, multidisciplinary teams can provide comprehensive care to patients. In this case multidisicplinarity might involve having providers from different clinical disciplines—for example, medical doctor (MD), registered nurse (RN), occupational therapist (OT), physical therapist (PT), social worker (SW)—working alongside each other (Zwarenstein, Goldman, and Reeves 2009). A care coordination team or a medical home might be examples of this.

Interdisciplinarity means something more. Interdisciplinarity is problem-solving perspective that integrates the knowledge and insights from many disciplines working together to achieve creative solutions (Armstrong 2006; Choi and Pak 2006; Fairbairn and Fulton 2000). To paraphrase Choi and Pak's (Choi and Pak 2006) metaphor, multi-disicplinarity is additive (for example, 2 + 5 =7), in which different types of knowledge are mixed together side by side but essentially remain distinct, whereas interdisciplinarity can be thought of as multiplicative or more (for example, $2 \times 5 = 10$). In interdisciplinary collaborations not only do team members come from disparate fields but the whole of the endeavor becomes more than the sum of its parts. The knowledge developed transcends the boundaries between disciplines, producing new forms of knowledge (Moran 2010).

As shown in many of the preceding chapters, effective interdisciplinary collaboration requires more than simply putting people from different disciplines in the same room together and hoping for the best (Klein 2000). In many ways, interdisciplinary collaboration is a paradigm for all collaboration, "a process through which parties who see different aspects of a problem can constructively explore their differences and search for solutions that go beyond their own limited vision of what is possible" (Gray 1989). To be effective, not only do different knowledge domains need to be bridged but also worldviews (Porter and Rossini 1984). Philadelphia University recognized this in the creation of their integrated college (DEC) and therefore crafted a core curriculum to establish common tools and language across the integrating disciplines. These tools were designed to facilitate collaboration and enable interdisciplinarity, as opposed to melding disciplines into a single viewpoint or simply coordinating a more streamlined multidisciplinary approach.

In healthcare, many differences in perspective can be traced to the distinct discipline (Leipzig 2002), which can root them in different problem-solving approaches (Choi and Pak 2006, 2007), or a person's role in the healthcare system (Glouberman and Mintzberg 2001a, 2001b), which gives them different stakes in the outcomes.

Facilitating Interdisciplinarity

In 2011, we conducted a workshop (Radcliffe Center) on facilitating (Witteman and Stahl 2013). The key tools were drawn from a wide variety of disciplines and were focused on facilitating interaction and communication among a diverse group (clinicians, industrial engineers, economists, industrial designers, human factors engineers, social scientists, entrepreneurs, nurses, psychologists, and others) to solve "wicked problems" in healthcare. "Wicked problems" are problems that are notably intractable due to their being subject to multiple competing and cross-influencing inputs and feedback mechanisms. In fact, the teams were not only tasked to map and solve the solution space around a wicked problem but also map and define the problems themselves. The problems identified and tackled in this workshop were patient-clinician communication and hand hygiene.

These were the key elements:

- **Frameworks and tools:** It is important to set up an explicitly interdisciplinary framework and tools for problem solving and problematizing.
- **Deep dives:** This is a technique popularized by IDEO, an industrial design firm. Deep dives are a form of immersive facilitated brainstorming usually targeted at specific end-user needs, often making use of tools and frameworks.

- **Improvisational games:** We used improvisational games, specifically, along the lines of the work of Viola Spolin. These improvisational games are about unearthing creative responses in the context of tight constraints and building team communication, for example, the "Yes, but…" game. Similar to the "Yes, and" improvisational game described in Chapter 9, "Navigating Spaces—Tools for Discovery," which focuses on building, here every individual must start every interaction with "Yes, but…." This forces the person speaking to explicitly accept what the previous person said and then explicitly turn it into something else.

- **Rapid visualization:** We had a team of industrial design students attend whose sole job was to rapidly draw and visually articulate on walls covered with paper for this purpose, ideas verbalized by the teams. This created an external object/representation, which all team members could respond to, add to, or edit. This helps answer the question "Do you see what I see?" and helps bridge inter-disciplinary gaps in language (Lattuca 2001).

Even the best techniques and tools can only go so far. Other key considerations in successful interdisciplinary collaborations to consider are personality types as described in Chapter 5, "The Role of Learning Styles in Innovation Team Design," and communi-cation styles and problem-solving styles as described in Chapter 6, "Your Team Dynamics and the Dynamics of Your Team." Solving complex problems by adopting interdisciplinary, systems-level perspectives often requires challenging the usual ways of approaching problems. Significant previous work on problem-structuring methods has shown the potential of interdisciplinary approaches, but has noted the difficulty of orient-ing people to new ways of tackling long-standing challenges (Mingers and Rosenhead 2004). This kind of shift in attitudes and methods can be difficult in any context, and healthcare presents particular challenges related to disciplinary roles at the professional, administrative, and academic levels (Glouberman and Mintzberg 2001a, 2001b). Participants in these exercises must be willing, engaged, and to some degree open to new ideas and approaches if the process is to succeed, hence establishing an explicit interdis-ciplinary framework before starting.

We suggest that setting teams off on the right track and giving them the tools they need to adapt to change might help, and the concepts and tools explored in our workshop do precisely that. These four techniques are designed to be used at the beginning and formative part of a project and also intermittently through the project to catalyze break-throughs, get out of dead ends, or take a project in new directions as more is learned, which is inevitable with complex problems.

Innovation, Technology Adoption, and Change in Healthcare

One way to define technology is that it is any instrumentality that facilitates the end-users' ability to achieve their goals. By this definition, technology can be a device, a test, or even a policy or process. Innovation is another word that means different things to different people. Traditionally, innovation implies a new or different solution to a problem or set of needs, a new technology that meets the new or changing goals of the end users. Recently, though, the word has often been conflated with process improvement, which is doing the same task more efficiently.

A new technology thus falls into one of two broad categories: efficiency solutions and transformative solutions, or as described in Chapter 3, "Framing the Vision for Engagement," optimization innovation versus development or formulation innovation. An example of an efficiency solution is a new CT scanner that is 10% faster than its predecessor, which is aimed to help problems with episodes of high patient volume. The salient problem is time in the CT scanner, which the problem addresses through optimization. The deeper problem is why the CT scanner was having episodes of congestion in the first place. An example of a transformative solution is the use of real-time locations systems to get the patients to the right place at the right time with the right resources, such as the CT scanner. This is an example of more upstream innovation in the realm of discovery and formulation in the opportunity recognition phase. Here the solution changes how work is done by enabling end users to visualize, contact, and coordinate current resources to get more out of the same resources. It is also a new technology that at relatively little expense measures things we have not been able to measure before.

However, either type of solution is meaningless unless it is adopted, and technology adoption is usually an interdisciplinary problem. At the macro level every change in healthcare must satisfy the competing and cooperating groups that represent cure (MDs), care (RNs), control (managers), and community (trustees) (Glouberman and Mintzberg 2001a, 2001b). At the micro level no technology succeeds unless supported by the end users and intermediate managers. There is a wide literature on technology adoption and implementation science. For technology to be accepted, it must satisfy perceived usefulness, perceived ease-of-use, social norms, and many other constraints imposed by competing groups. In our own work of rolling out a clinical RTLS, we found "trust" in how the technology is to be used and "trust" in the person promoting or supplying it is essential.

Trust is gained in several ways. One important way in healthcare is through evidence. Based in both science and art, healthcare responds to outcomes or activities that can be validated. However, the evidentiary demands vary from stakeholder to stakeholder. For example, a clinician may only accept evidence based on large experimental trials and will seek to optimize practice and wait for the evidence to come in before changing, whereas healthcare managers may choose to "satisfice," that is, make the best available choice with the information they have at the time the decision needs to be made for other reasons. The world of evidence medicine is too large to summarize here; however, suffice it to say that there are varying accepted degrees of evidence based on their source and reliability.

Two useful sources of evidence in interdisciplinary collaboration and innovation in healthcare are simulation and rapid prototyping. Simulation is the study of systems or technologies in which the system being studied reproduces the same cause-and-effect relationships found in the real-world example. Simulations can be in silico, that is, computer programs, or physical like simulation labs where clinical procedures are performed on mocked-up patients. Through experimentation such as sensitivity analysis and "what if" scenario experiments, the performance characteristics and boundaries of performance can then be explored. As discussed extensively in previous chapters, notably Chapters 9 and 10, rapid prototyping is the process building of physical prototypes that reproduce the solution being articulated, which then in turn receives immediate feedback on its success or failure by stakeholders. It is then iterated rapidly and repeatedly until a solution acceptable to the end users is identified.

We have used both methods extensively in a variety of projects.

The OR of the Future Project (ORF)

The ORF was aimed to address the problem of surgical demand. Demand for surgical services continues to rise faster than our ability to supply them (Hall and DeFrances 2003). In an increasingly resource-constrained environment, efficiency is critical for maintaining access to quality care. At the same time, we must maintain quality and safety without burning out our clinicians who supply these services.

Surgeons, nurses, and OR administrators often turn to new technologies to help solve this problem. However, in the OR setting, new technologies are usually introduced in an ad hoc manner without rigorous analysis of their potential costs and benefits. Our hypothesis was that by bringing an interdisciplinary team together, we could reinvent the OR both physically and organizationally to solve the OR-level constraints on surgical demand.

We designed the ORF to be a living laboratory where we could measure the effect of new staffing regimes, peri-operative systems (in-hospital systems surrounding and supporting surgical process), and equipment on the delivery of surgical care. This project was a collaboration among multiple stakeholders—Massachusetts General Hospital (MGH); Center for Integrated Medicine and Technology (CIMIT); a consortium of physicians, scientists, and engineers from the Harvard University Medical School teaching hospitals; Massachusetts Institute of Technology (MIT); and Charles Stark Draper Laboratory. The project team included surgeons, anesthesiologists, nurses, operating room (OR) administration, patients, bioengineering, operations researchers, and health outcomes researchers. The ORF team conducted a landscape survey of surgical state-of-the-art ORs in both the United States and Europe, searching for examples of best practices in OR and perioperative system design.

The main distinguishing feature of the ORF design was a central operating room with attached induction and recovery bays and a control room to provide a workspace for surgeons between cases. The operating room itself was equipped with an integrated OR system, mobile booms (suspending equipment from the ceiling, freeing floor space and allowing for flexible equipment configurations), and combined gurney/table systems. The redesigned perioperative process enables staff to care for patients in parallel or in an interleaved fashion, in contrast to the traditional sequential process, enabling up to three patients to be cared for simultaneously in the induction bay, the OR, and the recovery bay. However, this process change requires more staff (an additional 0.5 anesthesia FTE [full-time equivalent] and 1 nurse FTE) than in the standard OR process (Stahl et al. 2005; Stahl, Goldman, Rattner, and Gazelle 2007; Stahl et al. 2004; Stahl et al. 2006).

Before proceeding, however, decision makers in the hospital had to be convinced that it was worth the effort, that is, taking two operating rooms offline while constructing the new ORF, and had to be convinced that the new system would be worth the added expense after it was running.

Physical mock-ups were made to work out potential new clinical workflows, and the knowledge from these exercises and from the landscape survey were instantiated in a computer simulation model. This model was then used to adjust the physical design and test the boundaries of its behavior with regard to quality, safety, and cost (Stahl et al. 2004). These analyses were then used as evidence to build trust and help convince decision makers to build the ORF.

This process was taken full circle in that after the ORF was built and in operation, the initial model predictions were put to the test, and the computer simulation predictions did indeed predict future performance accurately.

This exercise in evidence-based design informed subsequent OR design in our hospital and other hospitals (see Figures 14.1a and 14.1b).

Standard Operating Room

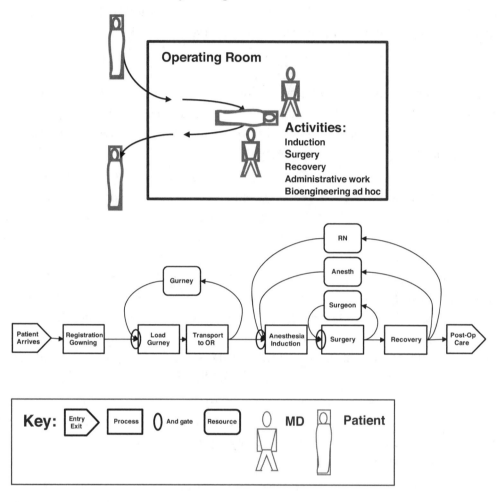

Figure 14.1a *Process flow for operating room of the future.*

New Operating Room

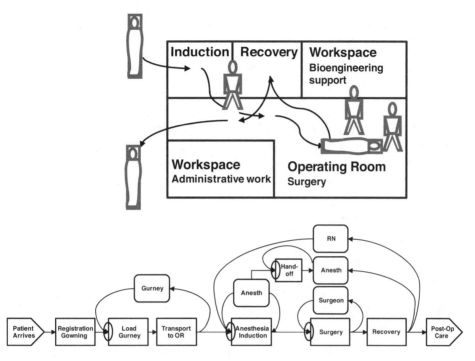

Figure 14.1b *Process flow for operating room of the future (continued).*

Evidence-based design is a developing field used by architects, industrial designers, and project planners in which designs are vetted based on the new structure's health outcomes, economic performance, productivity, customer satisfaction, and other measures. Specifically, in the context of healthcare, it explores what elements or systems of elements promote the organizational mission (usually, healthcare access, quality, and safety) of the healthcare facility. Lessons learned from these trials presumably can be transferred to other projects.

Interdisciplinarity enabled the team to explore the problem space and vet the solutions, generate ownership among a broad coalition of stakeholders and evidence for decision makers, and create something new in the difficult healthcare environment.

Aha! Moments

Reflecting on our efforts from the operating room of the future, we uncovered a series of key insights, notably the following:

- *Language and culture matter.*

  Assembling this interdisciplinary team was necessary but not sufficient. Once together, they had to be able to work together. Immediately, language became an issue. Each group had its own culture, its own language and way of approaching problems. Creating a unified language and goal was primarily achieved using a systems engineering perspective teaching the team as a whole how systems behave from their own individual piece to the integrated whole. With this came a new unifying language, which, in part because it was new to everyone, was acceptable by everyone.

- *Personalities matter.*

  As you can imagine, in a mix of these types of disciplines there were many strong personalities and several blocking personalities. Here, leadership and negotiating skills and understanding the nature of the competing-cooperating healthcare environment is essential.

- *Ownership matters.*

  In complex organizational environments ownership can be ambiguous, and when ambiguous often fraught with anxiety. Allowing people to take ownership gives them motivation to see the project succeed. The key solution in this case was to take a lesson from Harry Truman, who said, "It is amazing what you can accomplish if you do not care who gets the credit." This is often difficult in an academic setting; however, credit does seek its proper attribution with time.

- *Computer simulation does predict reality.*

  Simulation is a key method for bringing stakeholders together, improving design, identifying bugs before they happen, predicting future behavior, and generating evidence for decision makers (Stahl 2008).

Hand-Hygiene and Healthcare-Acquired Infections

This methodology has wide application. We are currently applying it to the hand-hygiene problem. Hand hygiene is a classic wicked problem, and has been for at least 150 years, since Ignaz Semmelweiss first identified it in Austria in the 1850s. There are likely more than 100,000 preventable hospital-acquired infections each year in this country, the majority of which could probably be eliminated if there was an effective, consistent way of decontaminating clinicians', and patients', hands between patient-clinician interactions.

The hand-hygiene problem has for the past 150 years been approached from the traditional single-domain perspective, repeatedly. Our soaps remove but don't kill the infectious agents; therefore, let's develop bactericidal soaps. It takes too long to clean our hands; therefore, let's develop desiccating agents such as alcohol-based gels. People don't know how to wash their hands properly or forget; therefore, we institute an education campaign; and so on. Yet hospital-acquired infection rates remain relatively static.

Our hypothesis was that any problem so resistant to change must be multidimensional and be a complex system of positive and negative feedback. To that end, we gathered an interdisciplinary team of infectious disease specialists, clinicians, industrial engineers, industrial designers, architects, behavioral and cognitive psychologists, patients, and others. The team was set the task of defining the problem space and mapping out the solution space with the specific goal of identifying the characteristics of key solutions.

Any complex system tends to be resilient. In the case of hand hygiene, the system is resilient at an undesirable system state. The key, then, is to find an achievable method to shift the state of the system.

Hand-hygiene activity is dependent on the workflow and physical space: Are there opportunities to clean your hands—for example, sinks available when you need them? It is dependent on perceptual, cognitive, and behavioral psychology factors. If I cannot see the dirt, I won't be prompted to wash it off. If my brain is occupied by too many other tasks, the hand-hygiene task gets bumped off the list. If my peers don't wash regularly, why should I? And so on. It is dependent on knowledge and skill: Do I know the circumstance in which to clean my hands and with what, soap or gel? Is it okay to wash my hands 30 seconds, 1 minute, half an hour before seeing the patient? And so on, to name a few of the complexities surrounding this behavior.

A key element to solving this problem is appropriate feedback based on reliable, trustworthy measurement. Our current state of the art is inadequate. The current gold standard, that is, having designated observers sampling behavior in clinical units, suffers from small sample size and the risk of modifying the behavior that the observers have been tasked to observe. Sending in "secret shoppers" suffers even worse sample-size considerations and often has even more limitations on the activities observed. Measuring the quantities of soap or gel used is rough at best. Results from these tools are fed back to the end users at often substantially delayed intervals (for example, monthly or quarterly) and often in aggregate. As a result, end-user behavior is challenged only intermittently and enough time has passed that the link between cause and effect has been attenuated and people don't know how relevant the feedback is to them.

One potential solution identified was to marry hand-hygiene measurement with real-time location systems to provide feedback at the time and place the patient-clinician activity is taking place. To this end, we developed a prototype system in which a signal is fed back to the clinician when the patient and the clinician are in the exam room together and an appropriate interval has passed.

We also developed a simulation model of the work flow and physical landscape in which this activity occurs, which we are using to explore issues of cost, benefit, and adherence. Results from this project should be published in 2014.

Discussion

The important challenges in healthcare are increasingly "wicked problems." New technologies and social trends such as point-of-care testing, ubiquitous sensing environments, the challenge of aging in place, new payment systems, and others offer new challenges that might transform what it means to deliver healthcare. If we are to bend the cost curve and maintain quality and safety, we can no longer constrain ourselves to in-the-box thinking. In fact, we need to reach across disciplines, across industries and modes of thought, to identify solutions. True interdisciplinarity offers a way to promote creativity and manage change. We need to have the courage to embrace change before we are forced to change.

Take-Away Points

From our experiences piloting learning launches of interdisciplinarity in healthcare, we note a set of key takeaway points, specifically the following:

- Interdisciplinarity offers a way of solving problems previously thought intractable.
- Avoid narrow teams.

  Avoid the trap of single-domain teams or even multidisciplinary teams, and include people who are stakeholders but might not normally interact and, if possible, people who are not stakeholders.

  The broader the range of perspectives, the more likely you'll truly understand the problem space.

  The broader the range of solution styles, the more likely you'll find a solution that is workable and sustainable.

- Putting teams together is not enough; they need the right tools to work successfully.
- Provide a safe environment with the space and time to experiment.
- Prototype solutions and use these prototypes to simulate the new experience if you want robust workable solutions.

- Be prepared to listen and have courage and perseverance.

  Interdisciplinary problem solving tends to be disruptive, and both exploring and solving a wicked problem will likely require challenging and changing the factors that make the problem resilient. These factors often include culture, political, and organizational structure.

References

Armstrong, P. 2006. Advancing Interdisciplinary Health Research: A Synergism Not to Be Denied. *Canadian Medical Association Journal, 175*(7), 761–762.

Care, P. S. A. a. N. S. f. (Ed.). 2003. Washington, DC.

Century, C. t. Q. C. A. N. H. S. f. t. s. (Ed.). 2001. Washington, DC.

Choi, B., and A. Pak. 2006. Multidisciplinarity, Interdisciplinarity and Transdisciplinarity in Health Research, Services, Education and Policy: 1. Definitions, Objectives, and Evidence of Effectiveness. *Clinical and Investigative Medicine, 29*(6), 351–364.

Choi, B., and A. Pak. 2007. Multidisciplinarity, Interdisciplinarity, and Transdisciplinarity in Health Research, Services, Education and Policy: 2. Promotors, Barriers, and Strategies of Enhancement. *Clinical and Investigative Medicine, 30*(6), 224–232.

Fairbairn, B., and M. Fulton. 2000. *Interdisciplinarity and the Transformation of the University.* Saskatchewan, Saskatoon: Centre for the Study of Co-operatives. University of Saskatchewan.

Glouberman, S., and H. Mintzberg. 2001a. Managing the Care of Health and the Cure of Disease—Part I: Differentiation. *Health Care Management Review, 26*(1), 56–69.

Glouberman, S., and H. Mintzberg. 2001b. Managing the Care of Health and the Cure of Disease—Part II: Integration. *Health Care Management Review, 26*(1), 70–84.

Gray, B. 1989. *Collaborating: Finding Common Ground for Multiparty Problems.* San Francisco: Jossey-Bass.

Hall, M., and C. DeFrances. 2003. National Hospital Discharge Survey. *Advance Data Vital and Health Statistics, 332.*

Klein, J. 2000. *A Conceptual Vocabulary of Interdisciplinary Science. In Practicing Interdisciplinarity.* Toronto: University of Toronto Press.

Lattuca, L. 2001. *Creating Interdisciplinarity: Interdisciplinary Research and Teaching among College and University Faculty.* Nashville, Tennessee: Vanderbilt University Press.

Leipzig, R. 2002. Attitudes Toward Working on Interdisciplinary Healthcare Teams: A Comparison by Discipline. *Journal of the American Geriatrics Society, 50*(6), 1141–1148.

Medicare, R. P. P. A. I. i. (Ed.). 2006. Washington, DC.

Mingers, J., and J. Rosenhead. 2004. Problem Structuring Methods in Action. *European Journal of Operational Research, 152*(3), 530–554.

Moran, J. 2010. *Interdisciplinarity: The New Critical Idiom.* London: Routledge.

Porter, A., and F. Rossini. 1984. Interdisciplinary Research Redefined: Multi-Skill, Problem-Focussed Research in the STRAP Framework. *R&D Management, 14*(2), 105–111.

Series, P. M. E. Q. C. (Ed.). 2006. Washington, DC.

Stahl, J. 2008. Modelling Methods for Pharmacoeconomics and Health Technology Assessment: An Overview and Guide. *Pharmacoeconomics, 26*(2), 131–148.

Stahl, J., M. Egan, J. Goldman, D. Tenney, R. Wiklund, W. Sandberg…D. Rattner. 2005. Introducing New Technology into the Operating Room: Measuring the Impact on Job Performance and Satisfaction. *Surgery, 137*(5), 518–526.

Stahl, J., J. Goldman, D. Rattner, and G. Gazelle. 2007. Adapting to a New System of Surgical Technologies and Perioperative Processes among Clinicians. *J Surg Res, 139*(1), 61–67.

Stahl, J., D. Rattner, R. Wiklund, J. Lester, M. Beinfeld, and G. Gazelle. 2004. Reorganizing the System of Care Surrounding Laparoscopic Surgery: A Cost-effectiveness Analysis Using Discrete-Event Simulation. *Medical Decision Making, 24*(5), 461–471.

Stahl, J., W. Sandberg, B. Daily, R. Wiklund, M. Egan, J. Goldman…D. Rattner. 2006. Reorganizing Patient Care and Workflow in the Operating Room: A Cost-effectiveness Study. *Surgery, 139*(6), 717–728.

System, T. E. i. H. B. A. S. H. (Ed.). 1999. Washington, DC.

Wilson, M., and D. Howcroft. 2005. Power, Politics and Persuasion in IS Evaluation: A Focus on Relevant Social Groups. *Journal of Strategic Information Systems, 14*(1), 17–43.

Witteman, H., and J. Stahl. 2013. Facilitating Interdisciplinary Collaboration to Tackle Complex Problems in Health Care: Report from an Exploratory Workshop. *Health Systems, 1*–9.

Zwarenstein, M., J. Goldman, and S. Reeves. 2009. Interprofessional Collaboration: Effects of Practice-Based Interventions on Professional Practice and Healthcare Outcomes. *Cochrane Database of Systematic Reviews Online 3*(3), CD000072. doi:000010.001002/14651858.CD14000072.pub14651852.

15

Disrupting Yourself—Launching New Business Models from Within Established Enterprises

Brandy Fowler has been an innovation consultant to Fortune 500 companies for the past 8 years, helping companies define their innovation strategy, build capabilities, and launch new businesses. Brandy is currently an Associate Director of Insights and Strategy at Smart Design, where she straddles the worlds of consumer-focused design and business design. She helps teams analyze and synthesize primary and secondary research and pull out the most compelling insights to inform developing new innovations. She received her master's from the Institute of Design in Chicago, where she studied user research methodologies, business strategy, and design.

Overview

Developing new innovative offerings is a must for companies that want to bring differentiated offerings to increasingly competitive markets, but it is no longer enough. The speed at which companies can imitate new offerings is increasing, as is the demand for companies to find new growth opportunities within older, saturated markets.

Innovating solely in products and services has become a more mature capability within many organizations, making it less of a differentiator. Fortune 500 companies have been using top-tier innovation consultancies for a considerable length of time now to bring new and different products and services to market. Also, many companies now have their own internal innovation groups to help infuse innovation throughout the company. There remains room for continual improvement within innovating on product offerings; but it is now table stakes to play and unless done extremely well it provides most companies with only a temporary edge.

Further, in industries where dated and broken business models are the norm, it becomes increasingly difficult for companies to find new growth. Two notable examples are the healthcare industry and the television industry. Established companies like pharmaceutical and cable providers have yet to break ground in new business models. Small, not-yet-established companies are experimenting with new business models and will mostly likely end up redefining the industry for large players who are unwilling to change.

The perfect storm of fear of steep competition within industries defined by unsustainable business forces has led companies to explore business model innovation as a safety net against these pressures. When executed well, business model innovation can be very disruptive to a company and an industry and can provide significant new revenue growth. For example, in the 1990s when personal computers were on the cusp of commoditization, Dell pioneered a unique business model for personal computing that dramatically increased its profitability. Its computers were not, in and of themselves, particularly innovative or cutting-edge products, but they became very profitable from the business model it was using to sell those computers. It sold its computers online and assembled them after it received the order, which enabled it to collect cash before it had to pay suppliers. This lowered the amount of capital it needed to run the business. The method of just-in-time production increased its inventory turns to 7 days versus the industry average at the time of almost 50 days, which led to a significant reduction in its operating costs.

Business model innovation is extremely difficult to do and almost always requires a company to change how it is structured and the processes it uses to monetize value. Product innovations, by themselves, often do not require the company to change their general way of doing business. Introducing a new business model to a company with a well-established existing business model can also pose cannibalization risks to existing businesses within the organization.

This section provides tools and strategies that can help mitigate the risks to the existing business, provides direction on where to innovate with business models, and offers considerations for developing new business model innovations.

Deciding Where to Innovate with New Business Models

After a company decides it wants to explore business model innovation, it first needs to establish where to innovate with new business models through assessing (1) how the business and industry are performing, (2) what market should be targeted, and (3) what type of offering should be brought to market, as illustrated in Figure 15.1.

PERFORMANCE	TARGET MARKET	OFFERING TYPE
How are the business and the industry performing?	What market should be targeted?	What type of offering should be brought to market?

Figure 15.1   *Three questions to explore to decide where to innovate with new business models.*

When a company starts looking into where to innovate with new business models, inevitably, the topic of cannibalization comes up. Most established companies have a strong fear of cannibalizing their existing offerings with new ones. But cannibalization is not always a negative strategy for a company to pursue. Furthermore, new growth without cannibalization can be achieved only under three conditions: (1) the company and industry are experiencing steady or growing performance, (2) a new target market is being addressed and/or (3) new highly differentiated offerings are being developed, as depicted in Figure 15.2.

PERFORMANCE	TARGET MARKET	OFFERING TYPE
1. Steady or Growing The industry and company are remaining steady or growing	**2. New Target Market** The company creates offerings for markets they currently do not target	**3. New Differentiated Offering** The company creates offerings that are clearly differentiated from current offerings

Figure 15.2   *Three conditions need to exist for a company to avoid cannibalization of existing offerings with new ones.*

If the first condition is not true and the company or industry is in fact shrinking, then it is worth considering whether a company should cannibalize offerings that are underperforming before deciding on the target market and offering type. In this case, business model innovation could be used to launch new offerings that replace areas of the business that are shrinking. The risk that cannibalization poses to a company is far less when replacing a shrinking business than if it were to launch business model innovations within parts of the business that were remaining steady or growing.

In assessing performance, it is important to look at the industry, the business, and individual business units to see which are shrinking, remaining steady, or growing, as depicted in Figure 15.3.

	How is the **industry** performing?	How is the **business** performing?	How are **business units** performing?			
▲ GROWING						
▬ STEADY						
▼ SHRINKING						

Figure 15.3 *A closer look at the first condition: assessing industry and business performance.*

If a company and the industry are performing well, but only one or more business units is underperforming, then a company has a choice to let those business units flame out or replace them with new ones. It really depends on how critical the business units are in providing revenue to the overall company and whether business model innovation efforts could potentially provide lift in those areas. An additional consideration is the strategic fit of the business unit to the company. Some companies maintain business units that offer strategic fit and advantage to other business units while not providing significant revenue.

A couple of shrinking industries where companies should consider cannibalizing existing businesses are the print newspaper and magazine industries, as illustrated in Figure 15.4. Many newspaper and magazine organizations have for years provided print papers and magazines to people's homes and offices and have been reluctant and slow to move into the digital age even when all the numbers are clearly pointing to a downward spiral.

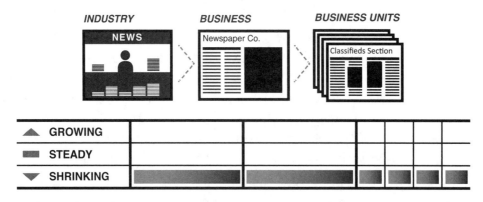

Figure 15.4 *Current state of the print newspaper industry and individual businesses.*

The *New York Times* is an example of an organization making some headway in moving from the print business to the digital business, but it is taking a pretty conservative approach. It was only in 2011 that the *New York Times* started experimenting with digital business models as it instituted a pay wall for access to digital content. It has increased revenues from its digital business, but like many newspaper organizations, it is reticent to go too far for fear of cannibalizing its print business, because its print business, while shrinking, still provides the *Times* with superior ad revenues compared to digital. This is where decades of development and optimization around the core offering has led to superior profitability. Businesses are often reluctant to explore new frontiers in discovery and formulation especially when it could compete with their carefully honed and optimized business.

The *Atlantic* magazine took a bolder approach, which was to fully invest in digital whether that meant cannibalizing its print business or not. It had been faced with ongoing financial failure and realized it had to make major changes to survive. Two notable changes it instituted were to (1) allow the sales team to hit their advertising sales targets regardless of whether it was for print or digital and (2) focus on creating engaging digital content that would draw in both consumers and advertisers. The impact of this strategy is that now the *Atlantic*'s digital advertising revenues account for a little over half of its total revenues. It is one of the few companies that has had financial success transitioning from print to digital. Now that it has a strong foothold in the digital business, it is experimenting with providing paid premium content to supplement existing advertising revenues.

Although time will tell how successful transitioning to new digital business models will be for newspaper and magazine organizations, some of the more innovative ones such as the *Atlantic* are at least starting to see their business turn the corner from shrinking to growing through exploring digital business models.

It is important for companies to take a more proactive approach in assessing whether all the industry, business, and/or parts of their business are shrinking, remaining steady, or growing. They can then get in front of the problem to decide whether they need to find new incremental growth to replace the losses or cannibalize current businesses to stay relevant.

We have looked in detail at the first condition to assess whether an opportunity exists to cannibalize poorly performing offerings in shrinking industries. But if a company is in a healthy industry and all or most of the company is performing steadily or growing, then finding new growth through business model innovation that will not cannibalize the business can come from the second two conditions: new target market(s) and/or new differentiated offerings.

Companies often struggle when trying to go after a market they currently do not target and creating offerings that are truly differentiated from their current offerings (Figure 15.5). They inadvertently end up cannibalizing existing offerings because they did not stretch far enough out from their existing market and offerings. At a minimum, companies not looking to cannibalize existing offerings should target markets and offerings that are new to the company.

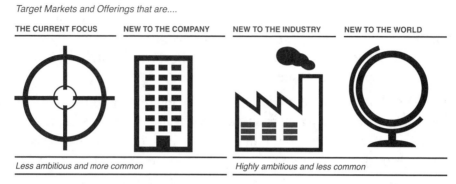

Figure 15.5 *Assessing how far to stretch into new markets and offering types.*

LAN airlines avoided cannibalization through business model innovation that targeted very different markets. What is unique about LAN airlines is that it operates these two distinct businesses using the same type of aircraft. One airplane can deliver high-end cargo while also functioning as a normal passenger airline. Its passenger business is roughly 70% of its revenues, with the cargo business providing close to 30% of its revenues.[1] The cargo business has created incremental revenue growth that does not erode its passenger business and allows LAN to weather business fluctuations more effectively than its competition because of its additional revenue stream.

What LAN pulled off is very hard to do. A company has to be extremely nimble to run two distinct businesses that are closely intertwined. Most companies either fail at reaching a new market because it is too unknown to them, or create offerings they think are differentiated, but to consumers and customers are not, and end up replacing versus adding revenue.

Getting a Business Model Innovation through the Company

Figuring out where to innovate with new business models is actually much easier than pushing the innovation through a large, long-standing company. Most established companies have become very efficient at streamlining, developing, and optimizing their processes to create the offerings they are known for delivering. What they are not good at is changing the status quo, committing resources and cross-organizational collaboration in order to deliver innovative offerings. It would be similar to asking a physician to stop practicing medicine and instead become a personal trainer. Physicians have a lot of knowledge on how the body works, but they would still have to learn new skills to be successful in that job.

When implementing new business models, the company needs to decide whether it should develop the offering internally, externally, or through a hybrid model (see Figure 15.6).

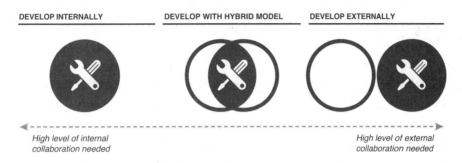

Figure 15.6 *Developing internally, using a hybrid model or externally.*

Most companies that are not highly innovative are best suited to develop externally or use a hybrid model in which internal resources are leveraged, but the new business model innovation does not need to fit within an existing business unit. Otherwise, their ingrained processes and orthodoxies for the way business is done will usually squash anything remotely innovative that needs to be developed using different processes and assessed by different metrics. Highly innovative companies like Google are good at internally developing and launching new innovations because their culture is infused with innovation capabilities. It is part of their DNA. However, most established companies need help in thinking through how to develop new business model innovations that will make it past ideation all the way to launch.

A notable example of internally developing and launching a business model innovation is Procter & Gamble. It wanted to sell razor blades in India. Emerging markets such as India, China, and Brazil have become a focus for many Western companies as a new market to penetrate. Emerging markets have complex dynamics and distinct user behaviors, which go beyond selling their existing products more cheaply. The product has to change, as well as how it gets delivered to market. Rather than strip down any of their many existing or prior offerings, Proctor & Gamble sent a team of designers, engineers, and ethnographers to India to understand how the product is distributed, purchased, used, and discarded. They integrated all of these considerations of both the design of the product and the business model. In the year following the launch of the Gillette Guard, the product achieved 50% market share.[2] P&G is great at developing new business model innovations internally because it has heavily invested in building up its innovation capabilities and processes. It has an internal group called FutureWorks, which focuses on developing transformational new business models. FutureWorks collaborates across the organization and is connected to P&G leaders and the overall company strategy, which helps ensure its success.

In contrast, Apple's insularity has hurt it in being able to successfully launch some of its new business model innovations. Apple is notorious for its secrecy, developing everything in-house and posing many third-party limitations. Apple's tendency toward tight control has been extremely successful in the Western world, but less so in emerging markets where its competitors have been more successful. Most people living in emerging markets use prepaid plans versus in the U.S., where plans are contract-based. Because of this, Apple is unable to get subsidies from wireless carriers in emerging markets to offset its cellphone costs for consumers. The product is too expensive and the business model is new to Apple. Apple is currently trying out new business model strategies such as allowing users to pay in installments to make the iPhone more affordable, but it still has some major ground to cover in catching up to competitors like Samsung and Nokia. Apple probably would have benefited from developing its emerging market products more externally through a separate development team and leveraging external partnerships. It just goes to show that even a company as innovative as Apple can also struggle with developing new business model innovations.

Case Example: New Business Model Opportunity for a Pharmaceutical Company

It is not news that the healthcare industry is broken and struggling, as detailed in Chapter 14, "Interdisciplinarity, Innovation, and Transforming Healthcare." The fee-for-service business model puts the wrong incentives in place, and if anyone has to pay out-of-pocket for healthcare services, they soon find their pockets empty. Several years ago, I did work with a pharmaceutical company that was very worried about its short-term and long-term growth opportunities through the traditional model of selling blockbuster prescription drugs, especially for primary care. Prescription drugs for primary care have reached a saturation point, with many pharmaceutical companies wondering how much growth is attainable in that space. To make matters worse, blockbuster drugs that provide so much revenue to pharmaceutical companies, within 20 years, all come off patent and go generic. Faced with a saturated space and impending loss of several key patents, the company wanted to explore how to bring a new innovation to launch that used a different business model.

Looking at the first condition of assessing whether the industry and company business were growing, remaining steady, or shrinking was the easy part because the client company was already acutely aware of the performance of the industry and its business. The pharmaceutical industry and its business were remaining steady; however, that was not going to hold for long, and it was already seeing shrinking performance in its primary care business. It knew it was not going to go out of business tomorrow, but the longer-term outlook was not too rosy, as depicted in Figure 15.7.

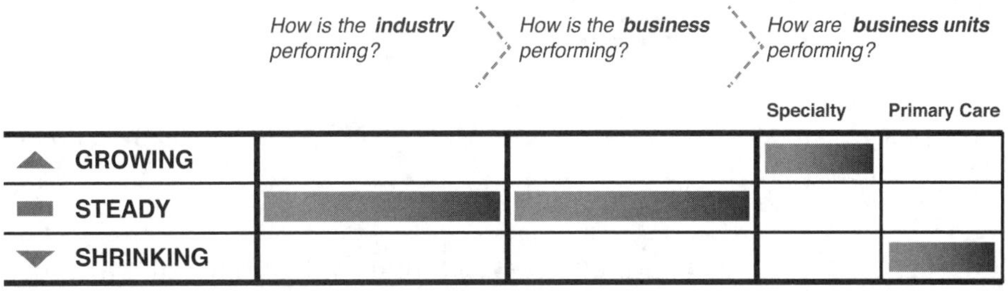

	How is the **industry** performing?	How is the **business** performing?	How are **business units** performing?	
			Specialty	Primary Care
▲ GROWING			▓▓▓▓	
▬ STEADY	▓▓▓▓▓▓▓	▓▓▓▓▓▓▓		
▼ SHRINKING				▓▓▓▓

Figure 15.7 *The performance of the pharmaceutical industry and the client organization.*

Since the client had already framed the performance issues it was faced with, we helped it think through the next two conditions: what market to target and what offering type to bring to market.

Because primary care drugs were shrinking, the client was not concerned with cannibalizing these existing offerings as long as the new offerings had good margins and revenue. Therefore, we decided to focus on a chronic condition market the company currently targets through its primary care business. Although the target market would be an existing focus for the client, the offering type was new to the company (see Figure 15.8). Instead of selling a prescription pill, the offering would be a holistic lifestyle program offered to employees of large employers to help with specific chronic conditions. If this program worked well and helped people get a handle on their chronic conditions, they would no longer need the type of prescription medication the pharmaceutical company makes.

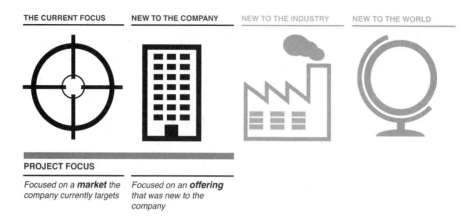

| THE CURRENT FOCUS | NEW TO THE COMPANY | NEW TO THE INDUSTRY | NEW TO THE WORLD |

PROJECT FOCUS

Focused on a **market** the company currently targets

Focused on an **offering** that was new to the company

Figure 15.8 *Business model innovation focused on an existing market, but with an offering that was new to the company.*

The offering type and business model were extremely different from the core capabilities of the organization. Instead of selling a prescription pill paid for by insurers, they would be selling a health-and-wellness program to large employers. The main revenue stream would be from a per-member-per-month fee (PMPM) for those employees who enrolled.

Because this was a big stretch for a company that spent so many years optimizing cost and revenue structures around selling drugs, the last phase of the project was to support it in thinking through how it was going to bring the new business model innovation to market and run the business after it was launched. It was self-aware enough to realize that if the business model innovation was developed internally, it likely would not make it through the organization's stage gate processes. The organization would essentially kill it before launch. It also recognized that it did not have a great history of developing initiatives solely externally using agencies and establishing partners. Therefore, the best fit for this company was to use a hybrid model (see Figure 15.9).

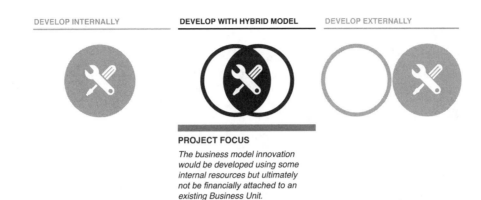

DEVELOP INTERNALLY   DEVELOP WITH HYBRID MODEL   DEVELOP EXTERNALLY

PROJECT FOCUS

The business model innovation would be developed using some internal resources but ultimately not be financially attached to an existing Business Unit.

Figure 15.9   *Developing a new business model innovation through a hybrid model.*

By using a hybrid model, it could leverage its internal innovation group to act as the project champion with oversight from business unit leaders. It would still do some development externally through partner agencies to help develop aspects of the program and oversee establishing partnerships. After the business was launched, it would still have oversight from business unit leaders, but it would not financially be attached to an existing business unit.

Conclusion

As the case example shows, these tools are meant to provide guidance in tailoring an approach to identifying and launching new business model innovations within a company. Developing new business model innovations is a challenge for even the most innovative companies. But through making clear assessments of where to innovate and by assessing performance, and then by choosing both appropriate markets and offerings, the company can help mitigate the inherent risks.

Endnotes

1. "When One Business Model Isn't Enough," *Harvard Business Review,* January-February 2012.
2. *P&G 2011 Annual Report,* http://www.pg.com/annualreport2011/ innovating/gillette.shtml.

16

Opportunities in Branding— Benefits of Cross-Functional Collaboration in Driving Identity

 **Maryann Finiw** has more than 20 years of experience managing innovation, research, and strategy programs. She is currently Senior Manager of Research and Marketing Strategy at SapientNitro and is also an Adjunct Professor at Philadelphia University, Emerson College, and Massachusetts College of Art and Design. In her previous position as a Principal at Continuum, she led innovation strategy projects for major corporate clients, including Ford Motor Company, Procter & Gamble, Coca-Cola, Andersen Windows, Master Lock, L.L.Bean, and American Express. With an M.B.A. from Harvard Business School and a Bachelor of Industrial Design from Pratt Institute, she thrives at the intersection of design and business; research and development; creativity and strategy.

Context

I began my education and career as an industrial designer, gaining experience in a field where the benefits of cross-functional teams for product innovation are now well known. Marketers, designers, and engineers working together on interdisciplinary teams have become the norm in new product development. In my professional evolution as a branding consultant and as a professor, I've found that applying those design-thinking principles and collaborative best practices to branding endeavors drives disruptive innovation and enables superior outcomes from the brand strategy process.

Why Use Innovation Teams? Four Key Benefits for Branding

Using truly collaborative teams that incorporate design thinking into their process can create brand strategies that are more relevant, holistic, impactful, and actionable. I call these cross-disciplinary collaborators innovation teams. To illustrate the effectiveness of this approach, I'll share real-world case studies, my personal experiences, and interviews with key project collaborators that will reveal why these interdisciplinary teams create better brand strategies. I'll include process examples that highlight some of the innovative methods that made these projects successful in order to illustrate how well-managed teams can create brands that consumers love, build brand loyalty, and increase profits.

More Holistic

Innovation teams create brand propositions that are more holistic and have a broader appeal

Market segmentation is a primary tool used by marketers. To create a sound brand strategy, marketers identify multiple customer segments within a market, select the segments to target, and then seek an understanding as to how their particular brand can uniquely meet the needs of, and resonate with, those specific customer groups. A common challenge that marketers face is how to speak to each segment without alienating the members of other segments. In companies that employ a more functionally siloed process, the segment and competitive perspective might also be more siloed and is likely to fail to elicit more innovative strategies. An interdisciplinary approach to brand strategy can uniquely facilitate identifying the glue that unifies one brand to meet the needs of seemingly disparate segments.

Employing a familiar term, a traditionally siloed marketing process employs a "left-brain" perspective. Left-brain thinking is seen as being primarily calculative—one plus two equals three—whereas right-brain thinking is considered to be more holistic—it sees the answer three and doesn't care whether it was derived from one plus two, four minus one, or nine divided by three. In the past, a more functionally siloed brand strategy process would often fail to find the solution to making the entire brand greater than the sum of its parts because of its basis in quantitative analysis. By involving interdisciplinary teams in a brand strategy program, we can employ a "whole-brained" and holistic perspective, an approach that has become known as "design thinking." Design thinking resolves the seemingly conflicting needs of diverse market segments to create a holistic brand image. By using interdisciplinary teams, we create a creative-process ecosystem that encourages and engages whole-brain thinking and enables the team to see the entirety of the brand value proposition.

An example of a design-thinking approach to brand strategy is illustrated in the launch of Merrill Edge. Merrill Lynch is the world's largest investment brokerage, with more than 15,000 financial advisors and $2.2 trillion in client assets.[1] Bank of America is the second-largest bank holding company in the U.S. by assets, operating in all 50 states and in more than 40 countries around the globe.[2] The merger of Bank of America and Merrill Lynch in January of 2009 created an opportunity for these two financial powerhouses to offer an integrated and uniquely powerful banking and investing capability. Complementing the Merrill Lynch Wealth Management business that serves affluent and high-net-worth individuals, there was an opportunity to broaden access to integrated banking and investing solutions for the next generation of affluent individuals, the mass affluent consumer. As shown in Figure 16.1, mass affluent is a marketing term that refers to investors who have household incomes over $75,000 per year and $50,000 to $250,000 in investable assets. The challenge for the cross-functional team developing the new integrated banking and investing solution from Bank of America/Merrill Lynch was how to appropriately marry the combined *brand equities* brought to the mass affluent target consumer by Bank of America and Merrill Lynch without alienating core Merrill Lynch Wealth Management clients.

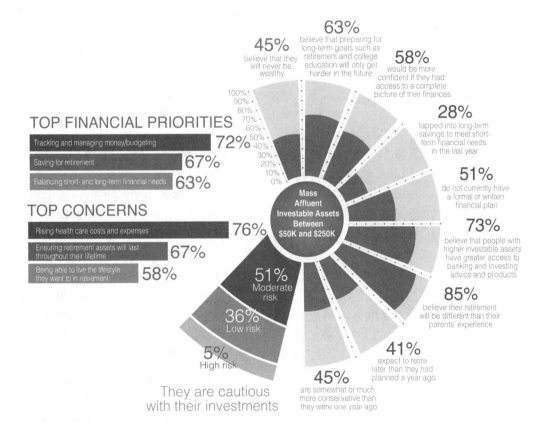

http://newsroom.bankofamerica.com/files/press_kit/additional/WhoAreTheMassAffluent012411.pdf
Image courtesy of Bank of America Merrill Lynch.

Figure 16.1   *Who are the mass affluent?*

The team that developed the Merrill Edge name and offering included product, platform, and marketing representatives from Merrill Lynch and Bank of America, and from third-party agencies in strategy, branding, and digital design. My role was to focus on customer insights and innovation strategy as an embedded consultant on the internal team at Bank of America. Besides the typical challenges of managing an interdisciplinary team, this team faced additional integration challenges. Since the merger between Bank of America and Merrill Lynch was new, the team had to forge working relationships between two formerly separate corporate cultures. Additionally, because banking and investing are both highly regulated industries (each operating under different sets of rules), legal and compliance experts were also integral to the team.

Tony Hitchman, SVP, Head of Merrill Edge Marketing at Bank of America Merrill Lynch, describes the critical glue that would unify these disparate perspectives as, "Be true to the clients." Our challenge was to balance the needs of the mass affluent prospects—for an offering that did not yet exist—against the brand perceptions of core Bank of America and Merrill Lynch clients. Our interdisciplinary team conducted multiple rounds of research with these diverse client constituencies to identify opportunities for naming, positioning, and differentiation.

The resulting name, Merrill Edge, successfully balances the equities of Bank of America and Merrill Lynch in ways that resonated with both client segments. Launched in 2010 on the heels of the 2008 financial service industry crisis, Merrill Edge was given important stability by Bank of America, so as shown in Figure 16.2, we used "Bank of America Corporation" in the logo as a visual foundational baseline. "Merrill" brought important investing credibility to the offering, but for the mass affluent customer, the full name of "Merrill Lynch Wealth Management" was perceived as being for someone wealthier than a member of the target demographic. To appeal to a more youthful mass affluent demographic, the name "Edge" was created to express an offering that was younger, hipper, and cooler. Merrill Edge was not their parents' Merrill Lynch solution. For the core Merrill Lynch Wealth Management client, the word "Edge" reassured them that this was a new offering from the company that wouldn't jeopardize their brand relationship with Merrill Lynch Wealth Management. As SVP Tony Hitchman explains, "Merrill Edge unites the banking strength of Bank of America with the insights of Merrill Lynch."

By creating an integrated team that enlisted multiple disciplines across several agencies and that spanned the newly merged companies, Merrill Edge delivers a value proposition that is holistic and has broad appeal. As illustrated in the mobile app shown in Figure 16.3, Merrill Edge offers the ability to easily move money between banking and investing in one online platform and includes available investment guidance. As Justine Metz, head of Global Wealth Management Marketing at Bank of America, explains, "The potential benefits to the customer and the business, of providing better solutions to the client, far outweigh the team integration challenges. It may take longer, but you get to a better result."

Bank of America Corporation

Image courtesy of Bank of America Merrill Lynch.

Figure 16.2 *Merill Edge logo.*

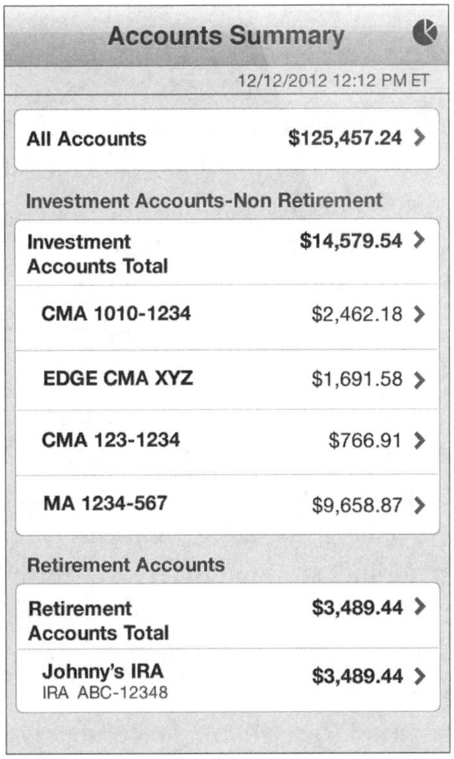

Accounts Summary	
12/12/2012 12:12 PM ET	
All Accounts	**$125,457.24** >
Investment Accounts-Non Retirement	
Investment Accounts Total	**$14,579.54** >
CMA 1010-1234	$2,462.18 >
EDGE CMA XYZ	$1,691.58 >
CMA 123-1234	$766.91 >
MA 1234-567	$9,658.87 >
Retirement Accounts	
Retirement Accounts Total	**$3,489.44** >
Johnny's IRA IRA ABC-12348	**$3,489.44** >

Image courtesy of Bank of America Merrill Lynch.

Figure 16.3 *Merill Edge Mobile.*

Chapter 16: Opportunities in Branding—Benefits of Cross-Functional Collaboration in   239
Driving Identity

Merrill Edge successfully launched in June 2010 and continues to grow, both in customer awareness and in number of accounts added. By July 2013, Merrill Edge had more than 1.5 million accounts and over $87 billion in brokerage assets. The awareness of Merrill Edge has seen double-digit percentage increases each year from 2011 to 2013, adding to the brand's potential growth.

More Relevant

Innovation teams help make brands more relevant to consumers by connecting on deeper values

In the preceding example, we discussed how teams can identify the glue that unifies one brand and leverage it to meet the needs of seemingly disparate market segments. Another key benefit of using interdisciplinary teams for branding is their ability to uncover and identify the glue that bonds consumers to a brand. Truly collaborative teams are better at identifying and embodying the brand core values that connect with consumers at multiple levels: functionally, emotionally, and culturally. By focusing on deeper brand values, they can build deep-seated brand loyalty.

Brand loyalty is strong when consumers are aware that some of the values they hold most dearly are shared by a brand whose products they buy. Examples of these brand values are the triple bottom line commitments at companies like Ben & Jerry's or Newman's Own. Having corporate values in common with values held by your customers is the ultimate glue that bonds a consumer to a brand. As Simon Sinek proposes in his TED Talk on "How Great Leaders Inspire Action," "People don't buy what you do; people buy why you do it—your purpose, your belief."

L.L.Bean is one of the nation's most respected and best-known manufacturers and distributors of outdoor clothing and equipment. L.L.Bean is headquartered in Freeport, Maine, and its legendary flagship store, shown in Figure 16.4, has no locks on the entry doors, since it is open 24 hours a day, all year long. As an outdoor lifestyle brand, L.L.Bean's product lines and customers range from outdoor equipment for serious enthusiasts engaged in hunting and fishing, to selling, at the other end of the spectrum, outdoorsy home goods and apparel that are more likely to be used in backyards than in the backwoods. In a previous brand strategy project sponsored by L.L.Bean, a traditionally siloed brand consulting firm had recommended that L.L Bean split the company into two brands: one brand focused on equipment that would compete against companies like REI and North Face, and another brand focused on apparel that would compete against companies like Gap and Polo. L.L.Bean wisely rejected this recommendation, instinctively understanding that these seemingly incompatible segments had coexisted for almost a century within one of the most beloved companies in America. Its unifying brand attributes—although difficult to articulate—had given L.L.Bean a track record of deep consumer loyalty and unparalleled business longevity.

Photo courtesy of L.L.Bean.

Figure 16.4 *L.L.Bean flagship store.*

In 2005, as a Principal in the Design Strategy Group at Continuum, I led a project team tasked with the dual goals of understanding L.L.Bean's deep brand heritage and identifying how to leverage its brand legacy and iconic products in ways that would be relevant to today's consumers. We called it Project DNA. The internal core team for L.L.Bean's brand DNA project included a diagonal slice across a matrix of disciplines and management levels from both the client and Continuum. We drew team members from middle to senior management, and from marketing, strategy, merchandising, product design, and communications design groups. Consequently, the most important stakeholders at L.L.Bean all had their interests represented. Beyond their involvement in the brand DNA project team, they were ultimately responsible for embodying the brand in the design and merchandising of products. When L.L.Bean used this highly collaborative interdisciplinary team to help articulate and leverage its brand heritage, they were able to find the common threads that strongly connected the brand to both the devout outdoor sportsmen and the casual outdoor apparel consumers.

In direct contradiction to the traditional branding firm's previous attempt to split the company into "backyards" and "deep woods" market segments, our team was able to identify 16 shared values that emotionally connected the brand to both of those seemingly disparate segments within L.L.Bean's customer base. For example, one of the shared values we identified is "reliable." The L.L.Bean brand is valued as "reliable" across all varied segments, but the "reliable" brand attribute gets embodied differently to meet the needs of each segment. An outdoor enthusiast can rely on L.L.Bean's outdoor equipment to keep them safe and warm even in harsh outdoor conditions, and an apparel customer can rely on L.L.Bean clothing to not fade, even after repeated washings. The company also reinforces reliability with its legendary 100% satisfaction guarantee.

By the end of the brand DNA project, we had provided L.L.Bean with a powerful tool. As Marcia Minter, VP Creative Director at L.L.Bean describes, "These are not just product attributes or brand values; they're our corporate values. They're what the company is all about—how we do things and why we do it." Marcia says the level of clarity provided by these brand values is broadly applied within the company, and she routinely shares the core brand values with L.L.Bean's outside collaborators—from large firms to individual contributors, and advertising agencies, design firms, and photo stylists. Marcia even refers to these values in job interviews and on a new hire's first day. Minter concludes, "It fundamentally comes down to already having a moral position on how to engage with people."

In 2012, L.L.Bean celebrated its centennial anniversary, a significant milestone in the life of a brand whose values continue to resonate with its diverse consumer segments. As illustrated in Figure 16.5, L.L.Bean reinterpreted some of the iconic catalog covers that helped define the company's unique character to help commemorate this important anniversary. As Tom Armstrong, CMO of L.L.Bean, explains, "These shared values are customer-relevant and timeless. They ground us and act as a foundational touchstone that orients people to who we are."

Photo courtesy of L.L.Bean.

Figure 16.5 *L.L.Bean iconic catalog cover.*

More Impactful

Innovation teams achieve superior business results by identifying more meaningful brand differentiation

Teams help achieve superior results for both the end user and the business. The multiple perspectives help identify meaningful attributes on which to differentiate that are more relevant to consumers and more impactful to the business. Emily Bowden, Brand Strategist at Sapient Nitro, explains it best: "Where mere cross-functional connections can be effective in working towards a common goal, a truly collaborative process invites disruptive innovation."

Some of the world's strongest brands offer iconic products that would be recognized if even a fragment of that product were found by an archaeologist. Any industrial designer dreams of his professional legacy containing a product as iconic as Coca-Cola's bottle, Apple's iPod, L.L.Bean's Maine Hunting Shoe, or Master Lock's laminated padlock. Master Lock's laminated padlock is so iconic that a graphic abstraction of a laminated lock is used as an onscreen symbol by many software developers to indicate whether a file is locked. Master Lock's laminated padlock is one of the most successful products in history, though the patents on the laminated padlocks expired decades ago. In the mid-1990s, Master Lock was not innovating. Widely recalled for its Tough Under Fire "shot lock" commercials, as shown in Figure 16.6, the Master Lock name elicits an enviable 98% unaided brand awareness, but in the mid-1990s that brand recognition was not translating into sales, so mass merchant retailers were threatening to reduce Master Lock's shelf space allocation. In addition, Master Lock wasn't doing a good job of differentiating its products; mass merchant shoppers no longer perceived the added value of the Master Lock brand compared to the cheap Asian knockoffs displayed on the same shelves.

Photo courtesy of The Master Lock Company.

Figure 16.6 *Master Lock advertisement.*

Traditional management consultants recommended that Master Lock had no choice but to compete on price in what was becoming a commodity market. John Heppner, CMO at the time (now CEO), rejected this recommendation and decided to employ an innovative design-thinking approach to identify differentiation opportunities that would allow the company to continue to command a premium market position and preserve shelf space. As a Principal at Continuum, I led the research and strategy project for Master Lock's innovation and differentiation initiative.

Heppner summarizes his philosophy about investing in capacity-building and focusing on growing innovation capability: "It's all about how you use the consulting relationship, whether you are expecting an answer from them, or using them as input, collaborating with them. Way too many just ask for the answer, but the company's got to execute, so I want to learn what I don't know. If you just delegate to consultants as a crutch, it falls apart. It's an investment to gain a competency."

During its previous product development programs, Master Lock had used a siloed research approach that primarily focused on getting feedback from locksmiths. To innovate on meaningful attributes, Master Lock needed to understand what mass merchant shoppers valued when shopping for padlocks. At mass merchants, it was particularly important to understand what women shoppers valued when shopping for security products, since 72% of shopping trips to mass merchandisers are made by women.[3] Consistent with Yvonne Lin's findings in Chapter 13, "Broad Thinking—Connecting Design and Innovation with What Women Want," women, as the main purchasers of consumer products, care more about what a product or service will do for them and their families than they care about the technical features offered. Consequently, the multidisciplinary team needed to understand what would motivate women at Walmart to choose a Master Lock padlock over a cheap Asian knockoff. During ethnographic in-store shop-a-longs with consumers at mass merchants, our team experienced a key "ah-ha moment." We discovered that shoppers expected bike locks to be in the bike aisle and luggage locks to be in the luggage aisle, but Master Lock's padlocks were (at the time) merchandised exclusively in the hardware aisle. People are not emotionally connected to padlocks; they are emotionally connected to what they want to protect. This key consumer insight translated into a market segmentation plan and channel strategy for Master Lock that showed them how to look "beyond hardware" and broaden distribution beyond the hardware aisle and hardware store. A collateral piece from this segmentation plan is shown in Figure 16.7. The company even used "Beyond Hardware" as a campaign theme for Master Lock's booth at that year's annual industry trade show.

Photo courtesy of The Master Lock Company.

Figure 16.7 *Master Lock market segmentation.*

The new differentiation strategy created significant business growth opportunities. With innovative new designs targeting key users and applications, Master Lock successfully gained distribution not only in new aisles, but also in new channels such as Target, Pep Boys, and AutoZone. Heppner clarifies, "One of the ancillary benefits we achieved in looking 'Beyond Hardware' was the ability to better understand the full extendibility of our brand—where it could potentially play and be successful. The segmentation exercise, combined with ultimate acceptance of the brand outside hardware, provided not only a stronger foundation for organic growth, but also strategic direction for where we might make acquisitions and utilize the brand as a key differentiator in an underrepresented segment or category."

More Actionable

Innovation teams gain greater consensus and buy-in from the client

The diversity of talent in interdisciplinary teams generates creative energy that fosters actionable brand strategies. These teams help gain stronger consensus, because they can offer a more richly layered set of reasons to support a position. Strategic directions are pressure-tested against multiple perspectives to manage trade-offs and reach compromises that create the strongest total system design. Core team members become evangelists throughout the client organization so that functional peers see that their perspectives were anticipated and addressed for greater buy-in and smoother implementation.

For Master Lock, the extended team even collaborated with retailers. Traditionally, if a product failed, retailers were stuck with liquidating inventory, so retailers might have been hesitant to embrace the innovative products and differentiation strategy that Master Lock was proposing. Master Lock reorganized its sales organization around the new segments, since it would be calling on buyers "Beyond Hardware." Master Lock then previewed prototypes with retailers to bring in its point-of-sale perspective and tested sales by rolling out new products to a hundred stores to evaluate their success before executing nationwide.

If the category was becoming commoditized, Master Lock, as the category leader, wanted to lead the fix of the entire category. The goal was to change retailers' brand perception—to see Master Lock as a fresh, innovative partner. Heppner explains the strategy: "Being first is good for the brand. Now, we continuously bring freshness to the brand with so many new products that customers turn some down, but then they don't look elsewhere. That adds strength to the brand."

Leveraging the foundational work of this innovation team, Master Lock has launched a steady stream of innovative new products that are selling well and winning awards. Master Lock's Titanium series of padlocks was one of the first products launched from the product road map we envisioned. The Titanium series of padlocks, shown in Figure 16.8, won recognition in *Business Week* magazine's annual Industrial Design Excellence Awards with a Gold IDEA in 2002 for product design and in 2007 as a finalist for a Catalyst IDEA, a competition that recognizes a product design's impact on market success and business transformation. The CEO of Master Lock tied its sales goals to the project innovation goals with the objective of reaching 25% of current-year total sales to be generated by products introduced over the previous three years. Master Lock now consistently exceeds that 25% new product sales metric with a continuous stream of award-winning innovative new product launches, such as the Speed Dial combination padlock that won a silver Edison Award in 2011.

Photo courtesy of The Master Lock Company.

Figure 16.8 *Master Lock Titanium series.*

How to Drive Innovation Teams: Process Best Practices for Branding

The previous case studies have illustrated why interdisciplinary teams are better at achieving brand innovation. These teams create brand strategies that are more holistic, relevant, actionable, and impactful while generating meaningful results for both customers and the bottom line. It's important now to share some of the behind-the-scenes details of the processes that made these project teams so successful.

Convene a matrixed team composition: The most effective cross-functional teams are taken from a "diagonal slice" through the management chart of the organization, and should include younger managers with fresher perspectives, as well as people with a greater stakeholder position who can execute on initiatives downstream. If possible, teams should include critical consumer and customer/retailer perspectives as well. As

Mike Arney, Principal at Continuum, explains, "The challenge is to get people to live at both altitudes; to represent their function, and also to rise above it."

Recruit pairs of research respondents: To evoke deeper and more interesting insights during the research phase, recruit teams of research respondents in pairs, such as couples or best friends. Conducting in-context ethnographic interviews with pairs of respondents elicits a more natural dialogue. These participant pairs keep each other honest and build on each other's comments, guiding the conversations toward identifying a brand's most significant emotional connections to the user. For our outdoor lifestyle brand research, we even included recruits from multiple generations of families. They gave us a layered perspective on interactions with the L.L.Bean brand, from holiday gift giving to using the brand's outdoor equipment on family vacations.

Use immersive research techniques: Nothing is less interesting for a research subject than being shown pictures of products while seated at a table in a windowless office building. During our L.L.Bean consumer research phase, our team conducted immersive activities with research subjects that were often done either at the subject's home or at a family cottage on a lake. We demonstrated tactile product interactions in a context designed to vividly express the core L.L.Bean brand values that consumers love, while tapping into memories and evoking stories that would elicit deeper insights into the unique qualities of the brand.

Create an immersive team space: Provide a dedicated war room that is a casual yet compelling environment that will help move the project forward. Office cubicles and conference rooms maintain hierarchy and status quo, but when people interact in a more casual environment, like a kitchen, a living room, or at the proverbial water cooler, they're relaxed and more likely to exchange and embrace different perspectives. The immersive environment should also be an inviting space where team members can come to work and think critically about the project.

The L.L.Bean team created an immersive project war room that we called "Base Camp." The goal was to "live" the brand and immerse ourselves in an outdoor lifestyle so that when we met as a team we would be closer to the mind-set of the outdoor enthusiast consumer. As shown in Figure 16.9, to immerse ourselves in the brand heritage, we surrounded ourselves with antique products and catalogs and collected the personal stories from sellers on eBay who were auctioning off their well-worn L.L.Bean heirlooms. The Base Camp war room was so effective a tool for collaborative meetings that when it came time to socialize the brand values and launch the training process throughout the L.L.Bean organization, the company moved the contents of the war room, as shown in Figure 16.10, from Newton, Massachusetts, to the Freeport, Maine, headquarters.

Photo courtesy of L.L.Bean.

Figure 16.9   *L.L.Bean war room.*

Prototype strategy: Prototyping isn't just for products—it should also be used to envision, visualize, and test the entire brand strategy. Create experiential models so that you can simulate and evaluate the user experience. Incorporating prototyping into the brand development process improves quality and focus. As illustrated in Chapters 9, "Navigating Spaces—Tools for Discovery," and 10, "Value Creation through Shaping Opportunity—The Business Model," a key element of the design-thinking process is prototyping. In a traditional business process, people are rewarded for success, whereas prototyping, by definition, expects failure again and again until the design direction and details are fully vetted. It is important to note the difference between mistake and failure. Mistake is an error disconnected from theory. A failure includes theory. Each failure then represents learning, or "failing forward." Prototypes are iterations in a design process that provide learning moments that improve results. Evaluation of prototypes focuses criticism on the prototype, not on individuals, so that all team members can align on making the best strategy for the consumer and build on each other's ideas. When critiquing prototypes, team members are not in it for themselves; they are, ideally, advocates for the end user.

Photo courtesy of L.L.Bean.

Figure 16.10 *L.L.Bean war room: a blend of archaeology and anthropology.*

Master Lock and Continuum's multidimensional team prototyped a ten-year road map for the product and package designs, and also envisioned what the business would look like if it pursued the market segmentation and channel strategy opportunities identified to move "Beyond Hardware." Master Lock then enlarged the road map in order to refine and update product development and launch plans for each target segment and retail channel, and to make the segmentation strategy road map an actionable living prototype.

Encourage healthy debate: Foster true collaboration among team members by promoting vigorous, healthy debate. Debate pressure-tests ideas, exposing and resolving conflicts; it also creates a better experience for the end user and drives better outcomes for business. To refocus attention away from disparaging a teammate's ideas and onto improving the user experience, direct the debate toward customer needs, data (including soft data such as consumer anecdotes and stories), and evaluating and improving prototypes.

Heppner explains, "Collaboration is a very intense exercise to get to the 'ah-ha' experience. It's the rigor of the process to constantly iterate, honestly talk through issues, and collaboratively work through them together. People think and express themselves in different and unique ways. To get the full value of that input, you need to create creative tension. Not every team member contributes at the same level at first—you must yell, offend, and take no prisoners to achieve total collaboration and best thinking."

Conclusions and Recommendations

This chapter examined several real-world case studies in which cross-functional teams developed powerful brand strategies for a range of industries, from outdoor apparel and security devices to financial services. A truly collaborative team can create a brand strategy that is more holistic, relevant, and actionable, offering more meaningful results for customers and improving a company's financial health. We consistently saw these benefits across a range of brand challenges, from launching a new brand offering to articulating and leveraging the core DNA of existing brands. The reader is encouraged to recognize and leverage the unique capability of cross-functional teams and apply the process tips for effectively managing collaborative teams in a brand strategy program. The result can be the creation of a stronger brand that consumers will love, with increased brand loyalty and greater company profits. Specifically, in summary:

Why to Use Innovation Teams: Four Key Benefits of Teams for Branding

- More holistic
- More relevant
- More actionable
- More impactful

How to Drive Innovation Teams: Process Best Practices for Branding

- Convene a matrixed team composition
- Recruit pairs of research respondents
- Create immersive spaces and activities
- Prototype strategy
- Encourage healthy debate

Endnotes

1. Wikipedia, Merrill Lynch size.
2. Wikipedia, Bank of America size.
3. Nielsen, Share of U.S. Retail Channel Shopping Trips by Gender, 2012.

Afterword

As we look back at our experiences with disruptive innovation from our viewpoints as investors, advisors, educators, and leaders, consistent hurdles stand out. Historically, companies were formed around a singular innovation—they were able to do something different, better, faster, or cheaper than the competition. After the market supported the innovation, the company tended to focus on developing incremental improvements and optimizing the innovation for maximum monetization and eventually profit. Risk aversion impacts organizational structure. Indeed, organizational structure…and behavior…morph into organizational stricture, often with a focus on reduced risk and uncertainty. The consequence is that the organization cannot easily discover new ideas and formulate new value propositions in a manner that is easily integrated into the optimization machine. To be successful with disruptive innovation, the organization needs to dedicate thought, time, and space to the discovery of new opportunity spaces and formulation of new value propositions. We have found that most companies successful with disruptive innovation have a cultural support of innovation teams and well-integrated leadership to nurture new ideas and then to move them from the discovery and formulation stages into development and optimization to continually redefine the company's leadership position in the market. This perspective is supported by the recent McKinsey Global Study on innovation structures, which found that "where innovation is fully integrated into strategy, executives are six times as likely as those without integrated strategy to say their separate functions meet their financial objectives effectively."[1]

At Philadelphia University the President consistently used his bully pulpit to support and reinforce the Provost office as a shelter in which to discover and formulate the new curriculum and organizational structure for the Kanbar College of Design, Engineering and Commerce. We incubated the early ideas with key faculty partners, fellows, and advisors and tested ideas through charrettes and learning launches with students and broader faculty. After the curriculum architecture was sketched out, we built curriculum development teams composed of diverse sets of faculty and administration to develop the curriculum and make it their own, and brought in new deans to lead the new organizational structure. This method worked well in an academic environment where building consensus is essential.

Today, we witness companies stumble in their innovation initiatives as the tension between maximizing the known opportunities of the day pulls against the efforts for formulating the value propositions for the new tomorrow. We believe that the key to a successful balance lies in a cultural understanding of innovation as a core competency, organizational structure that facilitates rather than obfuscates, dedicated time and effort, and integrated leadership.

Endnotes

1. McKinsey Global Survey Results, "Making Innovation Structures Work," 2012, page 3. Contributing authors: Marla M. Capozzi, a senior expert in McKinsey's Boston office; Ari Kellen, a director in the New Jersey office; and Rebecca Somers, a consultant in the Washington, D.C., office.

Glossary and Resources

Glossary

Bodystorming is a kinesthetic form of brainstorming in which participants imagine that the product or service actually exists and physically interact with the imaginary product; gaps in function and form come to light. The consulting firm IDEO uses bodystorming as a tool in its innovation work.

Brainstorming is an activity in which multiple ideas are generated about a given topic, by freely sharing initial, undeveloped ideas. Typically, a constraint such as time or a word restriction helps to galvanize more creative ideas. Quantity of ideas is the goal. This activity should ideally be followed up with an action plan of how to apply the ideas that have been netted.

Brand equity describes the value of having a well-known brand name. The owner of a well-known brand name can generate more money from products with that brand name than from products with a less-well-known name. Some marketing researchers have concluded that brands are one of the most valuable assets a company has, because brand equity can increase the financial value of a brand to the brand owner.

Brand loyalty refers to a consumer's commitment to repurchase a brand's product or otherwise continue to support a brand with positive behaviors such as word-of-mouth advocacy.

Breakup Letters is a tool used by Smart Design to elicit customers' true feelings about products, services, and businesses. Smart asks customers to imagine its product, service, or business as a past relationship and to write a breakup letter detailing what first attracted them, why they are leaving, and who took their place. Some interesting examples can be found in this video link: http://vimeo.com/11854531.

Broad Thinking refers to strategies and tools to understand women and to analyze their needs. The end goal is to design products and services that women appreciate. See *Femme Den* in the "Resources" section.

Charrette is a structured brainstorming process historically used in the architecture and design professions that brings together diverse stakeholders working toward consensus on a complex challenge.

Clanning refers to the perspective of a group of people of a common connection that can be race, religion, profession, or another means of establishing a shared culture. The term *clanning* was made popular by the futurist Faith Popcorn.

Comorbidity is the presence of one or more disorders or diseases beyond the primary disorder or disease.

Connect + Develop is the name for Procter & Gamble's open innovation model, founded under CEO A.G. Lafley in 2001. It was built on the belief that "sustaining solutions would be found in collaboration, not isolation," and that 50% of new ideas would come from outside of the company: www.pgconnectdevelop.com.

Convergence-divergence refers to the process of expanding and contracting focus in brainstorming. Divergence is any process in which there is multiple idea generation and diffusion of ideas often deviating from the main focus. Convergence is the sorting and sifting of ideas to narrow the scope back to the focus. The convergence-divergence process is dynamic and ebbs and flows during the process of creating, iterating, and developing a project.

Creative abrasion is a type of cognitive dissonance typically found in teams in which the friction caused by differences in approaches is valued and leveraged to develop more innovative outcomes.

Customer Development Model is a concept for start-ups advanced by Steve Blank and consisting of four stages: Customer Discovery, Customer Validation, Customer Creation, and Company Building.

Customer Journey Mapping is a tool to visually chart the physical and emotional touch points a customer experiences when interacting with a service or product; includes pre- and post-interactions.

Customer Validation is the second stage within the Customer Development Model proposed by Steve Blank. It is a business process aiming at building a repeatable sales road map that can be scaled up by sales and marketing teams hired later.

DELI, or Deeply Embedded Life Interests, is a concept that refers to a series of long-held, emotionally driven passions, intricately entwined with personality—a blend of nature and nurture. Identified in the work "Job Sculpting: The Art of Retaining Your Best People," *Harvard Business Review,* there are eight DELIs, and tapping into your team's DELIs is a way to cement their engagement to the project or the firm.

Doblin Ten Types of Innovation is a framework first proposed in 1998 that expanded innovation beyond the traditional product innovation and showed that companies that combine multiple types of innovation are more successful than those that don't: www.doblin.com/tentypes/#framework.

Ecosystem of Design refers to organic interdependencies within an organization.

ESG (Environmental, Social, and Governance) refers to the three main areas of concern that have developed as central factors in measuring the sustainability and ethical impact of an investment in a company or business. ESG is the catchall term for the criteria used in what has become known as socially responsible investing. Socially responsible investing, including ESG, is among several related concepts and approaches that influence and, in some cases, govern how asset managers invest portfolios.)

Foresight is a "systematic, participatory, future intelligence gathering and medium-to-long-term vision-building process aimed at present-day decisions and mobilizing joint actions." Contrary to forecasting, foresight provides projections of multiple plausible futures that form the basis for scenario planning: www.millennium-project.org/.

Gearing Up Framework is a framework proposed by Avastone Consulting that includes five interconnected gears: (1) Comply, (2) Volunteer, (3) Partner, (4) Integrate, and (5) Redesign: www.avastoneconsulting.com/MindsetsInAction.pdf.

Improvisation is the practice of acting, dancing, singing, creating artworks, problem solving, or reacting in the moment and in response to the stimulus of one's immediate environment and inner feelings. Improvisation has been proven helpful in building collaborative teams and sparking innovation because it stresses listening, agreement, an open stance, and building on what has come before.

Integrative thinking is the ability to constructively face the tensions of opposing models, and instead of choosing one at the expense of the other, generating a creative resolution of the tension in the form of a new model that contains elements of the individual models, but is superior to each.[1] Roger Martin, Dean of the Rotman School of Management, made this concept popular.

Interdisciplinarity is a problem-solving perspective that integrates the knowledge and insights from many disciplines working together to achieve creative solutions far greater than that which can be crafted from any single domain or coordinated domain perspective. Also referred to as transdisciplinary.

IOM is an acronym for the Institute of Medicine.

Kanbar, Maurice (born 1930) is an American entrepreneur, inventor, and philanthropist who is particularly well known for his creation of Skyy Vodka and 36 patents and is credited with inventing the multiplex movie theater in NYC. Kanbar is a graduate of Philadelphia University.

Latent ROI (Return on Investment) refers to budgeting money in project management to allow for lag time, mistakes, and testing out ideas in iterative ways.

Learning launch is the process of generating increased revenues through conducting small experiments in the marketplace that provide knowledge for testing and improving (or abandoning) a new business idea quickly and inexpensively.[2] The term has been made popular by the work of Dr. Jeanne Liedtka.

Long Tail pattern is a business model pattern characterized by selling smaller quantities of niche offerings instead of focusing on selling high quantities of a few bestsellers. The aggregation of sales to all the niche markets can be as lucrative as the revenues from a best-selling product. Amazon.com is a good example of a long-tail business model pattern.

Low-fidelity prototype is a prototype that is a quick and crude example of a product, an idea, or a service. It is not meant to exactly replicate reality, but rather serve as a proxy to give a sense of what could be and help identify stumbling blocks early on during the ideation and development process. The benefits of a low-fidelity prototype are that it is quick to make, cheap to produce, and accessible.

Market segmentation is a strategic marketing approach that involves dividing a broad group of targeted consumers into subsets of users who share common needs and interests. Marketers then design and implement strategies to target those needs using media channels and retail touch points. (See also *target market*.)

Marketing strategy is a guide, constructed by an entity, to concentrate its resources on its optimal market opportunities. The goal of a marketing strategy is to increase sales and achieve a sustainable and long-term competitive advantage. A marketing strategy includes all process activities, including analysis of the company, and the formulation, evaluation, and selection of the strategic tools that will contribute to the marketing objectives of the company.

Mass affluent is a marketing term used to refer to the wealthiest population demographic. *Mass affluent* is used by marketers of consumer products to refer to consumers with an annual household income of about US$75,000 and up; in the financial services industry, *mass affluent* commonly refers to individuals with US$50,000 to $250,000 or US$100,000 to US$1,000,000 of liquid financial assets. Investable assets include investments in retirement plans, college savings plans, individual stocks and bonds, mutual funds, exchange traded funds (ETFs), annuities, money market accounts, savings in cash, and other assets. The value of real estate owned is typically not included in liquid investments.

Mass merchandiser or **mass merchant** is a large retail store that offers a wide range of products and seeks to sell large quantities of goods quickly through such means as discounting and customer self-service. Examples of mass merchandisers include discount retailers such as Walmart, Kmart, and Target.

Medical home is a team-based primary-care health delivery model aimed at providing comprehensive and continuous medical care and maximizing health outcomes.

Mind map is a visual outline of information. A mind map is often created around a single word or text, placed in the center, to which associated ideas, words, and concepts are added. Major categories radiate from a central node, and lesser categories are subbranches of larger branches.

Mixed market economy is an economy in which the government has a role to ensure that equity/fairness takes place and that everything runs smoothly. Also, the government plays the role of a market/economy watcher, sitting back and intervening only when needed between producers and consumers.

Motivational drivers, as described In the article "Employee Motivation: A Powerful New Model" (Nohria, Groysberg, and Lee, 2008) from *Harvard Business Review,* proposes that individuals are driven by four main motivators: to acquire, defend, comprehend, and bond.

Multi-Sided Platform pattern is a business model pattern that brings together two or more distinct but interdependent groups of customers. The business model is of value to one group of customers only if the other groups are also present. The credit card provides a good example of a multisided platform: It brings together consumers and vendors. Only if there are many consumers participating is it of value to vendors, and only if vendors are participating is it of value to consumers.

NAE is an acronym for National Academy of Engineering.

Nordic Innovation is a Nordic institution promoting cross-border trade and innovation. Home to the Green Business Model Innovation project: www.nordicinnovation.org/.

Open Innovation is a term promoted by Henry Chesbrough, a professor and executive director at the Center for Open Innovation at the University of California, Berkeley, in his book *Open Innovation: The New Imperative for Creating and Profiting from Technology*. "Open innovation is a paradigm that assumes that firms can and should use external ideas as well as internal ideas, and internal and external paths to market, as the firms look to advance their technology."[3] Procter & Gamble's Connect + Develop is a very successful example of open innovation.

Peri-operative systems are the technological and organizational systems surrounding the three phases of care surrounding surgery: preoperative (admission, anesthesia induction), intraoperative (surgery), and postoperative (recovery).

Qualitative data refers to the research findings that are generated through the process of interviews, observation during onsite visits, and participant-observation (participating in the process you have observed).

Quantitative data refers to research findings that are generated through the process of surveys and statistical analysis.

Social Return on Investment (SROI) is a principles-based method for measuring extra-financial value (that is, environmental and social value not currently reflected in conventional financial accounts) relative to resources invested. It can be used by any entity to evaluate impact on stakeholders, identify ways to improve performance, and enhance the performance of investments:[4] www.thesroinetwork.org/ and www.sroi-canada.ca/.

Strategic intuition is the practice of tactically mining your team's collective memory and integrating memory, observation, and raw data to build a plan of action.

Target market is a group of customers at which a business has aimed its marketing efforts. A well-defined target market is the primary element of a marketing strategy. Target markets are groups of individuals separated by distinguishing characteristics, such as geographic segmentation, demographic/socioeconomic segmentation (gender, age, income, occupation, education, household size, and stage in the family life cycle), psychographic segmentation (similar attitudes, values, and lifestyles), behavioral segmentation (occasions, degree of loyalty), or product-related segmentation (relationship to a product).

Transmedia storytelling is a concept that utilizes multiple platforms to tell a brand's story and is annotated by the user in (for example) a movie, a novel, a graphic novel, a website, and an animated short film.

Triple bottom line is a term for measuring progress that considers equally the "people, planet, and profit." "People" pertains to fair and beneficial business practices toward labor and the community in which a corporation conducts its business. A triple-bottom-line company conceives a reciprocal social structure in which the well-being of corporate, labor, and other stakeholder interests are interdependent. "Planet" refers to sustainable environmental practices. A triple-bottom-line company endeavors to benefit the natural order as much as possible, or at the least, minimize its environmental impact. Within a sustainability framework, the "profit" aspect is characterized as the real economic benefit enjoyed by the host society, or the real economic impact the organization has on its economic environment.

T-Shaped Thinkers is a concept popularized by IDEO CEO Tim Brown to describe individuals who have both great depth of expertise and great breadth and ability to apply knowledge in areas of expertise other than their own.

Types of capital is a concept that acknowledges three asset classes—not just financial. The sustainable development debate is based on the assumption that societies need to manage three types of capital (natural, social, and economic), which can be nonsubstitutable and whose consumption might be irreversible.

> **Natural capital** is the extension of the economic notion of capital (manufactured means of production) to goods and services relating to the natural environment. Natural capital is thus the stock of natural ecosystems that yields a flow of valuable ecosystem goods or services into the future.[5]

> **Social capital** is the expected collective or economic benefits derived from the preferential treatment and cooperation between individuals and groups. Just as a screwdriver (physical capital) or a university education (cultural capital or human capital) can increase productivity (both individual and collective), so do social contacts affect the productivity of individuals and groups.[6]

> **Financial or economic capital** comprises physical goods that assist in the production of other goods and services—for example, shovels for gravediggers, sewing machines for tailors, or machinery and tooling for factories.[7]

Value proposition is a promise of value to be delivered to a consumer and that consumer's belief that he will experience that value. A value proposition can apply to an entire organization, to parts thereof, to customer accounts, or to products or services. Offering a value proposition is critical to a successful business strategy. Kaplan and Norton say, "Strategy is based on a differentiated customer value proposition. Satisfying customers is the source of sustainable value creation."

VUCA, or Volatile, Uncertain, Complex, and Ambiguous, is a term that began in the late 1990s and derives from military vocabulary. It has subsequently become popular in strategic leadership in a wide range of organizations, including everything from for-profit corporations to education.

White space exploration (sometimes just referred to as white space) is a term for undiscovered areas of opportunity that might be outside the business current offerings, part of an immature market, dependent on emerging technologies, reliant on shifting cultural norms, or a combination of these factors. The term *white space in innovation* became popular with the seminal book *Seizing the White Space: Business Model Innovation for Growth and Renewal,* by A. G. Lafley and Mark W. Johnson.

Resources

Notable Think Tanks and Consulting Firms

Avastone Consulting provides executive, leadership, and organizational development services to Fortune 500 companies and other complex organizations, enabling them to realize the potential of people and the human system at work:[8]

www.avastoneconsulting.com/

Bob Willard is a leading expert on quantifying and selling the business value of corporate sustainability strategies. Bob used his 34-year career at IBM Canada to engage the business community in proactively avoiding risks and capturing opportunities by using smart environmental, social, and governance (ESG) strategies. Notable offerings include the Sustainability Advantage, www.sustainabilityadvantage.com/, and Business Case Simulators, www.sustainabilityadvantage.com/products/index.html.

Business Innovation Factory (BIF) is a platform for transforming our most intractable systems, like healthcare, education, entrepreneurship, and energy, where players—both private and public—can design and test new solutions in a real-world environment.[9] BIF holds an annual, always-sold-out conference that highlights innovators from around the globe. BIF Labs tackle complex challenges such as aging, healthcare, and entrepreneurship: www.businessinnovationfactory.com.

Claro Partners is a Barcelona-based, global innovation consulting firm that explores disruptions in society, technology, and business in three ways: They make sense of these big shifts for your company, they define your unique business opportunities, and they design services that respond to disruptions: www.claropartners.com.

Continuum is a 30-year-old global design and innovation consultancy that partners with clients to discover powerful ideas and realize them as products, services, and brand experiences. Continuum has offices in the U.S., Asia, and Europe. Notable innovations born or advanced through Continuum include the Reebok Pump, the Swiffer, and One Laptop Per Child: http://continuuminnovation.com.

Femme Den is a design lab focused on the female consumer, powered by Smart Design, that integrates designers, researchers, strategists, and engineers who bridge the gap between assumptions and realities about design for women. Women buy or influence up to 85% of consumer purchases: www.femmeden.com.

Forum for the Future is a think tank that focuses on action for a sustainable world: www.forumforthefuture.org/.

Four B (4B) is named for their target audience, the four billion women in the world. 4B is a collective of researchers, designers, and engineers who improve women's lives through design. They help companies and organizations consider gender while developing compelling and functional solutions to complex design and innovation problems: http://four-b.com.

Green Business Model Innovation is a project of the Nordic Innovation organization: www.nordicinnovation.org/Publications/green-business-model-innovation-business-case-study-compendium/.

IDEO is an international design firm and innovation consultancy founded in Palo Alto, California, in 1991 through the merger of four established design firms. The company helps design products, services, environments, and digital experiences and has become increasingly involved in management consulting and organizational design. IDEO was very influential in the formation of the Stanford D School and the rise of the concept of "design thinking" in business. Notable IDEO leadership includes David Kelley (founder of IDEO and founder of the D School), Bill Moggridge (founder of IDEO, pioneer of human-centered design, former director of the Cooper-Hewitt Museum), and Tim Brown (current CEO): www.ideo.com.

Innosight is a global strategy and innovation consulting firm that collaborates with senior leaders at the world's top companies to identify and pursue new growth opportunities, build innovation capabilities, and create disruptive new products, services, and businesses. Innosight was cofounded by Dr. Clay Christensen, Harvard Business School professor and *New York Times* best-selling author of *Innovator's Dilemma*, *Innovator's Solution*, and *Disrupting Class*: http://www.innosight.com.

The Martin Prosperity Institute is the world's leading think tank on the role of subnational factors—location, place, and city-regions—in global economic prosperity. The institute takes an integrated view of prosperity, looking beyond economic measures to include the importance of quality of place and the development of people's creative potential: http://martinprosperity.org.

The Natural Step is a "nonprofit organization with over a decade of experience helping organizations and individuals understand and make meaningful progress toward sustainability": www.naturalstep.org/en/canada and www.naturalstep.ca/.

Rotman Design Works is the business design studio at the Rotman School of Management that teaches students how to tackle complex business challenges using Business Design, a human-centered, creative problem-solving methodology. Design Works was founded by Heather Fraser and Roger Martin. Heather is the author of the book *Design Works,* a guide to business design: http://fraserdesignworks.com.

Sarah Singer & Company works with teams, leaders, and educators to accelerate learning, spark insights, and maximize the ripple impact of every interaction. Steeped in the mastery of high-impact teaching and the latest data on how the brain best learns, we move people past their perceived boundaries to create transformative change. Paying close attention to dynamics in communication, natural talent, learning style, and perception, we help clients see themselves more clearly, then give them tools to increase their impact quickly. Individually, on teams, in professional or educational worlds, and in daily life, Sarah Singer & Company bridges the gap between the research and daily results in energized performance and growth. Find Sarah at sarah@singerlearning.com, and her latest thinking and work at www.singerlearning.com.

Smart Design is an award-winning innovation consulting firm with studios in New York, San Francisco, and Barcelona offering business design, consumer insights, product design, service and experience design, and complete realization services from prototype to production. The Femme Den was founded at Smart Design: http://smartdesignworldwide.com.

Strongly Sustainable Business Models Group (SSBMG) is a multi-institution and multidisciplinary research group within sLab whose objective is to support SMEs in shifting significantly toward a strongly sustainable mode: http://slab.ocad.ca/the-strongly-sustainable-business-model-group-ssbmg.

See also the LinkedIn Group: Strongly Sustainable Business Models: www.linkedin.com/groups/Strongly-Sustainable-Business-Models-5005769/about.

Notable Integrated Education Programs

Aalto University is a Finnish university established on January 1, 2010, in the merger of the Helsinki University of Technology, the Helsinki School of Economics, and the University of Art and Design Helsinki. The university is internationally recognized as a leader in interdisciplinary collaboration, pioneering education, surpassing traditional boundaries, and enabling renewal: www.aalto.fi/en/.

Babson College is a highly selective business school that has been ranked the number one M.B.A. program in entrepreneurship for 20 consecutive years by *U.S. News & World Report.* Babson's undergraduate and graduate programs offer collaboration with nearby Wellesley College and Olin College, as well as integrated product development courses with Rhode Island School of Design: www.babson.edu.

California College of the Arts, Design M.B.A. Programs were founded by academic entrepreneur Nathan Shedroff, and all offer business education rooted in design thinking and social and environmental responsibility. Each Design M.B.A. program offers the integration of learning of pragmatic skills with outside projects and working with real organizations headquartered from the San Francisco Bay Area. Programs include Design Strategy M.B.A., Public Policy M.B.A., and Strategic Foresight M.B.A.: www.cca.edu/academics/graduate/design-mba.

College for America at Southern New Hampshire University is an example of disruptive innovation in higher education as it breaks the norms of cost and credit hour and focuses on the development of competencies. From its website, CFA states, "The

College for America (CFA) delivers an innovative solution to the most pressing problems of cost, access, and quality in higher education throughout the United States and around the world. CFA seeks to create a talent pipeline that addresses retention, succession, and economic prosperity." The executive director of CFA is interviewed in Section 4 of this book: http://collegeforamerica.org.

The Franklin W. Olin College of Engineering (Olin) is a private undergraduate engineering college located in Needham, Massachusetts, adjacent to and affiliated with Babson College. Olin College is noted in the engineering community for its integrated, project-based curriculum, and large endowment funded primarily by the F. W. Olin Foundation that enables it to offer deeply discounted tuition. Unlike many institutions, Olin College does not have separate academic departments, and faculty members hold five-year renewable contracts with no opportunity for tenure: www.olin.edu.

Hasso Plattner Institute of Design ("D School" or "d.school") is a design school based in Stanford University, in cooperation with the University of Potsdam. The school was founded by Stanford mechanical engineering professor and IDEO Founder David Kelley in 2004. Like some other design schools, it integrates business and management training into more traditional engineering and product design. Students who study at the D School must be first accepted into one of Stanford's graduate schools: http://dschool.stanford.edu.

Ontario College of Art and Design offers a Master of Design in Strategic Foresight and Innovation to create a new kind of designer: a strategist who sees the world from a human perspective and rethinks what is possible; an innovator who can imagine, plan, and develop a better world: www.ocadu.ca/graduate-studies/programs/strategic-foresight-and-innovation.

Philadelphia University (PhilaU), founded in 1884, is a private university in Philadelphia, Pennsylvania. Academic programs are divided among the integrated colleges, including the College of Architecture and the Built Environment; the Kanbar College of Design, Engineering and Commerce; the College of Science, Health and the Liberal Arts; and the School of Continuing and Professional Studies. Courses are also offered via PhilaU Online. The Kanbar College of Design, Engineering and Commerce has won multiple awards for its innovative curriculum and teaching pedagogy, notably the Strategic Design M.B.A., the M.B.A. in Innovation, and the Master's in Industrial Design: www.philau.edu/designengineeringandcommerce/index.html#/academicPrograms.

Rotman School of Management, or just Rotman, is the University of Toronto's graduate business school named after Joseph L. Rotman. Through the deanship of Roger Martin (1998–2013), the school rose in prominence and attention with the institutionalization of "integrated thinking," which infused design thinking in the M.B.A. program. Designworks and Martin Prosperity Institute were both born at Rotman.

Strategic Innovation Lab (sLab) is a lab at OCAD University practicing concepts of strategic foresight and innovation: http://slab.ocadu.ca or http://slab.ocad.ca.

University of California at Berkeley's Institute for Design Innovation was launched in 2013 out of the Engineering School with a $20 million gift from the Paul and Stacy Jacobs Foundation. The focus of this emerging innovation institute is to expand the role of design in engineering education, emphasizing rapid design and prototyping for manufacturability. Dr. Sarah Beckman is the Chief Learning Office of this new institute.

The University of Pennsylvania's Integrated Product Design master's program merges the disciplines of design, engineering, and business for the purpose of creating compelling new products and experiences. The program draws on three schools within the University: the School of Engineering and Applied Science, the Wharton School, and the School of Design:[10] www.me.upenn.edu/ipd/.

Endnotes

1. "Definition of Integrative Thinking," Rotman School of Management website, University of Toronto.
2. Dr. Jeanne Liedtka, "Designing Learning Launches," University of Virginia–Darden School of Business, April 5, 2010. http://papers.ssrn.com/sol3/papers.cfm?abstract_id=1583278.
3. Henry William Chesbrough, *Open Innovation: The New Imperative for Creating and Profiting from Technology* (Boston: Harvard Business School Press, 2003).
4. "Social return on investment" definition from Wikipedia: http://en.wikipedia.org/wiki/Social_return_on_investment.
5. "Natural Capital" definition from Wikipedia: http://en.wikipedia.org/wiki/Natural_capital.
6. "Social Capital" definition from Wikipedia: http://en.wikipedia.org/wiki/Social_capital.
7. "Financial Capital" definition from Wikipedia: http://en.wikipedia.org/wiki/Financial_capital.
8. Avastone Consulting Web site: www.avastoneconsulting.com.
9. Business Innovation Factory Web site: www.businessinnovationfactory.com.
10. University of Pennsylvania IPD Web site: www.me.upenn.edu/ipd/.

Index

C

cable providers, 224

California College of the Arts, 40, 267

Cambridge University Autism Research Centre, 206

cannibalization
   avoiding, 227
   risks, 224
   of underperforming offerings, 225

capabilities, collective, 191–192

capital, 151
   access to, 150
   financial or economic, 263
   natural, 263
   social, 263
   types, 172, 263

capital requirements, assessing, 162

career trajectories, 36–37

cars as cultural norm shift examples, 101

Catalyst IDEA, 247

Center for Integrated Medicine and Technology (CIMIT), 215

Center for Open Innovation, 262

Centers for Disease Control, 11

CEO, authority to pivot, 189

CFA (College for America), 143, 145

chalkboard drawing, 134

champions, in strategic plan implementation, 24

Chang, Annie, 133, 135, 141

change, rapid response to, 150

channel strategies, 245

channels
   distribution, access to, 150
   as element of Business Model Canvas, 168

Channels (CH), 155–156

charitable organizations, 168

Charles Stark Draper Laboratory, 215

charrettes, 38–39, 41, 131, 255, 258
   definition, 130

Charron, David, 144, 147, 170, 179

chat as tool, 198

Chesbrough, Henry, 262

chief innovation officers (CINOs), 50

Cho, Sooyoung, 109

Chobani, 130, 134, 138, 141

Christensen, Clayton, 116, 266

Cindy Tripp & Company, LLC, 142

CINOs (chief innovation officers), 50

clanning, 35, 258

Claro Partners, 95, 98, 265

Clerkin, Kris, 143, 145–146

Cloud Gehshan Associates, 113

Coca-Cola bottle as iconic product, 243

COCE, 146

code of honor, 88

cognitive barriers to innovation, 60

cognitive biases, 62, 189

cognitive categories, identifying, 102

cognitive dissonance, 107, 258

collaboration
   belated, 35, 37
   interdisciplinary, 3–4, 211
   as result of successful strategic planning, 24

collaborative courses and degree programs, 31–32

collaborative education, 12

collaborative teams, 240, 251

collective capabilities, understanding, 191–192

College for America (CFA), 143, 145, 267

College Unbound: The Future of Higher Education and What It Means for Students, 37

colleges, creating integrated, 32

commitment, escalation of, 189

commodity business, 152

common sense as self-created filter, 90

communication
   during strategic planning, 24, 26
   human, evolution of, 5
   facilitating, 211

F

F. W. Olin Foundation, 268
facilities, university master plans for, 19
failing, better, 114
failure
  common elements of, 116
  role in opportunity recognition, 10
  versus mistake, 250
failures
  as design tools, 114
  leveraging strategic, 114
  manageable, 115
Fallacy of Detachment, 17
familiarity as key to innovation, 60
Fast Company, 143–144
fear
  as barrier to innovation, 60
  iteration, 124
  as motivator for business model innovation, 224
feasibility, 163
Federal-Mogul Corporation, 14–16
fee-for-service business model, 230
Femme Den, 196, 265, 267
Fenelon, Manoj, 130, 134, 139, 141
fidelity prototypes, 118, 132
fieldwork, 97, 132
fight-or-flight response, 57
filter, design process as, 120
financial capital, 263
Financial Components, 155
financial model, 151, 161
financial proxies, developing, 174
Finiw, Maryann, 191–192, 235
Fischer, Jordan, 133, 141
fit
  internal and external, 149
  as opportunity dimension, 149
  strategic, 226
flexibility in strategic plan implementation, 26

focus
  attention, maintaining, 93
  expanding and contracting, 258
focused strategy, 146
forecasting, 259
foresight, 172, 259
formulation innovation, 213
formulation phase, areas of focus, 38–39, 41
Forum for the Future, 174–175, 265
Four Actions framework, 170
Four B (4B), 265
Four Steps to Epiphany, The, 1, 123
Fowler, Brandy, 192–193, 223
Fowler, Mark, 122
frameworks, 68, 96
  Blue Ocean, 170
  Business Model Canvas, 153, 168
  business models as, 151
  discovery-driven planning, 160
  Four Actions, 170
  Gearing Up, 175
  Innovation Bull's-Eye, 162–163
  innovation process, 30
  iteration stimulus, 165
  objectivity of, 151
  opportunity evaluation, 149
  screening matrices, 164
  SSBMG (Strongly Sustainable Business Model Group), 175
  sustainability, 263
  sustainable business, 174–177
  TRIZ, 159
  using to assess maturity, 177
  versus tools, 140
frameworks phase of innovation process, 69
framing errors, 97
framing effect bias, 189
Franklin W. Olin College of Engineering, 268
Fraser, Heather, 266
functional organization, 51

Minter, Marcia, 242
mission statements
  Google, 20
  IBM, 19
  revising, importance in strategic planning, 19
Mission-Strategy-Critical Long-Term
  Initiatives, 8
mistake versus failure, 250
misunderstandings, revealing, 8
mixed market economy, 209, 261
model
  business. *See* business model
  financial, 151, 161
Model Viability, 170
Moggridge, Bill, 265
Morris, Doug, 116
motivational drivers, 57–58, 261
multidisciplinarity, 210
multidisciplinary, 4, 6
multidisciplinary teams, 16, 45, 169
multisided platform pattern, 169, 261
myths, revealing, 8

N

NAE (National Academy of Engineering),
  209, 262
name change as reflection of mission
  revision, 20
narrow teams, 220
National Academy of Engineering (NAE), 209
natural capital, 172, 175–176, 263
Natural Step, The, 175, 266
needs
  emotional, 57
  latent, 137
  women versus men, 197, 200–207
Net Present Value, 162
network effects, 150
New Sustainability Advantage, The, 176
New Venture Creation, 3
New York Times, 226

Newman's Own, 240
Nexus Learning Approach, Philadelphia
  University, 42, 45
Nguyen, Mai, 135–136, 141
Nixon, Natalie, 10, 34, 38, 97, 127
Nohria, N., 57
Nordic Innovation, 177, 262, 265
normatives, 100
norms
  communication, 100
  cultural, 99, 101–105, 108, 111
North Face, 240
Norton, 264
NSF Innovation Corps, 1

O

objectives, integrating as part of strategic
  plan, 23
observation, 132
observations phase (innovation process),
  68–69
OCAD University, 175, 269
occupational therapist (OT), 210
offerings
  breadth of, 150
  quality of, 150
Olin College, 268
online education, 143
online educational model, 144
Ontario College of Art and Design, 40, 268
open innovation, 262
*Open Innovation: The New Imperative for
  Creating and Profiting from
  Technology,* 262
opportunities
  identifying cultural norm shifts, 100–101
  as reasons to pivot, 186
  scoring with screening matrices, 165
opportunity
  crafting, 8
  four main dimensions, 149